D0096597

TYCOON

About the Author: Peter Jones

Peter Jones is a Tycoon and is one of the leading lights of his generation in the world of modern business.

He is a man with many missions, but there are two causes that have become priorities in recent years. Firstly, he has led a revolution to change the way the world of business is perceived by the masses. Some years ago, in a comment article he authored for the BBC, he described business as the new rock 'n' roll, claiming that being an entrepreneur was just as sexy and alluring now as being a pop star has been for decades. Teenagers in particular, he argued, are just as likely to pick up a laptop and a business guidebook as they are a guitar to set them on the path to riches, fame and glory. The increase in the number of television shows in primetime entertainment slots with a business slant is also testament to the fact that there is a growing appetite to understand the mechanics of setting up and running a company.

Secondly, Peter wants to make business accessible to the many, rather than the few. His own television shows are a key driver in encouraging a broader range of people to try their own hand at becoming entrepreneurs, but he is also working hard at establishing Britain's first Tycoon academy, where people can get the skills and confidence needed to make their own business dreams a reality.

His own business journey started early. Peter's ambition of running a multi-million-pound company can be traced back to his early childhood, dreaming of entrepreneurial success while sitting in his father's executive leather chair.

At the age of 16, he completed the Lawn Tennis Association's coaching examinations, and at 17 he set up his first company, a successful tennis academy at a local club. He started his first major business at just 19, providing computers and services to corporate clients. He went on to make that dream a reality, building a £200 million business by the age of 35. He is owner, chairman and chief executive officer of a large portfolio of businesses, ranging from telecoms and leisure to publishing, media, recruitment and property.

Beyond the business community, Peter has become a regular face on television and is now one of the foremost business personalities in the UK and abroad.

His television career began in 2005, when he appeared as an investor on BBC2's groundbreaking business television show *Dragons' Den*, which is now in its fourth series and has become one of the most watched shows in its genre and has ratings that continue to grow.

In 2006, Peter launched his own TV media company, Peter Jones TV, and its first commission, *American Inventor*, became an instant hit for America's largest TV network, ABC. When the show aired on 16 March 2006, it was ABC's biggest success for years on a Thursday night. The show has been recommissioned for another series in 2007 and has now been sold to many other countries around the world, including France and Russia. It will soon be seen in the UK.

The same year, Peter signed a multi-million-pound deal with ITV to produce and star in business-style TV programmes over the next two years. The first of these, *Tycoon*, airs in the summer of 2007 and sees Peter searching the UK for the next big business success story.

PETER JONES

TYCOON

HODDER &
STOUGHTON

First published in Great Britain in 2007 by
Hodder & Stoughton
An Hachette Livre UK company

First published in paperback in 2008

1

A CIP catalogue record for this title is available from the British Library

ISBN 978 0 34095235 1

Typeset in Sabon by Hewer Text UK Ltd, Edinburgh
Printed and bound by Mackays of Chatham Plc, Chatham, Kent

Hodder & Stoughton policy is to use papers that are natural, renewable and recyclable products
and made from wood grown in sustainable forests. The logging and manufacturing processes are
expected to conform to the environmental regulations of the country of origin.

Hodder & Stoughton Ltd
338 Euston Road
London NW1 3BH

www.hodder.co.uk

DEDICATION

To those of you who are determined to make your dreams reality. . . But most of all to my family, especially my children, who I have no doubt will make their own mark on this world by acting on their dreams.

ACKNOWLEDGEMENTS

I have never read a business book. Crazy as it may sound, although many people have given them to me as presents, I've never found the time to sit down and read one. I'm not sure if this is a good thing or a bad thing. It is a bit worrying, especially now I've written my own book, because I have nothing to compare it against. I am going to have to leave this judgement to you!

Because of this, I asked a couple of people in the journalistic world to help me; to keep me on the straight and narrow and look over what I have written. So, thank you, Rachel Bridge, for all those hours reviewing, editing and listening to me in the early days of writing my first few chapters. A big thank you to Cheryl Rickman, who has spent many weeks working with me and interviewing me to make sure I have captured everything about my mindset so that it can be included in this book.

Thanks also to John Eastaff and Eric White at Peter Jones TV for their hard work in keeping the pressure on me, even when I didn't feel up to writing because I had already done a 16-hour day. Thank you, strangely, for allowing me less sleep than normal but motivating me to complete the book. Thank you to Rowena Webb and Helen Coyle at Hodder & Stoughton, the publishers of this book – I hope it proves a hit!

My thanks to Stephen and George for all of their support and dedication over many years in helping to build our business. Thank you to Jonathan Groves for always being on hand on the commercial side of my TV business. And to everyone who works for the companies that I have an interest in. Without you, our success would be small. You make it happen and have the most important job of all. Thank you.

To my parents, David and Eileen, who have supported me unconditionally in everything I have done. You are not just loved by me but adored by me – I will never forget what you have done in helping me create a new life for many more generations of our family to come. THE JONES lives on!

To all my friends – thank you for being you. For helping me stay the person I will always be and true to myself. I know you would love it if I mentioned you all individually: so here goes – thank you to Bobby and Jo, Phil and Anne, Tarik and Suzie, Richard and Ali, Simon and Paula, Ben and Jilly, David and Kate, Rob and Sarah, Greg and Sam, Stafford and Sarah, Andy and Stephanie, Daryl and Sarah and not to mention all your great kids. You are my extended family.

Finally, thank you to my gorgeous Tara, the person I turn to and the one I love, who has been there from the days of having nothing but encouraged and supported me to live my dream. You call me your angel but you have been more of one to me, and from the bottom of my heart I thank you for your support and unwavering love. I love you, *always*. To my children – Annabelle, William, Natalia, Isabella and Tallulah – the little ones I cherish as much as anything else in this world for they are sparks that light the flame. I love you to the moon, the stars and back again, and hope all your dreams will become reality as you find your way through this amazing world we live in.

CONTENTS

INTRODUCTION

'For a dream to become reality, make it real enough to believe in'

PETER JONES

---

ty•coon

• noun. **1** a wealthy, powerful person in business or industry; **2** magnate.

I never really thought I would write a book. I'm not much of a bookworm. Frankly, I never seem to have the time to read books. These days, emails, business and trade press, briefings, proposals and contracts make up the majority of my reading material. However, as I've not read any of the self-help business books on the shelves, my book is not based on previous people's secrets-of-success theories, so I hope it makes refreshing reading.

I've had a serious interest in business since I was just 11 years old, but my vision of running my own business began even earlier, when I was only seven. I would sit in my father's office chair and pretend I was in charge of a big company – a big dream for a schoolboy, but one that ultimately came true.

Aged 16, I saw the chance to start a small business, and after completing the Lawn Tennis Association's coaching exams, I set up my own tennis coaching academy when I was just 17 years old. Since then, when my main motivation had been to buy a car, I've set up and invested in many businesses providing a variety of services and products.

I've achieved great success, lost everything, bounced back and achieved even greater success. And it certainly hasn't been easy.

1

Of the many businesses that I've started up or invested in, a few didn't quite make it. This book gives you the opportunity to learn not only from my methods of making things happen, but also from my own, sometimes costly, mistakes.

ANYBODY CAN BECOME A TYCOON

Part of the premise of the *Tycoon* series on ITV is that with the right mental attitude, the right idea and the stamina to succeed, anyone can become a Tycoon. I don't believe entrepreneurs are born. I firmly believe that with the right application, anyone can develop the qualities necessary to succeed in business, especially when they adopt a certain mindset and a set of Golden Rules. In fact, I believe the UK is an innovative and entrepreneurial nation at heart, but we don't do enough to nurture talented people and help them turn their business dreams into reality.

This book and the *Tycoon* series are about achieving that objective: making dreams come true!

The truth is that anyone can do it! People end up as entrepreneurs from totally different starting points, but anybody can learn the process of thinking and behaving like a Tycoon. Sure, circumstances at home and the environment we grow up in play a vital part in shaping who we are, but whether you are born into a poor family or an entrepreneurial one, I believe anyone can make it.

In this book, I will reveal the key components that make up the Mindset of a Tycoon, but first let me dispel a myth about being an entrepreneur; let's go against the grain of popular thinking.

Do you agree or disagree with this statement: 'You've either got it or you haven't'? If you agree, I'm afraid to say I believe you are wrong. Certainly, there are hundreds of examples of people who clearly do have 'it': Woods, Beckham, Gates, Trump, Schumacher, Jobs, Churchill . . . The list is endless. And it's fair to say that some people have incredible and exceptional talent. Let's face it, we can't all bend it like Beckham. But the fact is, we *can* all kick the ball. In fact, with a bit of practice, we might become half

2

decent, even exceptional with enough dedication, focus and determination.

You've either got it or you haven't? Rubbish! I believe we've all got some 'it' – maybe in different measures, but we all have 'it'. However, the majority of people haven't had the time or the inclination to reach inside themselves to find 'it'. Most of us don't even bother looking.

When you read this book, though, you will be able to replace this myth with a fabulous new realisation: that you have 'it', that everyone does. 'It' is the entrepreneurial talent you never knew you had. Until now. It just needs to be woken up and animated.

There is a sleeping giant entrepreneur inside you. It's there, and I hope you're going to start looking for it. There's no time to waste – you need to take action to be successful. So many people go through their lives saying, 'What if . . . ?' or, 'If only . . .' and it drives me mad. These people never move forward; they just continue to focus on the past. It is far better to try and to not succeed than to wonder, 'What if . . . ?' And that is the first train of thought that all Tycoons follow, to act when others wouldn't. Action is a core component of the Mindset of every Tycoon.

THE TYCOON MINDSET

The Oxford dictionary definition of 'tycoon' is 'a wealthy, powerful person in business or industry; magnate'. But what interests me is not the definition of a Tycoon per se (which, for the record, I define as a successful serial entrepreneur or, for a bit of fun, an 'ultrapreneur'). No, I'm much more interested in the definition of a Tycoon's Mindset. How does a Tycoon think, act and behave, and why? Achieving prosperity is something many wish for, but Tycoons actually achieve it. Why is that? What goes on in the mind of a Tycoon that doesn't in the minds of others?

I know that identikit Tycoons do not exist. Each Tycoon has a unique methodology. However, there are many notable qualities that all Tycoons appear to share, and there are some similar schools of thought that they follow to achieve their goals.

Sadly, Tycoons don't have the best reputations and are often stereotyped as arrogant, cocky or tyrannical. I believe, in general, that this is a misconception. Confidence and self-belief are mistaken for arrogance. Only those who are not hungry to learn, who think they know everything are arrogant, and Tycoons are open to learning and readily admit they don't know it all. Confidence and self-belief are, however, vital parts of the Mindset of a Tycoon. Furthermore, tyranny gets you nowhere in business; it's counterproductive, and Tycoons know this.

Tycoons are not always the best-educated, best-dressed, most organised or cleverest people. Charm is not always a prerequisite for 'Tycoonism'. Some are sour-faced, some are warm, some are extrovert, some are introvert, some are tidy, and some are messy. In my experience, the similarities lie less within the personality or character of an individual, and more within the mindset.

> 'In the middle of difficulty lies opportunity'
> ALBERT EINSTEIN

Successful people in all walks of life have a certain mindset, an inner set of beliefs that guide them in the right direction towards achieving their goals. This inner wiring to succeed gives them the focus and approach to make things happen. The great news is, by adopting the Mindset of a Tycoon, I believe that anyone can programme and rewire themselves for success.

In this book, you'll discover how to think like a Tycoon, how to see the opportunity when others miss it. The Tycoon Mindset is magnetic. It draws in more opportunities and resources in order to succeed. As you learn how to develop the Mindset of a Tycoon, you'll create a more focused, positive attitude, enhance your belief and determination, and use the results you gain as a springboard to further and bigger achievements. You'll learn how to develop your imagination, create a vision and turn your dreams into reality.

IMAGINATION IS THE KEY

So, are you pursuing your dreams right now? Every one? The biggest one? Do you know what your dreams and ambitions are? If not, when did the entrepreneur inside you fall asleep or start dozing off? Before you answer that, let's go back to school . . .

When we are children at junior school, anything's possible, isn't it? We may not be a trained pilot at the age of seven or even have a plane, but we can run around with our friends with our arms outstretched like wings making 'whooooosh' noises, flying at the speed of sound. That's because our imagination takes over to build elaborate worlds around whatever we choose. At that age, our imaginations are our world. 'Let's pretend' is a powerful prefix to any sentence, because it gives you the power to explore a whole new world of possibilities simply by using your imagination.

At playtime, we could invent people, situations, games, scenarios and come up with complex plots and schemes. We could even join in with other kids and mould the imaginary world we've built with ourselves with someone else's. We all indulged in imaginary play when we were children. Some of us even had imaginary friends, but we all pretended to be something, be someone or be somewhere to make our games real.

How many of you do that now? How many of you play imaginary games? If you're over 16, I expect few of you to say you do. Shame, isn't it? Where does all that imagination go? It seems to dry up as we leave school and enter the 'real' world. People become too busy to pause for thought, too caught up in the routine of daily life to escape into their imagination.

I believe that a vibrant imagination is the lifeblood of a successful entrepreneur. It is the key component in a Tycoon's Mindset. My imagination runs wild all the time. I encourage it, and I would encourage you to let your imagination do the same. Let it loose and you'll wake the entrepreneurial giant inside, I promise you. The more you let your imagination flow, the wider awake that sleeping giant will become. This is because imagination sparks an idea and helps to create a powerful vision to work towards. Passion and belief fuel that vision. No wonder, then, that Tycoons have passion, belief and vision in very large doses.

You might be a little sceptical, and I can appreciate that. 'Peter, you've gone mad,' you might be thinking. Well, maybe you should give it a try before you close your mind to the possibility that I could be right.

It's imagination that lights the flame; it's the spark that leads to becoming an entrepreneur! To me, imagination is the true starting point on the road to becoming a Tycoon.

After all, ideas impact the world we live in and it is imagination that creates every one of them.

WHAT'S IN THIS BOOK?

To maximise success, you need to work on the internal (the mindset) and the external factors (team, tools, logistics, finance, and so on). So this book combines practical principles and examples with action steps – from testing an idea and making an effective pitch to securing investment, marketing, taking on staff and growing a business.

It has taken me 25 years to accumulate the knowledge and approach that make up the Mindset of a Tycoon. And here I will share it with you. Over the pages that follow I am going to share with you my personal insight into the qualities and skills I believe every successful entrepreneur possesses, and I'll provide as many examples as possible, so you can gain an insight into my decision-making process.

Personally, I never start or invest in a business that doesn't adhere to certain criteria. I will reveal these criteria, but, more than that, I will show you how to go about securing investment from someone like me and other investors.

I've done well for myself and now I'm keen to encourage others to do what I have done, to succeed, to win and to make their dreams a reality. This book gives me a great chance to share the many truths I've learned along my own journey and to provide insight into my business philosophy.

Investing in creating the Mindset of a Tycoon takes nothing but time and a willingness to learn and practice. You've already taken the first step, by investing in this book. I promise to make that investment worthwhile.

There are many paths in life for us to choose. I hope this book helps set you on a path to fulfil your dreams and make success happen for you. Success is a euphoric feeling. I hope, through reading this book, you are able to experience that feeling and encourage others to do the same.

If you don't try, you cannot succeed. So . . . are you hungry?

'Never give in! Never give in! Never, never, never, never – in nothing great or small, large or petty. Never give in except to convictions of honour and good sense'
WINSTON CHURCHILL

1

THE TEN GOLDEN RULES

I truly believe that anyone has it within them to become a successful entrepreneur. In order to take the first step, however, you need to have some key building blocks in place. These are the critical success factors for entrepreneurial brilliance. I call them my **Ten Golden Rules**. They form a vital part in creating a **Tycoon Mindset** and I know they are a winning formula for business success.

RULE 1: Have a vision.
RULE 2: Use your influence.
RULE 3: Build your confidence.
RULE 4: Make a commitment.
RULE 5: Take action.
RULE 6: Aim for results.
RULE 7: Get your timing right.
RULE 8: Persevere.
RULE 9: Be caring.
RULE 10: Use your intuition.

RULE 1: Have a Vision

All entrepreneurs, myself included, love to dream – and we love to dream *big*. In our dreams, we visualise what we want to see happening for real and we imagine what it feels like to have succeeded already, as if that vision has already come true. Then we set our goals and objectives, and employ strategies to get the results we see in our dreams. Those goals and objectives will be different for different entrepreneurs, but what unites us is that we all have an engaging vision of where we want to get to, and we all take action to get there.

I believe that in order to achieve success, you need a clear and compelling vision of what success means to you. It's far easier to be and remain passionate about the future if you can visualise where you want to go and how to get there. Your vision is your destination. You'll need a map to help you reach that destination, which will be made up of goals and results. The vision is the vital part, otherwise you won't know where you are heading and your goals will be irrelevant.

To create a Tycoon Mindset for yourself, you need to:

1. Dream big!
2. Visualise your success as if you've already achieved it.
3. Set objectives and results-oriented goals that build to those objectives.

True entrepreneurs are driven by the pursuit of success. It is what defines them. That success might be measured in terms of greater monetary gain and the freedom to choose a certain lifestyle, or in terms of a sense of personal achievement, respect from peers or simple contentment. There are many ways of defining success, but a typical Tycoon will always be harbouring another vision of some sort, a vision beyond the vision he or she is currently focused on – a bigger picture.

TYCOON TIP: Aim high, think positive and make your vision long-sighted. Go as far as you can see, and when you get there, you will always be able to see further.

In fact, as entrepreneurs move closer to their goals, something very odd happens. As we perpetually visualise new and expanding opportunities, our goals shift too. Literally, as one horizon is reached, a new horizon is revealed. The truth is that success is like an exciting, addictive, adrenaline-fuelled drug. As one vision becomes real and the success visualised is actually achieved, the next idea takes root, the next vision takes shape, and the adrenaline continues to pump. The initial 'hit' of success becomes a driver towards the next 'hit'. Tycoons are highly driven, highly motivated, success-oriented people. If a Tycoon's vision is the destination, having set objectives, achieving success and reaching goals are the fuel that helps them get there.

So be warned: pursuing a vision of success is not a path for the faint-hearted, lazy or unimaginative. It will involve effort and sacrifice. It will involve effort because if you do not try, you cannot succeed, and it will involve sacrifice because realising a vision will mean something has to give. It's not easy. You don't tend to see entrepreneurs going on holiday very often in the early stages. However, as someone who has been there and done that – and who is still there – I can promise you that no day will ever be dull and the rewards on every level will be immense. These days, I take more holidays than I used to, but I still put 100 per cent effort into everything I do to make my vision happen.

TYCOON TIP: Focus on your dream achievements. Think. What makes you tick? What is it that you'd choose to be successful doing?

TYCOON TALE: WALT DISNEY *The world's media were invited to be present on the first day that Disneyworld, in Orlando, Florida, was opened to the public. Partway through the day, a reporter said to one of the Disneyland executives, 'Isn't it a shame that Walt isn't here to see this?' to which the executive replied, 'The great thing is that Walt has seen all this; he saw it before anyone else . . . He created it in his mind before he decided to have it built.'*

My Mindset

I created my business vision when I was just seven. After two years at state school, my parents, who, like all parents, wanted the best for me, had sent me to private school, even though they couldn't really afford it. However, from the minute I arrived I felt like a fish out of water. Consequently, I would frequently play truant and walk two miles into Windsor, where my dad worked.

I loved going to his office because it was the only place I could play my absolute favourite game. I played it every time I went there, which was often. I used to sit in his large swivel chair, push his papers around his desk (which probably infuriated him at the time), pick up his green 1960s telephone and pretend to be in charge of this big company. I would issue instructions down the phone to imaginary business people and pretend to send telexes (the fax in those days), handing papers over to a make-believe secretary. I would imagine this scenario so vividly, using all the props at my disposal, that it would seem real.

This was a serious game. I wanted to run my own business. I dreamed about it all the time. I visualised as a child that I would some day be a millionaire. I believed I could make it happen at seven, I really did. This was my vision!

Later, I would go on to set objectives and goals, and employ strategies to reach those goals and make that vivid vision real. But it is the importance I placed on the overall vision, on the bigger picture, that I believe has helped me to achieve success. It's the number-one rule in any Tycoon's rulebook – to visualise the possible, whilst believing in the impossible.

What *did* you dream about when you were seven? What do you dream about now? Being an entrepreneur is about taking those dreams and ideas, the seedlings of reality, and making them happen. It's about making imagined visions become fact, forging ideas into a real and tangible business. Whether it's moving abroad to run a business in the sun, setting up a lifestyle business around your favourite hobby or creating an empire, by having a clear vision you have put the key in the ignition and started the journey towards making it happen for real.

Do you have the Mindset of a Tycoon? Put yourself to the test. Visualise winning. Do it now.

TYCOON TIPS FOR SUCCESS
How to Visualise Effectively

1. Find somewhere quiet where you can relax and visualise in your mind's eye what you want from your life and business. Think big. Be far-sighted. Reach for the sky.
2. Imagine that this success has already happened . . . There you are, in your mind's eye, enjoying your success. Visualise it. Picture what you're wearing, who you are with, what you are doing, what you are saying.
3. Visualise yourself telling someone the story of your success, of what you have achieved. Make it real in your mind's eye. Now you are imagining what it feels like to have already succeeded in your chosen endeavours. You are painting a picture of your dream life and business.
4. Focus on all of this for a few minutes. Crystallise your vision.

Now you have a vision to work towards, a destination to plan a route to. Reach for the stars and achieve your full potential. Strive to be the best you can be. Commit to it. In doing so, your vision is closer than you may think.

RULE 2: Use Your Influence

Many unsuccessful entrepreneurs cajole and push others to reach heights they themselves are unable to reach, often with an overt stick-as-opposed-to-carrot approach. When you have an individual who runs their business with this forceful attitude, there is no staff empowerment whatsoever. This means the individual team member will never act on their own initiative because they're too frightened to make a mistake. The staff and boss become head-buriers and a blame culture arises. That is devastating for a company.

Bosses who lead by example are the most successful individuals. They're demonstrating exactly how to do it, why they're doing it, which encourages people to come with them and do their job well. The hard-line-boss strategy is very poor for the growth of the company; it's stifling.

Other unsuccessful business people take the view that 'If you want a job done properly, you have to do it yourself.' They assume there's no point in relying on others, as nobody will do as good a job as they'll do themselves. Well, a job is always worth doing properly (what other way is there to do anything?), but that job doesn't always have to be done by you. Delegation, learning from others and appreciating the key skills and qualities in others are all vital ingredients in the recipe for success. Perfectionism is a worthy quality, but it can be reached by using your influence wisely and harnessing the strengths others have alongside your own.

Tycoons know the importance of filling the gaps and weaknesses in their own skill set or business idea by finding the parts of the jigsaw puzzle to create the best chance of success.

> **TYCOON TIP:** Don't be so self-absorbed that you ignore the needs of those people around you or ignore opportunities to learn, share and grow.

Successful entrepreneurs realise that there is great wisdom in having individuals around them who they can rely on and trust to perform tasks better than they can. The reasons why are:

- Delegating key tasks frees the entrepreneur's time to do what they do best – namely to get on with creating more success by developing the business, building relationships and achieving goals.
- Sharing your vision inspires and influences people to do what is needed to make that vision become real. Transparency with those around you is vital in business. How can you expect to influence and drive your team in the right direction if you are not straight with them or do not let them in to share your vision?
- All successful businesses need business partners to move forward and grow.

'Our success has really been based on partnerships from the very beginning'
BILL GATES

Despite what the media would have us believe, successful entrepreneurs are very rarely one-man bands. Yes, we may have started out working on our own at the kitchen table, but, unless we are able to build a strong support group around us to help us on the way up, it is unlikely we will ever reach the top. The truth is, the ability to share your vision with the people who work for you and advise you is critical to achieving true success with any longevity. You ultimately need to get 'buy-in' to your vision from your team.

Many people who run businesses on their own don't surround themselves with other people. They spend ten hours a day cooped up in the office and think they have to dedicate every minute of the day to getting their company right. I think this is a mistake, because they end up being very narrowly focused. Even worse, they could be repeating mistakes by doing the same thing day in, day out. Instead, they should be talking about their experiences to other people in similar situations and discussing how to take the business forward. The learning opportunities from doing this are immense because networking gives you access to resources you didn't know you had.

To fledging and existing businesses alike, getting out there to network, share and learn is one of the most useful tools at your disposal. By networking, you have far more chance of using your influence to find out interesting market information, source contacts, skills and suppliers, and generate referrals and new business than if you keep yourself and your business hidden away. You will also get a lot more networking done if you delegate or outsource tasks effectively. People create opportunities and give you the chance to make connections. People provide links in the chain.

I used to network with like-minded individuals on the golf course, and would often play golf with some of the representatives and account managers from the mobile-phone networks we dealt with. This was a great way to build relationships and find out how we could help each other out in a relaxed and enjoyable setting. These days, I might be sitting round a table with some of the industry's best-known people at an entrepreneurs' dinner, with the chairman of the CBI (Confederation of British Industry), sitting opposite Gordon Brown, talking to Margaret Booth from the Department of Trade and Industry or, on the TV side, spending an evening with Simon Cowell, Paul McKenna or Gordon Ramsay. It's interesting, the kind of networking events and dinners you get invited to as your influence grows.

Certainly, getting an audience with people is much easier now. If I'd tried to phone the chairman of Asda three years ago, I'd probably have been pushed around their various departments. Whereas now, I could pick up the phone to Richard Branson, billionaire business-man Philip Green or Gordon Brown and speak to them – a great privilege. As your business grows, so does your network and so does your influence. You can help others to achieve their goals and have easier access to those who have the resources, contacts and knowl-edge to help you to achieve yours. Networking helps you to find partners, get advice, give advice, get contacts and supply contacts. In business, Tycoons use their influence to network.

Incidentally, it is important to make the distinction between 'influence' and 'manipulate'. Influence is about making sure that the people who work for you benefit from helping you to succeed. Manipulation, on the other hand, is all about 'me, me, me' and is never a wise idea. No one likes to feel manipulated or bullied into doing things. Taking time to understand others and their needs, then tapping into their values and motivators is a vastly underrated quality. Influence makes up a focal part in a Tycoon's Mindset. We understand the value in others, in our team and our network of business partners. It's important.

There is another important part of influence, and this can be put into practice as you build your network of business contacts and partners. The more contacts you have, the more you will be able to use your influence to help others achieve their objectives, by matching skills, knowledge and contacts with those in your network who are looking for skills, knowledge or contacts. By using your influence to help others, you will find favours returned, as you are provided with more knowledge and contacts in return.

A good example of this use of influence would be the opportunity I saw on the BBC show *Dragons' Den* to invest in Levi Roots and his marvellous Reggae Reggae Sauce. I saw the marketability of Levi as he's such a great character, a likeable guy with a huge personality. His product also tasted great. Where influence came into my decision to invest, however, was when I considered the contacts I have in my network. I'm friends with a couple of CEOs at major supermarkets. Knowing this made me believe I could help Levi bring his dream of having his sauce stocked on major supermarket shelves to fruition.

I was right. Levi had been trying for many years but couldn't get the doors to open. Like many entrepreneurs, he couldn't even get a meeting with the major supermarkets. The morning after the episode of *Dragons' Den* featuring Levi and his Reggae Reggae Sauce went out, I called the CEO of Sainsbury's. That same day, both Levi and I had a meeting, and, a week later, a contract was signed.

From that moment, my team and Levi together have moved mountains to get the product ready for launch across the stores and on the shelves in just three weeks. It's on the shelves now. Without influence, motivation, a great product and personality behind it, this result would have taken months, if not years to achieve, and may not have even happened. But we (and Levi) are hugely pleased it has. It's a prime example of what can happen by using your own influence, or using the influence of your investors, partners and contacts. The sauce sold hundreds of thousands of bottles (and still continues to do so). An amazing success, outselling many leading brands.

TYCOON TIP: Recognise that no matter how much self-belief you have, there are times when every entrepreneur needs others. As soon as you think you know it all, you'll realise you didn't know as much as you thought you did. Embrace influence.

TYCOON FABLE *I mentioned the counterproductive result of having a forceful attitude earlier in this chapter. Well, here is one of my favourite fables. It illustrates the strength in using the gentle approach to achieve objectives. It's the story of the sun and the wind.*

The sun and the wind decided to have a competition to see which was the more powerful. They would do this by seeing which of them was more successful at getting a man to take off his coat. The wind boasted that with his strength, he would simply create such blustery conditions it would blow the coat off the man. He started blowing an enormous gale, but, to his dismay, his blustery storm actually had the opposite effect because the man simply buttoned his coat and clutched it tighter to him. Eventually, the wind stepped aside and invited the sun to have a go. The sun simply shone brightly and soon it was so warm that the man unbuttoned his coat and took it off. The moral of the story is that sometimes the gentle approach can work wonders.

My Mindset

I started my first business when I was 17. It was a tennis academy. My main motivation for starting that business was because I wanted to buy a car. I was also intent on controlling my own destiny. So how did I manage to create a business at 17? Well, I first started earning money when I was just 11, by helping my English teacher during the school holidays. He was a qualified tennis coach and ran one of the most successful tennis camps in Berkshire. I would collect tennis balls for him, practise with his pupils and demonstrate shots. It was good for him and invaluable for me. I learned how to teach, motivate and encourage other people, and I had a little money in my pocket. I would spend weeks during the summer months being his assistant coach. (Well, that's what I called myself - he probably thought differently.) Having this experience at such a young age gave me confidence, and a real motivation to do it for myself one day. I'd been bitten by the proverbial business bug.

The youngest you could be to apply to become an official LTA (Lawn Tennis Association) coach was 16, and no sooner had that day arrived I was on the instructor's course. Because I had been coaching tennis for years, I passed the course with flying colours. In fact, I was confident that I would pass the minute I arrived simply because I had proved to myself through putting what I'd learned into action that I could do it.

That same summer, I started my own tennis academy, where I would provide tennis lessons to tennis-club members. Firstly, I negotiated the use of the courts at my local tennis club at weekends and holidays. I then created a flyer, including a tear-off slip for people to complete and return with payment to join the academy, and mailed it to every member at the club. Only £40 went on flyers because I printed and designed them myself, and £150 went on spare balls, equipment and rackets. I didn't really know the market that well, except as a tennis player, but I had a personal target of trying to get in 20 people to each lesson.

I was incredibly excited! About to start my A levels, I was running a small business, earning the money I always wanted to have, buying a car when most of my friends had bikes, and I remember that feeling of true independence. I was on my way!

As the academy became more popular, I had my first experience of using influence to pursue a goal when I asked one of the younger club team members if they wanted to earn pocket money by helping me. The value of this was enormous. I could coach far more people and earn more money. The value of bringing people into my business, teaching them and motivating them to be an integral part of the academy was something I learned at a very young age.

The Tycoon Mindset involves never standing still. It requires forward-thinking and moving forward constantly, onward and upwards. As such, the Tycoon knows they need others to build their vision.

TYCOON TIPS FOR SUCCESS
How to Use Your Influence

1. Use your skills to seize opportunities that create win-win relationships and situations.
2. Make the most of those opportunities. Be influenced to take action.
3. Learn. Never stop learning. Soak up knowledge, skills and contacts.

4. Put what you've learned into practice.
5. Use your influence. Motivate, persuade and impress others and get them on board.
6. Delegate tasks that are not the best use of your time. Use your influence to move others to take action with you.

RULE 3: Build Your Confidence

In business, we know it's vital to have a trustworthy and loyal team of advisors, but Tycoons also know the importance of what they themselves bring to the table. *You* and your people are your greatest allies, so you need a certain amount of confidence and self-belief to start a business and to keep going under pressure.

The bottom line is, if you don't believe in yourself or your idea, why should anyone else?

Tycoons often have a huge amount of self-confidence. This can manifest itself in several ways. For a start, it can mean that they will evaluate risk very differently to others. Their innate confidence gives them the ability to evaluate and test ideas extremely quickly in a way that often looks hasty to outsiders.

This confidence extends to all other areas too. If you succeed at something, it confirms that you were right – and the more this happens, the more your confidence grows. This is the reason why many hugely successful people have self-confidence in abundance. We've proved ourselves right. This success helps develop self-belief and the results can be very powerful. Some people think, 'I'll never be able to do that,' or, 'I can't do it,' and their lack of self-belief becomes a self-fulfilling prophecy and they'll prove themselves right, but Tycoons are different. If you believe you can achieve your goals and there's no reason why you can't succeed, you'll end up proving yourself right by making things happen. This will, in turn, perpetuate your belief in yourself and help you to keep on achieving.

It is, of course, important to get the right balance between self-belief and caution. It is crucial not to become overconfident, as this can lead to complacency and arrogance. Contrary to popular belief, the Tycoon is not an arrogant specimen. Quite the opposite. Confident, yes, but all Tycoons feel they are still learning. Arrogance means you think you know it all and act accordingly. The Tycoon knows they don't and is hungry to learn, always. Furthermore, Tycoons are flexible in their approach. Having the courage of your convictions and self-belief is neither arrogant nor complacent, but critical to success.

Don't race forward with blind arrogance; be prepared by minimising risks and learning all you can to maximise your confidence and your chances of achieving the desired result.

> **TYCOON TIP:** Break down challenges and obstacles to overcome each hurdle one by one.

So how do you boost your own self-confidence when you are just starting out on the road to becoming a Tycoon? Here are the ways I have boosted my own confidence. It basically comes down to two things:

1. **Gain experience, skills and knowledge.** If you are someone who doesn't have that natural in-built confidence and self-belief, then you *can* still acquire it. The first way of doing this is by gaining experience and learning different skills. Work for other people and become confident in a particular role – and then as many different roles as possible. Your goal should be to end up with a broad spectrum of understanding and skills, so you can feel confident about taking on any task.
2. **Change your perception of failure.** This is even more straightforward. Just don't acknowledge the existence of the word 'failure'. Personally, I avoid using 'failure' and prefer to use the word 'feedback' instead. In fact, I really believe that there are no failures in this world, only events that give you feedback. I see every outcome as having value, and if I do not get the result I set out to get, I take a look at the result I did get and explore

what it is telling me. I focus on what I did right and assess and alter what I didn't. This means I am better equipped to have another go; it also means I have learned something really valuable from a so-called failure that will help me in the future.

Failure equals feedback. To fail is to learn. In learning, we grow, we equip ourselves more effectively and go on to excel and succeed. This realisation is an instant confidence-booster to anyone who has made a mistake and learned from it. We all have. And if you know that you cannot fail, regardless of the outcome, you give yourself the freedom to have confidence, take the plunge and pursue success. Believing in yourself and your business and having the courage of your convictions equips you with confidence. Achieving your goals boosts that confidence and takes you on a journey on which you will conquer goals and achieve great success.

Learning is a business survival tool, an essential one. To paraphrase Darwin, 'Listen. Learn. Adapt. Survive.' There is no such thing as success without learning. Mistakes and failures (feedback from now on!) help you learn what not to do so you are better equipped to know what to do from that moment onwards.

Frankly, it is far better to try and get feedback (or 'fail') than not to bother trying and always wonder, 'What if . . . ?' With that realisation, you can make *big* things happen and learn an incredible amount on your journey toward your vision.

> **TYCOON TIP:** Remove the word 'failure' from your vocabulary and substitute it with 'feedback'.

If you want to be successful, you need the courage of your convictions, but you also need the courage to risk failing. Doing nothing at all means you'll certainly avoid failure, but it will also mean you'll avoid success.

As soon as you replace the word 'failure' with 'feedback' in your vocabulary, the things you say to yourself to boost your self-confidence immediately become much more positive and forward-focused. Confidence grows when it is nurtured and reinforced – remember how children thrive on it? Well, we adults are no different. When our confidence gets a boost, it enables us to shine.

The most important aspect about nurturing self-confidence is that confidence and self-belief are there for you, not just when things are going well, but also when things are going badly. It's important not to let obstacles, challenges or even the occasional mistake knock your confidence. Everybody makes mistakes. We are all human. As long as you learn from them, you use feedback to create a positive outcome. If you focus on what you've done right and change what you did wrong, you're further down the road towards succeeding and you will be better equipped with more specifics, more knowledge, enabling you to make more informed decisions. So do you still see failure as a bad thing now?

Ultimately, believing in yourself and your business and having the courage of your convictions equip you with more confidence. And if you know you cannot fail, regardless of the outcome (because it's all useful feedback), you can instantly feel more confident that you can succeed. Success will become your main focus. If you believe you'll achieve something, you are more than likely to do so.

Self-belief is a sustaining force. It acts as an anchor, validating your idea, proving its viability and gives you the self-belief to make it happen.

TYCOON TIP: Learn from mistakes and failures. Use them as feedback to know what not to do next time.

TYCOON TALE: THOMAS EDISON *Thomas Edison had literally thousands of attempts at inventing the first ever light bulb. When asked if he was tired of repeatedly failing in his attempts, he replied, 'On the contrary, I have successfully discovered over a thousand ways not to invent the light bulb.' You can be sure that he took each 'failure' as valuable feedback about what not to do next time, until he finally had it – the revolutionary light bulb. That was, quite literally, his 'light-bulb moment'. What will yours be?*

My Mindset

After setting up my tennis academy, I went to work for a small software company because I believed computers were the future. I set up a limited company when I was 19. However, I believed that in order to use my skills to seize opportunities for a second time, I needed to learn about computers and business before really launching forth with that company.

So, after six months working for a software company when I was just 20, I went to work for a company that built computers. I earned less from working nine till six every day during the week than I did when I was coaching tennis just at weekends, but I knew I needed to gain experience of computers and how to run a business in order to succeed in that industry. I learned fast, and, as it was a small company, I was given the responsibility of running the office. I learned about sales, marketing, how to build a computer, how to fix a computer. In fact, I learned as much as I could about everything. I call it being a 'sponge' – absorbing as much information as quickly as possible. Learning, soaking up skills and knowledge are, as I've said before, paramount to succeeding in life and in business.

This learning experience soon enabled me to create my own business, building, maintaining and supporting computers. Once again, I was putting what I had learned into practice. By the time I'd reached my 21st birthday, it had become a very successful business, thanks to me targeting corporate customers and one great account we won was one of Britain's most successful PR companies, Lowe Bell Communications, owned by Sir Tim Bell.

I really focused on giving them the optimum service, rather than trying to give a service to hundreds of other companies. We sold to other companies, but I concentrated on working with this company and that paid dividends. I ended up taking over all of their work. If they ordered a computer or needed any maintenance, they used me. I developed a great rapport with the main buyer, Bob Davison, and, although he and the business had very high expectations, we developed a strong working relationship. In fact, I really enjoyed working with him and we always did all that we could to keep our service levels high and our response to his requirements fast, often working weekends to deliver a solution. In just a few years, my business gave me the trappings of wealth: a nice house, a Porsche and a BMW, plus money in the bank.

I was only in my mid-20s, but I had secured exactly what I wanted. My vision had materialised. It had become real. When I was 22, I married my first girlfriend, whom I'd met at 17, and we had a beautiful daughter and son together. I was on top of the world. I had a business that was successful, a family and money, or so I thought . . .

When I was 26 years old, my whole business collapsed. I'd made many stupid mistakes. I'd been doing so well that I'd failed to protect the business. I hadn't bothered doing credit checks or insuring the business adequately. While I was living the life of a yuppie, swanning around in my Porsche with my portable mobile phone (hardly portable, more like carrying a phonebox), some of the companies we supplied went bust owing us lots of money. The final straw came when a large courier company who owed us a small fortune went out of business.

Consequently, we had to close the doors. My dream stopped dead in its tracks, and, a couple of years later, my marriage failed. I had it all and lost it all almost as fast as I had got it. I felt like somebody had just turned the light off to my world.

My saving grace was that I owned a small industrial office on a trading estate. I ended up living in a 12-foot-square office with nothing but a desk and a bed in it. I had no money, no car and, perhaps even worse, no hot water. Every day for six months I had to wash in cold water. I also spent a few weeks living back with my parents – it was a tough time. But even then, when I was right at the bottom, because I'd learned from my mistakes, I still had enough confidence and self-belief to give me the strength and the ability to turn the situation round. I'd created a successful business once: I could do it again. Tycoons never make the same mistake twice and I didn't intend to. I knew I had to commit to doing whatever was necessary to make success happen, equipped with more knowledge than I'd previously had.

TYCOON TIPS FOR SUCCESS
Confidence – How to Get the Balance Right

The lessons I learned from the failure of that business were
crucial to the success of my subsequent businesses, and I will
share them with you now. Even if you seize opportunities, make
the most of them and learn as much as you can in the process,
these are not the only pieces in the jigsaw that make a
successful business. I learned that to *sustain* a successful
business, it is also crucial to:

1. Avoid complacency. Markets change; business can be volatile.
   Confidence is paramount, but overconfidence can be
   counterproductive. The difference between natural and
   worthy confidence (a positive characteristic) and arrogance,
   complacency or overconfidence (negative characteristics) is
   that confident people know they don't know it all and have an
   openness to learning that arrogant, overconfident people do
   not have. Confident people aren't afraid to ask questions;
   arrogant people are.
2. Learn from your own mistakes and those made by others.
   Learn from my mistakes: protect your business. Get insurance
   and credit checks on customers, always. And don't put all your
   eggs in one basket. Spread your business income over a range
   of clients to limit potential damage to your own business.
3. Evaluate feedback continuously. Don't get so caught up in the
   day-to-day running of your business that you have no time to
   step back and check key areas, or are so busy that you
   forget to evaluate the risks.
4. Don't let overconfidence lead to over-indulgence. Don't spend
   money you haven't got by buying flash cars. Make money first.
   Watch what you spend money on. Keep costs to a minimum.
5. Feel your confidence flourish as you gain more feedback and
   equip yourself with more knowledge. Whether that's through
   failing or succeeding, feel confident that you are better
   equipped.

RULE 4: Make a Commitment

Tycoons know that you can't get away with doing anything half-heartedly if you run your own business. The truth is, becoming a successful entrepreneur requires huge commitment, both to yourself and to your vision of where you are going. You need to be aware of your responsibilities, be organised and driven. Commitment to succeeding is vital.

Remember, if you are your own boss, you will:

- Still be working when everyone else has gone home or, at the very least, still be thinking about work and the business after you've left the office.
- Not be paid when you go on holiday or are ill, at least not in the formative years.
- Need to optimise your time consistently.
- Need the ability to handle adversity and keep going against the odds.
- Not be able to blame others for any misfortune – the buck stops with you. Take action.

This doesn't mean you can never take time out to go on holiday, but it does mean that you will need to plan ahead and make sure your absence does not have a detrimental effect on your business. With commitment comes responsibility, not just to yourself, but to your staff, your customers and your suppliers. If you take time off from your business, you need to have the appropriate cover to deliver your promises in your absence.

I often hear entrepreneurs saying that they can never switch off. While this is undoubtedly true, the secret is to find something you believe in passionately and that you enjoy because then thinking or talking about new ideas, deals or other work-related topics after-hours won't bother you. That said, it is also important to find some work-life balance. This means you will need to make time to switch off, see family and friends, exercise and so on. You can be a committed Tycoon and still have a life. But you need to be prepared for some incredibly hard graft. Commitment requires good organisation and communication skills, so work on these areas.

> **TYCOON TIP:** Be prepared to work hard, take fewer holidays and struggle to switch off. Plan accordingly so you can make time for life as well as work. Set goals, even for a family holiday, and enjoy it when you achieve them.

The good news is that making a commitment can be incredibly empowering. My personal experience is that once someone has committed to do something, the simple act of making that commitment seems to create a momentum all of its own. True commitment starts at the point at which you are true to yourself and builds pace from there.

Vidal Sassoon once said, 'The only place where success comes before work is in the dictionary.' Indeed, Tycoons are in it for the long haul.

> **TYCOON TIP:** Committing to follow through once a decision is made is an invaluable ally on your road to success. That in itself will create momentum towards your ultimate destination.

TYCOON TALE: DAME ANITA RODDICK *Dame Anita Roddick is the founder of the Body Shop, one of the world's most successful retailers of cosmetics and related products. When she brought the Body Shop into existence in the 1970s, she decided to create cosmetics out of ingredients that she stored in her garage or had brought back from her travels. She opened her first shop in Brighton, England, with only 15 products and was able to finance it using the hotel she ran with her husband as collateral. Her products contained ingredients that women used in cleansing rituals that she had witnessed in her travels. She describes a woman's body as a canvas on which to paint stories. She was totally committed to social responsibility and wanted to create products that supported her beliefs. Customers wanted to sell the products, and in 1984 the company went public and spread franchises all* over England. Then Dame Anita empowered women across the world even further by creating the Body Shop @ Home to enable mums and women everywhere to sell Body Shop products at parties in the home. Today, the Body Shop has over 1,980 stores and more than 77 million customers in 50 different markets, serving customers in over 25 different languages. Its success has put Dame Anita's net worth at more than $200 million. She committed to a purpose and an ethos and was committed to change, to her staff and suppliers, and to her own vision and beliefs. There can be very few more committed individuals than Dame Anita Roddick.

My Mindset

If I hadn't committed wholeheartedly to starting another business back in 1998, I would not be writing a book now about the Mindset of a Tycoon. I wouldn't have anything to talk about. It took real personal commitment to do it all again, and even more commitment to build a £200 million business from nothing in six years. Committing to start up in business doesn't mean you can never take a break. However, taking time out requires effective organisational and communication skills.

A few years into my first business start-up, if I had to go on holiday with the family I didn't want people to know I was going to be away for two weeks: I thought I might lose their custom if they knew. As a result, I would leave my normal voicemail message on my phone. Sadly, this simply meant I was continually worried about how the business was doing and whether I was missing important calls or opportunities, so much so that I ended up being constantly on the phone. It wasn't much of a holiday for me or my family!

However, I gradually learned that the most practical way to deal with taking a break is to communicate with the people you deal with, so they know in advance where you are going to be and what you are going to be doing. People feel guilty about taking a holiday, but there is no reason anyone should. The only reason you should feel guilty is if you have failed to tell people that you are going away. Nowadays when I go on holiday, I still need to make phone calls, but I structure my day so that the people I am holidaying with know that I will only be spending a small set amount of time on the phone to deal with issues that arise. I let people know I am away and ask them to contact me only if it is something major that needs my help.

In the last 12 months, for the first time I'm now taking four to six weeks' holiday a year. The reason for that is I'm working even harder now, so I need to be careful. As much fun as I'm having, I'll just put myself into an early grave if I don't try to get some downtime. Now I try to take a few weeks out, whereas in the early days I wouldn't take any time off. Back then, holidays weren't just infrequent; they were nonexistent.

Now, because I've got even more business interests and things to do, I actually need a holiday. Also, I see taking a break as a positive thing to do, because I come back refreshed, with new ideas. And I don't stop when I'm away; the communication lines are always open. I'm on my BlackBerry and my mobile at certain times of the day, so it's like I'm working from home for a few weeks. It's not like I go away and put my BlackBerry in a cupboard and pick it up two weeks later. Even on holiday I do not switch off from my business completely. No Tycoon does. But I am thankful that I'm now able to take time out. I feel I've earned it.

You reap what you sow in business, as you do in life. By making a commitment, you will be rewarded in the long term.

TYCOON TIPS FOR SUCCESS
How to Be Committed

Commit to:

1. Your vision. Start taking action towards your vision as soon as you can.
2. Getting organised. Plan effectively. Communicate well with everyone, and ensure you can deliver on any promises you've made.
3. Prepared yourself for sacrifices, hard work and 100 per cent non-stop effort.
4. Your business. Always plan breaks in advance and keep your team, suppliers and customers in the loop about your whereabouts and availability.

5. Rewarding yourself and your team when you achieve targets. Everybody needs time out to recharge their batteries. Although holidays may be a distant memory in your first few years of trading, book yourself a holiday as soon as you achieve a major goal.

RULE 5: Take Action

Tycoons are big believers in the saying 'The early bird catches the worm.' You may have the best plans, the greatest strategies and the loftiest goals, but it all counts for nothing unless you create forward momentum and press the 'go' button.

Results are a vital part of the Mindset of a Tycoon and a key asset to all businesses. But you can't get results until you take action. Action is the bridge between your vision and results. Action comes straight after commitment. Action involves figuring out how to get from where you are now to where you want to be. What actions will you need to take? Where do you go from here? Write it all down. Commit your goals and actions to paper, and, in doing so, you've created a blueprint in both your mind's eye and on paper. That is the first step towards becoming extremely successful.

Your vision gives your goals clarity, and your goals are stepping stones towards your vision. As such, with no goals (or action) your vision will remain just that – a product of your imagination and nothing more. You need to take action to get results, and you need results to reach your destination – your vision of success.

And therein lies the reason why one of the Tycoon's most valuable tools is an action plan. A plan of action offers the Tycoon instant milestones to focus on and the goals they need to work towards. An action plan reveals the tasks needed to be actioned in order to achieve the result or get to the final destination.

TYCOON TIP: Plot the tasks and actions that need to be taken to reach your goals and make your vision real. Then go out there and do it. Actions speak louder than words!

When a Tycoon thinks of an idea that they believe is a winner, they act. They do something that 99 per cent of the population doesn't: take action. But they don't stumble forward blindly; they make informed decisions to act. It's the act of taking action that will separate you from the rest of the pack. By taking action, you commit yourself to starting your journey.

Remember, nothing happens unless you make it happen. Tycoons make things happen every single day. Initiative is a daily, even an hourly, matter. There are all sorts of things that require action. Many unsuccessful businesspeople procrastinate about taking action on critical matters. If you want the Mindset of a Tycoon, don't fall into that trap – take action today and do something that will change your life for ever. As Thomas Edison once said, 'Genius is 1 per cent inspiration and 99 per cent perspiration.'

Think about what you can do today that will bring you closer to your vision. Map it out step by step. Consider the actions you need to take. Done that? Congratulations, you're well on your way to thinking and acting like a Tycoon.

My favourite poem is 'If' by Rudyard Kipling. I was given a copy by my father when I was younger and it has pride of place on my desk at work. I hope you benefit from it in the same way I have. I have found it to be very motivational.

> If you can keep your head when all about you
> Are losing theirs and blaming it on you;
> If you can trust yourself when all men doubt you,
> But make allowance for their doubting too;
> If you can wait and not be tired by waiting,
> Or being lied about, don't deal in lies,
> Or being hated, don't give way to hating,
> And yet don't look too good, nor talk too wise:

If you can dream – and not make dreams your master;
If you can think – and not make thoughts your aim;
If you can meet with Triumph and Disaster
And treat those two imposters just the same;
If you can bear to hear the truth you've spoken
Twisted by knaves to make a trap for fools,
Or watch the things you gave your life to, broken,
And stoop and build 'em up with worn-out tools;

If you can make one heap of all your winnings
And risk it on one turn of pitch-and-toss,
And lose, and start again at your beginnings
And never breathe a word about your loss;
If you can force your heart and nerve and sinew
To serve your turn long after they are gone,
And so hold on when there is nothing in you
Except the Will which says to them: 'Hold on!'

If you can talk with crowds and keep your virtue,
Or walk with kings – nor lose the common touch,
If neither foes nor loving friends can hurt you,
If all men count with you, but none too much;
If you can fill the unforgiving minute
With sixty seconds' worth of distance run –
Yours is the Earth and everything that's in it,
And – which is more – you'll be a Man, my son!

TYCOON TIP: If . . . you can take action, you'll make something happen. You need to act now. You need to take action in order to 'talk with crowds' or 'walk with kings' or 'start again at your beginnings'. If you want something rather than nothing, you need to take action . . . today!

TYCOON TALE: STELIOS *Founder of easyGroup, Stelios Haji-Ioannou, a Tycoon and a good friend of mine, has always taken action in a number of* ways to pursue his dreams. Without taking action, taking risks and persisting, Stelios would not have launched 12 growing companies in the space of 12 years.

Initially, having sought out inefficient industries where he could rework the logistics to reduce prices for customers, he took action into uncharted territory to provide a budget option airline, easyJet, and take on the big boys.

He then realised he had two core assets: the 'easy' brand and the airline, so he took action to separate the airline from the brand by creating other companies with the same brand ethos as easyJet. He made sure each company he set up within the easyGroup brand was low cost for the customer. He outsourced distribution, gave power back to the consumer by letting them print their own tickets and choose to have less space in a hotel room for a better price, and went on to successfully establish easy-Cruise, easyCinema, easyMusic and easyHotel, among many others.

Finally, when a couple of his companies faced difficulties during their start-up period, he persisted to make sure they became profitable and made it through the hard times to become hugely successful companies. He took action when many less determined people wouldn't. None of his success would have happened without his ability to take risks, and, most importantly, to take action in the first place.

'You cannot delegate entrepreneurship'
STELIOS

My Mindset

Back in 1998, I decided that the time was right to start a telecoms business. It was a big risk because I didn't really have a lot of money to invest in it, and I was also earning good money working for another company at the time, but I instinctively knew the time was right because I had the self-belief and confidence to make it work.

So I took action. In 1998, after being employed for two years, I left the job I was in that had helped me get back on my feet, and within a month I was working from the same office I had once lived in. This time, though, things were different.

I took out a mortgage to buy a house and started to work for myself again. The first few months were very exciting, and within six months we were already overachieving our targets. I had a gut feeling that to succeed quickly, I needed to focus on something that differentiated us from our competitors. I needed to take action. It was a gut instinct, but I thought about only supplying Ericsson equipment.

I created something I called 'single-brand distribution' – supplying one manufacturer's product solely, but with the benefit of building a reputation of being the product champions. This paid off in a major way – not only did the company receive preferential treatment from the manufacturer, because we focused exclusively on their brand, but our customers received better service because we knew our product better than anyone else. Customers even began to think that we were actually Ericsson in the UK!

Our first-year sales topped £13.9 million and I was well on my way to making millions. I use this concept today with all our manufacturer suppliers, and our competitors have tried to copy us, which is the ultimate compliment. Taking action and making it happen was and still is a great asset to the way I live my life and run my businesses.

TYCOON TIPS FOR SUCCESS
How to Be Action-Focused

1. Think creatively and create a plan of action.
2. Build momentum. You will face many challenges in getting your idea off the ground; just be creative.
3. Focus on taking action on areas that will generate the best reward.
4. Talk to as many different people as you can. Take action and get on the phone. Go to events, network, get out there.

5. Learn from others and don't be afraid to ask questions. Seek out answers; take action to gain the knowledge and tools to proceed.

RULE 6: Aim for Results

Every Tycoon thrives on having aims, setting goals and hitting targets. We deal in results – undeniable, measurable, tangible results. In achieving the results you set out to achieve, you'll create new opportunities and horizons and widen the goal posts to enable even greater success. For a Tycoon, each time they achieve a goal they will build on those achievements to maximise their success. You should do the same in your entrepreneurial endeavours. For example, aim to improve the margin on your best-selling products and services or focus on a niche audience who are buying large amounts from you. Build, grow, leverage and optimise your most successful efforts for optimum results.

Human beings are conditioned to slot easily into a routine and stay there, but I find that dangerous. To be successful in business, you can't stand still. You need to be constantly improving. Some people say, 'If it ain't broke, don't fix it.' But it doesn't always work like that. You need to fix, tweak and change constantly to improve. If you decide something is working fine and doesn't need improving further, you can be sure that your competitors will be making improvements while you sit still.

TYCOON TIP: Set realistic goals. They have the best chance of succeeding.

Of course, in order to achieve results, it is important to determine exactly how such great results will be achieved. That means carefully planning the business idea and understanding the component parts that will contribute to a successful outcome.

For example, when I started Data Select, part of my telecoms businesses, I knew before I even began that the component parts to get right were:

- **Funding:** we needed to make sure we had the right funding in place.
- **The product set:** we focused on my 'single-brand distribution' concept (all efforts concentrated on distributing one brand instead of multiple brands) and making sure that concept was put in place effectively.
- **Operational infrastructure and systems:** a complete solution that would deliver end to end from processing an order to customer receipt.
- **Effective sales and marketing plans** with all our suppliers.
- **Focused market research:** we looked at targeting specific customers and uncovering who bought what, why and where.
- **Recruiting the right people to do specific jobs:** we focused on employing the specific people that we wanted from day one – from someone to look after our finance, marketing or sales, all of those areas were pre-planned.

I therefore devoted more time to these key component parts and broke down what needed to be done within each area before launching forth with the business. We had clarity in our goals long before we launched the business.

Everyone likes to set goals to work towards. It isn't only Tycoons or budding entrepreneurs who do so. However, where entrepreneurs win over others is in the energy and focus they put into achieving the result. The Tycoon is on a constant mission to achieve and always has something they are working towards . . . results!

TYCOON TIP: Be results-driven. Always. Having a clear focus on the results you want and a plan for how you intend to achieve them is a sure-fire ingredient of success. Resolve to get specific and measurable results and there's a greater chance you will.

It doesn't matter whether you are a sole trader or have a company with 1,000 employees; you have to be very specific if you want to achieve results.

Let's say you want to achieve £250,000 turnover over the next year. Now, that is a big target, and if you don't know precisely how you are going to achieve that, you will have a problem before you've even begun. So you need to break it down into smaller, more manageable goals.

1. To achieve £250,000 turnover in a year, for example, you will need to take roughly £20,000 per month, which is approximately £5,000 a week.
2. Then you need to start breaking down those figures further . . . If you are a florist, for example, you must start thinking about how many customers you will need in order to sell £5,000 in a week. It means you will need 200 customers (approximately £25 per customer) in a five-day week. That is equal to 40 a day, which means you need to sell flowers to 20 customers in the morning and 20 in the afternoon. If you are open 9 a.m. to 7 p.m., that is four customers an hour.
3. Then – and only then – you can start thinking about how you are going to do that. Perhaps you need to do some leaflet drops, or you need to start selling flowers via the Internet.

Whatever you decide, you have tangible, measurable tasks that you have to do in order to achieve the result you want. You have a map to guide you towards your destination – towards your vision. The secret is to break down the goal into small, manageable, comprehensible amounts and figure out the relevant result-oriented tasks to make it happen.

Everyone in my company is given specific key objectives to achieve, which we are measured against. Depending on their role within the business, this could be the number of phone calls a person makes in a day, or the number of presentations we need to make in a week, or the number of people we need to meet in a day. I make sure we measure the results consistently and frequently. Some companies look at financial performance weekly or monthly, but in my businesses we monitor performance daily and even by the hour. Some people may regard this as an exaggerated effort, but I think it is clearly one of the factors that has led to my business success. I learned that lesson from losing that first business, which has consequently proved valuable. Having a firm grasp of your figures, as well as the overall objectives, enables you to act quickly when things aren't going the way you planned. Speed in dealing with finances can be a business lifesaver. Logging, measuring and consistently improving results enable business growth.

The other reason that planning and knowing how to achieve results is so vital is simply this: planning for your success is as important as achieving success, because when you achieve success, you know exactly how you got there. This means your success can be duplicated, scaled up and multiplied, and it is that which turns an entrepreneur into a Tycoon.

TYCOON TIP: Set target dates for achieving your results. Analyse the results you are and aren't getting. How can you improve your results? What would it take to make those improvements?

TYCOON TALE: DONALD TRUMP *Donald Trump believes that in order to get results, you've got to think big and pace yourself. To get where you're going, develop a tempo that will enable you to get there. Chess players also use tempo, moving in relation to the number of moves required to gain an objective. Note that it refers to gaining an objective. We all know that chess is a game of strategy. So is business. Think about that and develop a tempo starting today. What are your business objectives? What results do you want? Which 'moves' do you need to take? Which strategies do you need to use?*

My Mindset

I have always aimed to get results. It is important to me that I know what I am trying to achieve and so I always write down my goals. Every year, since the age of 18, I and a group of friends have made a list of New

Year's resolutions. We sit in a restaurant and write down five things that we are going to achieve the following year. It might be to earn £100,000, or buy a new car, get a bigger house or learn a new skill. Whatever it is and however dreamy it might be, we commit to aim to achieve these goals. Some take it as a bit of fun (or so they say), but I certainly don't. Interestingly, the more we achieved and resolved to achieve, the more competitive we have all become. All my resolutions are about achieving success. They are very tangible, very specific and very results-oriented. And they always come with a reward if I succeed.

When I was 39, I said that if I achieved what I set out to achieve in 2005, then I would hire the whole of Necker Island, exclusively, from Sir Richard Branson and fly out my friends of over 20 years and their families (who I still see almost weekly) to spend a week in paradise with me and my family. Thanks to a lot of hard work, I achieved that goal and we had an amazing time. It was the pinnacle of rewards.

Even when my result-driven goals were more modest, I still wrote them down. As I said earlier, for example, back in 1983, when I established my own tennis academy, my goal was to earn enough money to buy a car. Once I'd got a car, the next item on my wish list was bricks and mortar. When I was 19, going into my 20th year, I remember having a resolution to buy a house. I achieved that resolution by the end of the year and was thrilled to be able to buy a three-bedroom semi-detached house in Tilehurst, Reading.

In 1998, I decided that my main New Year's resolution was for my business to achieve sales of £12 million. If I achieved that, then I would be allowed to go straight to Marinello's garage in Egham and buy myself a Ferrari 550. By April 1999 I had achieved sales of £12 million, in fact £13.9 million, and, needless to say, the Ferrari was mine, just after my 32nd birthday. I'll break down how we achieved such rapid growth in Chapter 5. However, in the meantime, it's important to recognise the value of having written-down goals that are results-oriented.

Goals that focus on specific results have served me well, and have helped to me regain success and sustain it the second time round. Results and goals have given me focus, direction and ambition. What will your resolutions be? There's no need to wait until the New Year to resolve to achieve certain results. Figure out what you want now, set yourself a target, commit it to paper and find a way to achieve it.

TYCOON TIPS FOR SUCCESS
How to Make Things Happen

1. Think big, but pace yourself. Develop your tempo.
2. Build a plan based upon the results you believe are actually possible to achieve.
3. Question your result-driven goals rigorously to test their believability. Make your goals and targets achievable. Uncover what your competitors are doing. How are they achieving success?
4. Work out ways in which to achieve those results and goals. Work out the 'moves' you need to take to gain your objectives.
5. Reward yourself and all involved in achieving results and hitting targets. Keep that momentum going.

RULE 7: Get Your Timing Right

What drives you to start your own business may depend on the stage you are currently at in your life. Timing is a very important aspect when planning and starting a business, and it is one that people often ignore. When I refer to 'timing' in this instance, I do not mean an opportune moment, I mean the stage at which the entrepreneur is at in their lives in terms of other priorities, such as job, family and available money.

The truth is that starting up a business requires enormous time, commitment and energy, and if you have too many other demands fighting for your attention at the same time, you'll be unable to give your business the best chance of success. Diversions or distractions, such as poor health or an unstable relationship, could turn a promising idea into one that fails before it has even got off the ground. Ultimately, your circumstances need to be right to improve your likelihood of succeeding.

So when you are planning to start your business, you must first carefully consider the effects it will have on your family. In fact, supportive partners, family circumstances and good health are critical success factors in the timing of your business, and you should ignore them at your peril. Be honest with yourself about potential distractions. At one point, my career and personal life had hit rock bottom, with me living out of my office and a failed marriage. But I had good health, and there's no better motivator to getting back the success you've previously enjoyed than being at the bottom. There were few distractions. I had no money, but I did have a very supportive girlfriend and parents who were always about for moral support. I made the most of those circumstances, picked myself up and launched forth.

You also need to make sure that you are using timing in the right way. If you are made redundant, for example, you might think that it is the perfect time to start up your own business. But if your confidence is at a low ebb and you are feeling forced into starting up your own business, the chances are you may be extremely unhappy and the business will fail. Conversely, you may have always dreamed of being your own boss, have a great bunch of contacts and feel you learned a lot during the job you've been made redundant from. In which case, redundancy might give you the push you need to spur you on and start that business. It could be the perfect opportunity and springboard to launch forth from. Only you will know whether your circumstances are right.

I have met many women who have given up a full-time job to have a baby and then decided that it would be the ideal time to start up a business. Now, for some women, they are right – having a baby need not be a barrier to running a successful business, but only if they passionately want to do it and genuinely have the time and energy to commit to it. The majority of new mothers will tell you they hardly have enough time to sneeze, let alone start up and run a demanding fledgling business. If anyone starts a business purely out of convenience, because they no longer have a job, then the business is unlikely to succeed unless they are prepared to make a lot of sacrifices. I've yet to meet a successful entrepreneur who hasn't sacrificed something – whether it's time with family or friends, their weekends or their sanity. (Only joking about the last one – honest.)

A business created soon after starting a family is most likely to become a lifestyle business (one that helps to pay the bills, but that's about it). Business is demanding, so are babies. Raising a child and starting up a business both require a huge amount of energy and commitment to be able to do them well. There are some that succeed at starting a business while caring for young children, but many fail. I defy any man or woman to try and look after the kids all day, run the home *and* establish a major business simultaneously. It isn't easy, so picking the right time (like waiting until they are old enough to go to playgroups so at least you have a few hours during the day) and doing it for the right reasons are vital to having any chance of success.

> **TYCOON TIP:** If you want to enjoy everything that matters to you in life – health, relationships, family and success – you need to take them into account when deciding when to start your business.

Timing is not only about when you choose to start your own business; it is also about market entry and making decisions at the right time to fast-track your success.

As well as being driven by their vision, Tycoons are driven by the needs and changes of the market they are operating in. This means good timing is part of a Tycoon's Mindset. They know when to act and when to hold fire.

Timing has always been a key driver behind the various successful directions in which I have steered my group of companies. Firstly, we started up at a time when most people would have considered it late to be entering such a fast-maturing marketplace, and yet we used this to our advantage: we added considerable value to our customer, network and manufacturer relationships in what was an industry first. We also made acquisitions with impeccable timing and entered and retreated from markets at just the right moment for maximum benefit.

Anticipating the changing needs of our partners has been central to achieving that result.

Timing is about:

- Anticipating the changing needs of partners, of the market, of your people and your customers.
- Entering or retreating from markets at the right time to maximise benefit.
- Focusing on core areas of business at a time when other industry players are not.
- Understanding your responsibilities and commitments and prioritising the things you must do effectively.
- Being realistic about circumstances, sacrifices and support. A budding entrepreneur needs to consider the life stage they are in as they start their business, and their additional priorities or considerations, such as family or health. Potential sacrifices incurred by entrepreneurial commitment must also be considered when planning the right time to start up.
- Considering effort and dedication. The amount of time devoted to core business areas needs consideration.

TYCOON TIP: Keep your finger on the pulse and your antennae alerted to stay in tune with what's going on in your market. Whether starting up a new business, entering a new market or targeting a new niche area, getting the timing right is key.

TYCOON TALE: DRAGONS' DEN *One of the people who appeared on* Dragons' Den *was a lady who wanted to start up her own tailoring business for women. Although her idea was good, I felt she had her timing completely wrong. She had just given up a very highly paid job and had a baby under 12 months old. Plus, she wanted to take from the business a salary to fund an equivalent lifestyle to the one she had enjoyed in her previous job. It was all too much, and for all the wrong reasons. I told her this and obviously didn't invest, although two of my fellow dragons did, much to my amazement. In fact, one of them said they would prove me wrong – on national TV! It is no surprise to learn that the* *business failed 12 months after the programme was aired and the dragons obviously lost all their money.*

My Mindset

My own experience in the restaurant trade illustrates the importance of timing. Like all mistakes, it's a valuable lesson in what not to do.

In my late 20s, I decided to open a bar and restaurant. Looking back, I think I thought it would be cool to own a bar and I relished escaping the real world. I didn't have much money, but I found a location that I could rent cheaply if I paid for the refurbishment. After only two years of operation, the business wasn't making any money. In fact, the business was losing money every week. I was managing the restaurant poorly, money was going missing from the tills, free drinks were being given out, and the restaurant, after an amazingly successful first year in the bar area, didn't go well at all. In fact, we hardly had any customers. The bar generated our income. It had already cost me a small fortune from the bank loans I took out, and I knew it was only going to cost more to keep it going. I decided to close the business down and concentrate on what I was good at – starting businesses I knew something about.

However, the importance of having a firm grasp on the market you are entering is not the only lesson I learned from that business closure. The importance of timing was also evident. At the time I decided to open that business, I was going through a divorce and I had children to support. The pressure was immense. I was concerned that if I kept losing money, I wouldn't be able to support my family. I didn't know the business well enough to turn it round. My timing was horrendous, so I had to make a tough decision:

1. I could spend the next six months trying to start up a business again without any money or income, and with a lot of pressure, or
2. I could bite the bullet and get a full-time job, which would enable me to keep on supporting my kids and build up a cash pile to start my own company again.

The timing and circumstances had clearly not been right, so I chose the second route. After two years of working for other people, I was eventually able to start my own business again and give it my full attention.

I now know that timing is crucial. It was the wrong time for me to start a business, especially one that I knew nothing about. By realising my mistake, I believe this is one of the most crucial decisions of my entire career. After those two years, earning a regular salary, building confidence, learning and thinking about my next challenge, I was able to properly plan my next business venture and gain focus with less pressure. I'd created the right circumstances, the right timing and learned some additional skills along the way.

As I said earlier, in 1998 I started my telecoms business (one of the key contributors to my fortune) and can honestly say I have never looked back since. This time, I made sure the timing was right. I persevered. I put the feedback I'd gleaned from my prior efforts to good use. This time, I knew about the competition and marketplace. I had contacts, skills and confidence. I had action plans and marketing strategies. I had a vision. This time round, I created a company that is worth over £50 million today, and I have interests in a further 20 or so businesses that I've either started or invested in.

TYCOON TIPS FOR SUCCESS
How to Get Your Timing Right

Before I own a bar and restaurant again, I will make sure I follow these lessons:

1. Research and review the local competition and the location to ensure that my timing is right. (Ensure the competition is not too fierce and the location has good footfall.)
2. Learn as much as possible about the industry and market to equip myself with knowledge and know when the right time to enter the market would be.
3. Take time to employ experienced people who are applying for the job at the right time in their own lives.
4. Take time to market the business cost-effectively.

5. Start the business at the right time from a personal perspective without distractions, but with a lot more experience.

6. Make sure the investment monies are available at any given time to properly cash-flow the business.

RULE 8: Persevere

Successful entrepreneurs have two fantastic qualities: determination and sheer perseverance. Tycoons know when to persevere and when not to. Most of the Tycoons I know, including myself, have all experienced failure at some stage or another, often more than once. Yet it hasn't stopped us from bouncing back and becoming very successful.

In fact, experiencing failure appears to act as a spur to succeeding next time. When I start a new business or invest in one, there is one trait that is always present – a determination to win and be successful. I will keep going when the going gets tough. Even roadblocks and dead ends don't discourage Tycoons. Tycoons learn to adapt and change goals and direction if necessary in order to achieve the success they want. Obstacles are there to be overcome. How boring would life be without any challenges?

For example, I persevered when we were becoming very successful with single-brand distribution after the first 12 months of trading, but I had to adapt it because I wanted to build and scale the business by bringing on other manufacturers, not just be remembered for selling one product. I needed a combination of perseverance and flexibility, so I adapted single-brand distribution for Nokia, Motorola, Siemens and Samsung. It was a case of persevering with that whole concept because it was working well, but adapting it slightly to fit the needs of my business, which resulted in it growing rapidly as a result.

Perseverance is about developing a keep-on-keeping-on attitude, while also flexibly adapting as you strive to grow and improve your business.

TYCOON TIP: Be flexible. The Tycoon has the ability to function outside of his or her comfort zone. It's not enough to do the same things over and over – you need to persevere *and* adapt.

Building a business takes time and hard work. The reason Tycoons succeed is because they act fast and push the boundaries. Tycoons refuse to take 'no' for an answer or give up. The Tycoon is relentless in the pursuit of his or her goals.

Making your dream come true is never as easy as you think it will be, and it can take years to develop before you reap the rewards. Tycoons go the extra mile.

Perseverance, sheer determination and tenacity are core characteristics of the Mindset of a Tycoon. Successful entrepreneurs battle against all the odds to build their business and always appreciate when it is time to get out, by selling the business, cutting losses or finding better management to take the company forward. There is a fine line between perseverance and being obstinate, though. Persevering sometimes means taking huge risks, but you continue at your peril if you fall on the wrong side of the line. Risks must always be highly calculated.

I believe that persistence is probably the most important aspect of the Mindset of any successful Tycoon, and my own. I will persevere and go that little bit further than others are prepared to go in order to achieve my goals. If it means working all the hours I can stay awake, seven days a week, 365 days a year, I would do it in order to succeed. It's a shame that this isn't physically possible.

In fact, I think my smartest business move was not giving up, because there have been times when I've created a business and things have not gone well. I could have quite easily just said, 'I can't do this, I'm giving up.' Most people would say my smartest business move was acquiring this business, or doing that type of deal. Well, for me it isn't. My smartest move in my business career has been a prevailing 'never giving up' strategy.

TYCOON TIP: Be persistent. Don't give up. Stay focused and don't take 'no' for an answer.

You need to have that persistent mindset from the outset when you are trying to secure your first customers. When you make calls to get appointments, rejection is common, but you're looking for that one needle in a haystack – getting a piece of business makes all those calls, appointments and rejections worth it.

In the thick-skinned Tycoon Mindset, there are only two ways to deal with rejection, and moping is not one of them. You either:

1. Move on, or
2. Turn it round.

Tycoons prefer the latter approach. When I hear rejection, I'm driven to make sure that one day I'll do business with them. I don't think, 'Ah, well, they're not interested, never mind.' I think, 'Why aren't you interested? How can I persuade you to be interested?' Break it down and make the relevant changes. I try and deal with those objections, because there are always objections. I'd then call back to tell them we've changed the product or service so it now fits their needs. It's worth going the extra mile to turn rejection round.

If rejected, I need a reason for that rejection. I never accept 'no' for an answer. It's not good enough. You've got to use your powers of persuasion to understand why that person doesn't want to use your product or service, so that you can learn from it, change it, adapt it, mould it and then get them as a customer.

Tycoons pursue an idea when others can't be bothered. They believe in an idea when others do not. They bounce back and deal with rejection when others don't. How do you respond to what you're confronted with? Do you recoil and move away, or do you take it on board and bounce back? How resilient are you?

TYCOON TIP: Be resilient. Don't dwell on rejection or lose confidence because of it.

TYCOON TALE OF HOPE *Remember these stories? There once was a man who tried everything to make it as a writer. He spent eight years writing short stories and articles for publication, but only ever got standard rejection letters in return. Then, one day, instead of sending a standard rejection letter, an editor sent a short note of encouragement, which simply said, 'Nice try.' The young writer was moved to tears and given new hope to keep on trying to write something that someone would want to publish. Finally, after many years of effort, he wrote a book that had a massive impact and was hugely successful. The book was called* Roots, *and the man's name was Alex Haley, who went on to become one of the most influential writers of the 1970s.*

Similarly, J. K. Rowling's first submission of Harry Potter and the Philosopher's Stone *to a publisher was rejected, so was the second one. Her perseverance paid off incredibly handsomely as the third publisher accepted the manuscript. J. K. Rowling has gone on to become the most successful children's author of all time. In fact, read any interview with any Tycoon, from businessperson to pop star to writer to sporting hero, and they will reveal their own experiences of rejection and persistence. In order to succeed in life and in business, you need to have a large dose of dedication and devotion.*

Every Tycoon has faced hindrance of some kind. Certainly, no Tycoon ever made it to the top without multiple rejection, failure or error. Apple Computer co-founder Steve Jobs made numerous attempts to get Atari and Hewlett-Packard interested in his and Steve Wozniak's personal Apple computer.

James Dyson never gave up either. It took him an entire decade of rejection before he got his product out there. These days, he's worth over £700 million. He once said, 'Success is made up of 99 per cent failure. You galvanise yourself, and you keep going, as a full optimist.'

My Mindset

In 2004, I appeared for the first time on television in what became the hit BBC2 show *Dragons' Den*. When I was building businesses, I never thought for a minute that I would see myself on TV. The BBC approached me about an idea where people pitch ideas to a panel of entrepreneurs in the hope of securing investment from one or more of them. It was supposed to be a one-off show for BBC2. Needless to say, within two years Dragons' Den had become a 'cult' hit show and one of the BBC's most successful programmes.

I loved the show and still do, but I believed there was a huge opportunity for a television show solely based around inventions. I thought it would be great to see thousands and thousands of people queuing up with their inventions ready to present to a panel of judges. A bit like *Pop Idol* meets *Dragons' Den*. The aim would be to find a great new invention, giving all those budding inventors out there a real chance for their idea to be seen on TV and the chance to win a million pounds. With this vision in mind, I had absolutely no idea of how to go about getting this show on TV, but I had made some good contacts so decided to use my strengths and pitch my idea to some of TV's most respected executives.

I first went to an executive producer who worked for the BBC, and, after presenting my idea, his feedback was that he couldn't ever see it being big enough to make primetime TV. His actual comment was 'It's OK, but it would struggle on BBC and probably only achieve two to three million viewers at most.' I was a bit disappointed, but didn't believe he was right. I knew that to have a hit show in the UK, depending on the channel of course, viewing figures needed to exceed 3 to 4 million. In America, they need to get over 8 million to ever have a chance of recommissioning.

Armed with this knowledge and passion for my vision, I decided to take my idea and pitch it to the head of commissioning at the BBC. It was a great meeting, but, in essence, he said the same thing. He thought it wasn't big enough and wasn't something for them. I was deflated, as I'd been rejected and knocked down twice.

I could have parked the idea at that point, but I wasn't prepared to give up that easily. I knew I had something. My intuition and research told me so. I believed it would work and had the courage of my convictions. A few months passed and I mentioned it to a few more people. Then I thought that the one person who might see my vision was Simon Cowell, the judge on *X Factor* and *American Idol* (America's biggest show). He was a client of Max Clifford Associates, the PR agency owned by Max Clifford, and, as his company handled our PR, I asked him to forward my idea to Simon. As a result, I had a meeting with Nigel Hall, who worked for Simon's TV business, and he loved the idea. He said he would show it to Simon the following week, as he was going to LA to see him.

A few weeks later, I picked up a voicemail from Simon Cowell, which said, 'To say I am excited is an understatement. I've got some ideas which I think could make the show even better but, more importantly, I think we could have a hit here in America let alone in the UK'.

Well, what can I say? I was dancing around! 'Simon Cowell thinks my idea is great,' I thought. I felt like a little boy who had just been told by his parents that he was getting an X-Box for his birthday. . . hand-delivered by David Beckham.

Within six months I had flown out to meet with ABC, the largest TV network in America, and, although Simon couldn't attend the meeting, I listened as I was told they wanted to commission the show. I couldn't believe it! My perseverance had paid off.

We hoped for a top-three hit. Amazing as it was, the show went out on 16 March 2006 at 8 p.m. and got 14.7 million viewers, making it ABC's biggest hit on a Thursday night for many years. Number one in America, it doesn't get better than that! We'll look at my TV programmes in more detail in Chapter 7.

TYCOON TIPS FOR SUCCESS
How to Persevere

1. Give yourself credit. You've already visualised your dreams, set goals and planned actions; you've made a commitment, so it's worth persevering with it.
2. Keep moving forward, always. Take action to get the results you want. Get yourself heard by the right people. Persist in doing so.
3. Persevere. Stay determined. Never give up unless circumstances dictate and you need to regroup.

4. Stay flexible enough to adjust actions accordingly when necessary. Sometimes you'll need to venture down a different path to reach your destination. In business, you need to be prepared to take a detour.

5. Believe and you *will* achieve.

RULE 9: Be Caring

I chose the word 'caring' carefully, because there is a place in every entrepreneur's life for taking care – of themselves, of the people close to them and of the people entrusted with responsibilities involving the business. Business can be ruthless, but, frankly, there is no need to be grumpy or greedy. Tycoons need not be tyrannical. In fact, genuinely successful Tycoons are far from the stereotypical ruthless tyrants (or dragons) we are made out to be. Yes, profit and success are key drivers, but people are the lifeblood of any business. Just as your vision is your destination and your achievements and successes are the fuel, your people are the engine that helps make your vision real. A great entrepreneur knows this and will never disrespect those he or she works with in any capacity, from staff and suppliers to partners and customers.

It is vital to care about the people who work with you – your staff and your business partners are your *biggest asset*. Tycoons know what their staff, partners and customers need and what drives them, what makes them tick. It is that understanding of people that spearheads success. So, yes, Tycoons care. Many want to make the world a better place, others want to give customers a better deal or service, but most of all they care about the members of their team.

In business, the biggest lesson I've learned is to treat others how you want to be treated yourself.

TYCOON TIP: Lead by example. Good people want to be inspired and want to work for good companies.

Tycoons invest considerable time, energy and money on areas such as training, development and incentives for the people who have key responsibilities in the business. In addition, a forward-thinking entrepreneur will take the time to understand the needs, wants, drivers, values and motivators of his or her 'key people', in order to treat and deal with them in a way that they know they are cared for. This attention to detail with people improves communication, productivity and results. Ultimately, caring about the individuals you employ begets loyalty and success.

> **TYCOON TIP:** Care about people. Relationships with people are key. Business and personal relationships should be cherished – your business partners or your best friends, all of them are equally important if you want to succeed.

Your team will only buy into your vision if they feel valued. You need their backing, so you have to earn it. You do this by delivering on what you promise, being honest, being true to yourself and being supportive to them. Feeling valued is motivational. Feeling free and able to contribute to the bigger picture helps instil that value. Therefore respect and communication are needed to ensure a caring approach in the workplace.

Caring does two key things:

1. **Caring begets loyalty.** It really is as simple as that. Caring helps to retain staff and build a winning team.
2. **Caring builds confidence** in individual team members and in yourself because it helps to build self-respect and self-regard. The more you give, the more you get back in return.

Part of caring about people is knowing exactly how to motivate and reward each individual member of a team. And this is what comes out of the analysis of individuals at interview stage. Everybody is different, and people are motivated by different things.

People aren't only motivated by the money that they earn. There are many different facets to why people are motivated to come to work: security, recognition, independence or work-life balance. Your job is to uncover what motivates the people you employ from the outset.

So many small businesses don't bother to properly introduce new employees into their business and throw them straight in at the deep end, believing they will just get on with it. Some people think that they only need to create this kind of introduction to their business when it is bigger. Believe me, they are wrong, very wrong. The first exciting moments for everyone starting a new job can never be recaptured. Having a well-thought-out programme of employee introduction that aims to give the new employee every possible tool in which to do their job effectively will enhance their job, performance and your business, and result in lower staff turnover and a happier, more loyal and productive team. Care for your staff and they will care for you and your business. It really is as simple as that.

Along with caring for other people, caring for yourself is vital as it means increased productivity, longevity and greater chance of an illness-free existence. So as well as having total commitment to being successful, you also need to underpin that with some solid foundations of healthy habits – such as eating well, getting enough sleep and relaxation, finding ways of dealing with stress and making time to develop fulfilling relationships with loved ones. One thing that all entrepreneurs have in common is the need for adrenaline, which is satisfied by the continuous need for challenge, goal-achievement and risk-taking. That means you need to make sure you have an appropriate exercise and nutritional programme in place to support this.

TYCOON TIP: Care about yourself. Make a conscious effort to keep your life in balance on all levels – physical, mental and emotional. One of nature's inescapable truths is that any extreme will at some stage need to be matched by an extreme of equal and opposite measure, so take care of how long you spend at any extreme.

TYCOON TALE: HOWARD SCHULTZ *Howard Schultz, who created the famous coffee shops Starbucks, said, 'Our mission statement about treating people with respect and dignity is not just words but a creed we live by every day. You can't expect your employees to exceed the expectations of your customers if you don't exceed the employees' expectations of management. That's the contract.'*

By taking care of the people who work for him, Schultz has created a more loyal and dedicated workforce and has encouraged a higher level of customer service. He has also saved the money that is normally required in that industry to attract, train and retain strong employees. 'My aim was to give our employees a vested interest in the company,' says Schultz. 'And that, I think, has made all the difference.'

My Mindset

Every business I have been involved with, and the businesses I own today, have a results-oriented ethos. I know that people need to deliver results in order for us to grow, so I focus on results. It doesn't matter if you are in sales, finance, facilities, HR or customer services, you must deliver the results-oriented objectives you have been given.

However, in order to help those who work with me to achieve results, I've introduced a culture that helps them to do so, and helps them to enjoy doing so.

Of course, sometimes the results don't happen and you go through tough times. Rather than just dismiss someone, I have often spent time with them, on occasions changing their job function to fit with their current mindset, whatever it may take to help them. Don't misinterpret me here. I wouldn't do this if I didn't believe in them. People without drive, passion and the determination to succeed, coupled with them achieving poor results, last two minutes in my businesses. But on quite a few occasions I have changed someone's job more than once to support them if I truly believe in them. More often than not, I use my gut instinct in driving this, and, so far, I have got it wrong just 1 or 2 per cent of the time, but, on the whole, I have been right.

Here's an example of a time I got it right. One of my employees had been head of a sales division. He had helped start it and had done a great job, but it needed a new set of skills and a different individual to take it to the next stage. I had that person, but I didn't want to lose a great asset. This person was very good, very talented and had been with me for a long time. I really felt that I should look at this individual's skills. His skills were coordination, planning, dedication and hard work, and he knew the marketplace and understood it, so I changed his role to look after projects. Subsequently, he became a project specialist, and he would head up and handle all the key projects in our business. The difference it made to our business was amazing! It meant that all our projects were properly coordinated and well thought through. They were delivered, he'd keep on top of them, so it was very effective and he was much happier too. We cared enough to create the right position for him. It paid him and the company great dividends.

TYCOON TIPS FOR SUCCESS
How to Motivate – Give Clear Direction

1. Take the time to understand what makes your people tick if you want to nurture loyalty. What are the real hooks and drivers for this individual? Think about what excites *them*, rather than what *you* think is an exciting way to motivate. What do they really enjoy doing? Focus staff on doing something they like to do that will also deliver a benefit to the business.

2. Have a well-planned, well-organised and well-written induction programme – something every new employee has to attend. It doesn't matter if it's for your first employee or your 1,000[th]; it is vital that you demonstrate from day one that you truly care about their success and have a clear plan for getting them familiar with your business.

3. Align what that person has been brought in to do against the motive and objectives you want them to fulfil. Clearly document and outline exactly what you want that individual to do. Give a clear job description and specific basic training in relation to their role. Then follow up to see how they are doing.

Send a strong message that you care about their well-being and have a personal vested interest in their success.

4. Motivate by giving very clear, focused objectives. Continually review ways matched to their character to drive them to achieve those results and fulfil expectations. People get demotivated when they don't have a firm understanding of what's expected of them. Match your expectation and theirs. Be clear. Be specific. This way, when an individual completes a task they feel happy they've met a challenge and achieved a goal.

5. Be personable and approachable. Chat informally to all employees, no matter how big your company grows. I genuinely believe a good CEO will talk and listen to everyone who has a stake in the business or the business's future, including all staff and business partners. Relationships are important to me and other successful entrepreneurs. Make sure they are to you.

6. Praise staff and say thank you. It's motivational. Show people you value their contribution to your vision.

RULE 10: Use Your Intuition

Over the many years I have been an entrepreneur, I have noticed that the role of intuition can be very significant in helping me to make decisions. Intuition is what we typically call gut feeling or instinct. Often, businesspeople give it little or no credence because of its apparent lack of objectivity and ability to be quantified. In corporate boardrooms, such a subjective topic is not widely encouraged or cultivated.

I think people are wrong to dismiss intuition so quickly. Whenever I have paid attention to how I feel about something, whenever I have tried it out inside my imagination, I have experienced a telling sensation of 'yes', 'no' or 'maybe'. We all get these sensations, but pay little or no attention to them. Well, now is the time to start noticing them.

Intuition should also be used in negotiation situations. Your gut instinct helps you know when to push harder and when to keep quiet. Intuition is when your mind marries events or feelings from the past with the present and creates an instinct. It's when your mind picks up on features it recognises from a previous event and gives you a sign based on that memory.

In nature, everything works on instinct. Every animal knows when to fight or run, when to eat or hibernate, when to procreate and when to sacrifice – there are no debates, no discussions, no caveats or conditions. It is totally in-built, instinctive, intuitive behaviour. Over the years, we humans have quietened our intuitive tendencies through our 'human intelligence'. Where we humans differ from the animal kingdom is in our ability to discriminate, choose, delay, ponder and question at will, but perhaps we have lost something on the way.

I encourage you to allow this intangible into the mix of all the factors you consider when making decisions and plotting your next success. It is all too easy to debate the merits – or otherwise – of a new idea, which can end up prejudicing the degree of success we experience. So if you are prone to a gut feeling or two from time to time, see what happens when you pay attention to them (and when you don't).

The way I do it is to connect back to the time I had that gut feeling and start listening to the messages it is telling me. I then start to visualise it in my mind, asking all kinds of different questions. Does it feel right? Do I know why? Does it make sense? You will notice that your body gives you a tremendous amount of useful, intuitive information. You might have noticed when you are about to do a major presentation and your stomach ties up in knots. When you felt passionate about something, you might have felt warm and open-minded and had those tingly feelings in your stomach. Body signals provide us with valuable information and are designed to let us know that we are having an intuitive moment. The next time you make an important decision, try and take note of the part your intuition plays and see if you recognise it. It is another invaluable tool and very much part of a Tycoon's Mindset. Practise using it.

TYCOON TIP: Give your gut feeling the airtime it merits when making your decisions.

TYCOON TALE: STEVE JOBS *Steve Jobs, the co-founder of Apple, has been incredibly successful and is a great believer in using intuition in business. He has been quoted as saying, 'Never let the noise of other people's opinions drown out your own inner voice. And, most important, have the courage to follow your own heart and intuition. They somehow know what you truly want to become.' One of his greatest product launches was Apple's digital music store, iTunes. When it was launched in late April 2003, iTunes became the first legal pay-as-you-go method for downloading individual tracks of recorded music. Music fans and the recording industry alike loved it, and, by the end of the year, more than 20 million songs had been purchased and downloaded from Apple's site. Soon the trade press was touting iTunes as 'revolutionary', 'groundbreaking' and a 'paradigm shift' for the market.* Time *magazine hailed it as the 'Coolest Invention of 2003'. Steve Jobs's intuition and abundant creativity are part of the reason why Apple is one of the most innovative successes of the modern age. His latest invention, the iPod, sold 18 million units in 2005. An amazing feat!*

My Mindset

When I entered the telecoms industry, there were a lot of service providers in the market trying to sell customers a range of services packaged around mobile phones. I knew that I didn't want to enter a market where there were lots of other people doing exactly the same thing: providing the same products and services to the same group of people and companies. So, in 2002, when I started Generation Telecom, I tried to find a way to be different. It is no good just doing something that somebody else does.

The market was overcrowded with service providers (companies billing airtime on behalf of the networks directly to the consumer or business customer), but there was an opportunity to acquire a business that sold exclusively to a specific industry: the rail industry. In fact, they had over 50 per cent of this market segment. Even the directors who worked with me didn't think it was a good idea, because it was a tough, overcrowded and competitive market.

The main question was the amount of money that we needed to put into the business to make the business work before we saw a level of return: it was going to drain cash. My financial director wasn't convinced that there was enough margin in this marketplace. There was low mobile-phone usage within the rail sector, as they didn't use their phones much, so the profit was small. However, this segment of the market was still large enough to target, and the company we intended to acquire had a large share of that market. My FD was concerned that we'd just be funding this continuously and wouldn't be able to make an annual operating profit.

However, my instinct said differently, and I decided to proceed with the acquisition. I knew that we could just get by on achieving a small annual profit, but the value of this business would be in the millions in a couple of years.

I can even remember saying at the time, 'In two years' time we will sell this business for millions.' I even said that it would be Vodafone themselves that would buy us. And that's exactly what happened because I knew exactly where the endgame was. I believed the acquisition would work because we would deal directly with a customer that relied on quality of service and I knew we could provide it. Furthermore, the contracts in place were for over a year and were solid.

I thought, 'The majority of people working in the rail sector have a mobile phone even if usage is low.' Also, because we had some large contracted corporates, I believed that if we focused on our quality of service, rather than increase our volume, we could sustain and then build a great business.

The rail industry, by its very nature, is staffed by many people who are continually on the move – so the ability to provide tools and equipment to exchange email, text messages with their roster, as well as voice calls in a cost effective way, backed by robust network connectivity, are vital elements to building great customer relationships.

As a result of that decision, we ended up as leaders in providing mobile services to the rail industry and, within just 18 months, sold the business to Vodafone, making millions in the process. Because I followed my instincts and focused on one area instead of trying to be all things to all people, I made a lot of money. I know it was risky, but my intuition was right and I am pleased it forms part of my make-up, and that of every Tycoon.

Tycoons take risks, but calculated ones. Tycoons do not make assumptions, but they do take notice of intuition. Trust that gut instinct – I do.

Of course, it's not only when making decisions about entering markets, negotiating deals or making acquisitions that intuition comes into play. It's also useful to use your intuition (along with other deciding factors) when taking on staff.

When it comes to hiring people, you must use that gut instinct. It's got to feel right. If you have reservations about hiring an individual, and your intuition says 'maybe' or 'no', you've got to take third-party advice or opt out of hiring him or her.

Mistakes are made when entrepreneurs are desperate to fill a role, have a gut instinct that the person isn't quite right but decide to hire anyway and deal with problems as and when they arise. Bad move. This means being unfair to the interviewee, and unfair to yourself, by putting unnecessary additional pressure on you and your team.

When all the analytical and psychometric testing has been completed (which is something we use to evaluate potential new employees), and you've matched the person's skills and experience with the role and expectations of that role, you ultimately need to ask yourself, 'Can I work with this person?' If you feel that you can't, you have to walk away from recruiting them, because there's going to be conflict. And conflict in a business just doesn't work.

TYCOON TIPS FOR SUCCESS
How to Use and Trust Your Intuition

1. Learn to recognise what your intuition is telling you. Practise using your gut instinct more often.
2. Use your intuition as your own unconscious perception

antennae. Let it guide you where to go next. Trust your gut feelings, your initial instinct to make decisions, and, when logic and intuition agree, you know you are definitely right.

3. Hear your intuition above the noise and data generated by the information age. Tune into it and better understand it.

4. Research to find evidence to support your intuition.

5. Use your intuition to understand when to push hard in negotiations and do the talking, and when to listen to the other person.

SUMMARY

You now know my Ten Golden Rules, and, to enable you to use them to good effect, I have created a summary below and some pointers to help you remember them:

RULE 1: Have a vision. Your vision is your destination. You'll need a map to help you reach that destination, which will be made up of goals and results. The vision is the vital part, otherwise you won't know where you are heading and your goals will be irrelevant.

RULE 2: Use your influence. All businesses need business partners to grow. Tycoons know the importance of filling the gaps and weaknesses in their own skill set or business idea by finding the parts of the jigsaw puzzle to create the best chance of success.

RULE 3: Build your confidence. If you don't believe in yourself or your idea, why should anyone else? Gain confidence through gaining experience, skills and knowledge. Change your perception of failure to realise that it gives you feedback. Feedback provides essential learning to help know what not to do next time.

RULE 4: Make a commitment. Committing to follow through once a decision is made is an invaluable ally on your road to success. Be prepared to work hard and make sacrifices. Commit to a common goal and make it happen, but commit to yourself and your health too.

RULE 5: Take action. Action is the bridge between your vision and results. Action involves figuring out how to get from where you are now to where you want to be and taking the necessary steps in order to get there. Without action, there would be no results.

RULE 6: Aim for results. Tycoons make things happen. They are driven by results. Planning for your success is as important as achieving it. You need to know exactly how you got there so your success can be duplicated, scaled up and multiplied, and it is that which turns an entrepreneur into a Tycoon.

RULE 7: Get your timing right. Anticipating the changing needs of the market and partners is crucial. Timing when to enter a market or not will help optimise success, as will knowing the right time and circumstances to start your business.

RULE 8: Persevere. Tycoons go the extra mile. Perseverance, sheer determination and tenacity are core characteristics of the Mindset of a Tycoon. Successful entrepreneurs battle against all the odds to build their business and always appreciate when it is time to get out. Try to have flexibility to work outside your own comfort zones in order to bring your dreams to fruition.

RULE 9: Be caring. Relationships with people are key. Business and personal relationships should be cherished. Treat people how you would want to be treated. Always remember that people are the lifeblood and engine room of any business.

RULE 10: Use your intuition. Listen to your instincts. They can protect you from making poor business decisions and guide you down the right path.

These key attributes are your tools for entrepreneurial brilliance. I am now going to talk to you about using your imagination, as it is this that fuels your vision – the first of the Ten Golden Rules. The next chapter will take you through making the best use of your imagination and creating a framework to use in pursuit of your dreams.

2

PUT YOUR IMAGINATION TO WORK

'Imagination is more important than knowledge'
ALBERT EINSTEIN

The majority of people live in a tangible world. They base their thoughts, their life, their capabilities and their ambitions on what they can actually see. I, on the other hand, live in a visual world, basing my thoughts, life, capabilities and ambitions on what is possible – on what I can do, on what might be. Not just what can be seen around me, with my eyes wide open, but what I can see in my mind's eye, when I have my eyes firmly closed. You see, Tycoons live in the realms of the possible rather than the actual.

As Albert Einstein said, 'Imagination is more important than knowledge. For while knowledge defines all we currently know and understand, imagination points to all we might yet discover and create.'

Einstein imagined what it might be like to ride a beam of light into space. The result? He discovered the theory of relativity. The knowledge he gained from his discoveries was immense, but, without the imagination in the first place, he would never have uncovered that knowledge and achieved those results.

Tycoons use their imagination more than most. In fact, the reason that Tycoons have such brilliant, money-spinning, industry-shaping concepts is because they have lots of ideas and act on them. They have mediocre ideas, bad ideas and fantastic ideas. The important thing is, they use their imagination frequently to create ideas. Lots! The Tycoon's imagination button is constantly set to 'on'.

I have ideas all the time. I believe we all have ideas. But only those who realise that anything is possible go on to make something from those ideas. Something we all know for certain is that, within the realms of our imagination, anything is possible. And that's where all successful entrepreneurs start the ball rolling – with their imagination.

I sometimes wish someone would invent the Entrepreneur's Mindset Imagination Recorder – EMIR for short. It would be a recording device that takes automatic notes when my imagination starts to go into overdrive. It can be hard to get it all down just using pen and paper, or even on to a Dictaphone, especially if my imagination fires up while I'm in the shower or drifting off to sleep. Unfortunately, until the EMIR, that's the way it will have to be. It's still worth the effort, though. Imagination is the greatest tool we have, and when nurtured, developed and properly used, it is potentially the most powerful tool in the world.

So how can *you* make your imagination work for you? Well, I suggest a very good place to start would be to follow these ten simple steps.

STEP 1: Fire Up Your Imagination

The first stepping stone on your journey towards success is to imagine. We all have the power to imagine. The problem is, not everyone knows how to use their imagination, so it often remains an untapped power. Yet creativity is seen as the single most important quality by many Tycoons, from Bill Gates to Sir Richard Branson. They favour creativity and imagination over any other factor in a Tycoon's Mindset. They know that it is ideas born from imagination that impact our world. Napoleon even famously declared that 'Imagination rules the world!' Creative thought is powered by imagination, and creative thought provides the key to unlocking potential. Without imagination and creative thought, there would be no books, no computers to type them on, no Internet, no MP3 players or X-Boxes, no light bulbs, no Nintendo Wiis, no electricity or transport. Frankly, without imagination, we'd all be stuffed!

Fortunately, then, it is not only the Gateses and the Einsteins of this world who have the capacity to imagine and create new ideas. I truly believe that everybody has an idea. Contrary to popular belief, I think British people are very entrepreneurial. We've all got ideas, but we're either too cocky and think we know more than anybody else, and fail to learn or test our ideas, or we limit our expectations and lack the confidence to believe in them. We don't take those dreams or creations forward, and we don't fulfil them. Tycoons, on the other hand, do.

Imagination helps you to blend calculated thoughts with feelings and visual expression to create what might be. If I asked you now to consider your future, to tell me what your future holds, you would automatically use your imagination to create a mental picture before you answer. One of the elements of a Tycoon's Mindset is this forward-thinking approach, creating a picture of perceived potential by harnessing the power of imagination.

Having spent many years actively using my imagination, I am now very adept at going into my own little world, and I can kick-start my creative mind with a few initial thoughts.

I remember on *Dragons' Den* when Imran Hakim pitched iTeddy. It was basically an MP3 player with a video inserted into a teddy bear's stomach. Whilst Imran was answering questions, I was thinking about how to improve his idea. Wouldn't it be better if it was detachable? That way, the bear could be washed. Also, kids don't always want to carry their teddy bear around with them all the time, but they do want to watch cartoons or listen to music. I also thought it would be great to persuade Disney to license cartoons and films via the iTeddy website and their own website, to Imran's concept. We might even be able to license iTeddy to Disney. I imagined the Web download for iTeddy – why couldn't we create a children's version of iTunes but for the iTeddy? I wondered who would sell it – I believed most retailers would, but would it be better to just sell it over the Web and keep all the margin, reinvesting it into the next version? What about the iTeddy family? A great idea.

Everyone loves the teddy bear, and to combine this with useful and engaging technology is exciting. You might think I'm going a bit overboard now, but this is how my mind thinks, this is how my imagination will take an initial thought or idea on a journey.

After investigation, I might find out that one or two of my ideas are off the mark, but you can see what I'm saying about my mind always being turned to 'on'. My imagination doesn't stop, especially when something sparks its interest. I'm sure you are the same. No surprise, then, that I actually invested in iTeddy and we are talking about how to turn these ideas and concepts created in my imagination and the imagination of Imran Hakim into reality. Together, we've brainstormed more ideas to make it even more exciting. We've used our imaginations to widen the opportunity.

Good imagination skills come from being observant, keeping your eyes open for opportunities and using those observations to fuel your imagination. Tycoons need a large dose of curiosity. Now, curiosity may have 'killed the cat', but, conversely, it animates the Tycoon. Curiosity rejuvenates ideas. It fuels them. Curiosity kick-starts the imagination.

TYCOON TIP: Be curious! Be inventive! Be creative!

You may be walking your dog one summer's evening and observe someone mowing their lawn, with sweat on their brow. You nod to them and smile. A few doors down, you notice another person mowing their lawn. 'It's the phone for you,' yells someone from inside the house, trying to shout above the noise of the mower. Those observations could be enough to jump-start your curiosity. It's 7.30 p.m. on a week night in the summer and you wonder whether these people have other things they'd rather be doing, from having a barbecue with friends to chatting on the phone or walking the dog. You ponder more on that. People generally think that having a gardener is an expensive luxury, so they cut their own lawn. So you question that further and your imagination goes into overdrive as you have an idea.

You could take on a street and hire a gardener for four hours to cut every lawn in the street. He might cost you £30 for those four hours, but he could cut 10 lawns. So would people pay just £4 for having their lawn cut? If so, you have created a viable business idea by observing, questioning and using your imagination. I might be slightly exaggerating the idea to get my point across, but I think you get what I'm saying. There really are endless opportunities to do things better than how they are already being done – the need for improvement is everywhere, across every market. There are so many problems awaiting solutions. Unfortunately, many people have forgotten how to use their imagination to its full potential and harness its power effectively.

It was my imagination that harvested my TV ideas and my observations about the telecoms industry and created Phones International Group. I can remember gazing out of the window one day, imagining what might happen if I went against the grain and pursued my idea. Now I've done just that. Our first order was for a few hundred pounds. Now the group turns over more than £100 million each year. See what can grow from our imaginations? We just need to water the shoots of our ideas and let them grow inside our mind. To have the Mindset of a Tycoon, you need to activate your own imagination, flick the 'on' switch and enter the realms of what could be.

TYCOON TIP: Be observant. Start practising using your imagination as you go about your daily life. Pause to ponder. Let your imagination flow. See where it takes you. Write it down.

You can also use your imagination to help you make key decisions by imagining scenarios. I did this when I needed to hire the right people to work for my telecoms businesses. I imagined my own interview technique. I pictured myself in the role of interviewer and then imagined the candidates that would be perfect for our business walking into the interview room. I painted a picture of the characters I would and wouldn't want. I then imagined I worked for a top recruitment agency and started questioning the inter-viewees on how they would do the job. As a result of this questioning, I realised that recruiting the best people for the relevant positions was in fact a full-time job and needed to be done by someone with the skill set to hire the right people. This momentary glimpse into my own little world created a spark that grew into a decision. I decided as there were already people hiring great staff for others, I would be far better off creating a recruitment agency that worked inside the company whose remit was to recruit staff alongside the key department heads. So that is what I did.

Imagination helps you to consider a multitude of possibilities very quickly. My imagination runs away with itself when I'm on *Dragons' Den* because there are ideas that make me think, 'What you have just pitched doesn't work, but if you were to change "x" and "y", this could be very exciting.' An idea often changes over time. The initial thought is only the spark that lights the flame and provides the 'eureka' moment. It is how to adapt and enhance the idea, how to create more innovative solutions going forward that keeps the fire burning, retains interest and makes an idea a potentially successful concept.

TYCOON TIP: Ignite your imagination by listening to other people's ideas or pitches, observing, questioning and being curious. Whatever fires up your imagination, uncover what it is and work with it. Let it stream like a movie in your mind.

STEP 2: Create Your Vision

'The beginning is the most important part of the work'
PLATO

Beginning with the end in mind is a rule that all Tycoons follow. And they not only begin with that end in mind, they keep that end result, that end vision, in mind at all times.

As George Bernard Shaw once said, 'Imagination is the beginning of creation.' It is from your imagination that your ultimate vision stems. And all successful people in all walks of life have a vision. Top athletes have learned to flex their imagination muscles as well as their physical ones. They visualise themselves at peak performance winning, breaking records, achieving their vision. Tycoons do the same. Both sets of individuals retain focus on their vision. In Chapter 1, you'll remember that vision is one of my Ten Golden Rules of a Tycoon's Mindset. Naturally, you can't have a clear vision without flexing your imagination muscles.

TYCOON TIP: Stick to your vision. Never lose sight of it. Tycoons are relentless in the pursuit of theirs.

Imagination is the origination of an idea. Your vision is what you have imagined and includes your dream of the successful result. Your vision is your desired outcome, so it gives you focus and direction, it gives life to your dreams, and, perhaps most importantly, it sustains you. In sustaining you when times are tough, your vision also makes you more resourceful than you ever thought possible. Indeed, vision is a powerful tool in any Tycoon's armoury.

For example, you'll find in any business that you set up that you'll need to go through walls and over hurdles to keep on track towards your vision. You'll need to adapt and be flexible, but you will remain focused on the wider vision, the bigger picture.

When I first established the Data Select part of my Phones International Group, I had a very clear vision. This was to become a top three player in the market. I pictured meetings with all the main networks; I visualised the business reaching its targets. And that vision empowered me to go out there and do it. Once the vision started to materialise and become real, I moved the goal posts, but I also adapted what had brought that vision to fruition. I then persisted with that vision by rolling out our winning strategies to other manufacturer and network partners. Because the long-term goals were so clear in my mind, I knew exactly what the objectives were, which gave me a firmer understanding of everything that would need to be put in place in order to achieve those objectives.

Your vision will empower you because it will trigger and sustain action. It will give you direction, make you resourceful, make you act and drive you to succeed. The vision is the very epicentre of the Tycoon Mindset, and, to succeed and excel in business, you are going to need a clear vision of your own.

Once you have fired up your imagination by observing, listening and questioning, you need to create a solid starting point to give your idea a presence. Do this by using visual stimuli. I often use colour to get started. Think about the colour of your idea, be it a brand, product or service. Imagine the brand name and personality. Give it a colour and a description. What does your product or service look, sound, smell, taste and feel like? You need to be able to see, hear and touch your idea to really paint your vision.

Whether you jot down your idea in words, draw pictures or sketches or record an audio description, your imagination will come into play and create a vision in your mind's eye. But you need to give yourself time to paint a mental picture of where you are headed. Running a business is an incredibly busy life, but it is important to make time to visualise your goals and picture yourself and your team achieving them. Picture your idea working; picture your own success. Draw it, describe it and get into it. That way, you'll have a far better idea of where you are headed, why you are headed there and what you need to do to get there.

Tycoons act on what they see and add to it by visualising. Practise working on and fine-tuning your vision regularly. Can you picture yourself five years from now dashing out to meet a delivery lorry containing your brand-new product line? Can you see your shop? Picture the décor, the products and the people? Capture the vibe, the personality and the aura of what you see, focus in on the details – the smiles as your customers leave your store, the plans on the table for an extension, then the move to larger premises, the networking dinner with the head honchos of your dream client company. Visualise it, use as much mental imagery as you can, bring it to life and dip into it throughout your entrepreneurial journey.

> **TYCOON TIP:** Harness the power of mental imagery to paint your vision.

STEP 3: Understand the Difference Between Imagination and Fantasy

> *'No idea is so outlandish that it should not be considered with a searching but at the same time steady eye'*
> WINSTON CHURCHILL

My imagination is my own private playroom where I can do what I please, where the only rules are my rules. However, it's not a complete fantasyland. Imagination and fantasy are, in my thinking, two completely different states of mind.

- Fantasy is often beyond the realms of the possible.
- Imagination is well within the realms of the possible.

That doesn't mean to say that ideas that seem completely outlandish at first should be disregarded. However, they need attention, they need to be questioned, and, in order to make them happen, they need to be possible. As Churchill says, keep a 'searching' yet 'steady eye' on your idea to make sure it is doable.

Ideas harvested by the imagination must be probable, rather than total fantasy; believable, rather than unlikely. I often say, 'For a dream to become reality, make it real enough to believe in.' So let your imagination run freely, without constraint, but still have viability in mind.

In the lair of the Dragons' Den, you can often hear me say, 'That's just pure fantasy,' usually to an entrepreneur who is not keeping their idea within the realms of the possible or has valued their business beyond all realms of reasonable possibilities.

As you'll have discovered in Chapter 1, I've been actively using my imagination to create a vision since I was seven years old, when I would cultivate my dream of running a multi-million-pound company by spending hours sitting in my father's leather swivel chair imagining my future. All of my friends at the time were pretending to be cowboys or spacemen or superheroes. Now I own my own company, yet none of those friends are busy riding horses across the plains of Colorado or flying to the moon. Their imaginations took them to a fantasyland. Mine took me to a world of possibilities within the realms of the actual.

It is when our imagination is able to hold on to beliefs that make total sense that we are able to take things to a higher level and move up a gear. We get more and more wrapped up in our idea and start imagining ever greater possibilities to make the idea even more real.

At the same time, having an idea that is believable gives you an incredible advantage because it means you think you can achieve it. A believable idea gives you the courage of your convictions, fuels self-belief and confidence. If you can truly imagine and believe in each stage of the journey to success, you'll be unwavering in your determination to get there.

I had two dreams as a child: one was to run my own business, the other was to become a tennis champion. In interviews, I'm often asked what I'd be doing now if I wasn't a successful entrepreneur. My answer is this: 'I would have been the world's number-one tennis player, without question. I dreamed about it. I've played against Björn Borg many times in my dreams and beat him.'

I chose the most probable of my two 'big picture' dreams. And I'm fortunate enough to be able to continue my tennis hobby and often play with GMTV presenter Andrew Castle, a good friend of mine, who used to be the UK's number one. I followed the most achievable path, but I've still enjoyed getting as close as possible to my tennis dream too.

There is nothing wrong with letting your imagination run wild, but you need to keep it within the bounds of reality. Our dreams will carry us amazingly long distances. To shut down this important aspect of the entrepreneurial mind is like closing our eyes to a whole new world of possibilities. But beware of straying from imagination to fantasy, as this can lead to confusion and disaster. Pursuing an unachievable vision is not wise.

> **TYCOON TIP:** For a dream to become reality, make it real enough to believe in.

STEP 4: Find the Missing Pieces

The best way to create a believable idea using your imagination is to find the missing pieces that will validate it and give it credibility. You'll have heard the phrase 'That idea is full of holes' used when a seemingly winning idea has some elements that need further thought. All new ideas need links in the chain that are missing completely. It's about finding the missing pieces in the jigsaw and putting them together in your mind.

There are also those times when the idea we have had is – in our own humble opinion – just too good to have any flaws whatsoever. Sometimes we can love our own idea so much that even the obvious cons to balance out all those pros are completely invisible to our optimistic eyes. That's why we need to rein it in and step back to re-evaluate and assess the idea with fresh eyes.

Entrepreneurs know when to stand back and review their ideas objectively. It's vital to appraise ideas honestly. A common mistake is to believe there are no flaws in an idea whatsoever, which often means missing obvious problematic areas. There will be links in the chain to fix and potential problems to smooth over, no matter how winning the idea is.

A good entrepreneur knows this, seeks out the missing pieces and focuses on the weaknesses of the idea as well as the strengths before fine-tuning the idea and proceeding. Once you've incubated your idea and used your imagination to illuminate it, you need to verify and validate it. It's time to reinvent your idea, play around with it and engage with it. Let the idea drift around your mind. Feel it grow. Seek out feedback and criticism.

TYCOON TIP: Immerse yourself in your idea. Put it under the spot-light, synthesise, question. Look for alternative possibilities and other ways of doing things.

Stepping back to filter information also helps to imagine the bigger picture and create this image in your mind's eye. For example, your imagination may drive you to think about up-selling (creating complementary additional related products, often more expensive, to sell to existing or new customers for repeat custom). You might imagine licensing and franchising possibilities or revenue-share potential. Think big. Who could you partner with on a revenue-share deal? How might you cut out the middleman? Where could you take this idea? The sky's the limit.

Now you've considered all the possibilities and angles, and have plugged into your imagination to take the idea forward, you need to take on the dual role of researcher and critic. View your idea not through the eyes of its creator, as you'd ordinarily do, but from a different perspective or range of different perspectives.

Standing back and really thinking about an idea we have had in realistic terms is an important skill. When we do this, we can appraise our ideas with more impartiality and fairness and provide our own honest feedback. If we do this properly, we are then at the vital first base of criticism that is so important for ironing out any initial glitches. At the same time, we will also see the missing pieces of our ideas coming together and linking up. If our idea is to stand up to scrutiny and become a success, we need to spend as much time thinking about its weaknesses as its strengths.

You need to organise backwards from your vision. When I make decisions about taking ideas forward, or about anything else for that matter, I'll seek out any missing links.

I like all the facts in front of me. I like them presented. I like to understand them. I like to know all the risks. I like to evaluate them. I like to know what the opportunity is. Once that information is there for me, I like to carry out a mental SWOT (strengths, weaknesses, opportunities and threats) analysis. So I ask myself, What are the strengths of this opportunity? What could we lose? What are the risks? What are the weaknesses in the idea that could break all this down and make this fail? I counterbalance my thoughts until the opportunity and reward outweigh the risk. In order to get to this point, as well as imagination, I need knowledge, research and facts. Tycoons need to make informed decisions; indeed, these are the only kind of decisions that Tycoons will make.

> **TYCOON TIP:** Tinker with your idea, investigate it, get a real insight into its strengths and weaknesses, opportunities and threats. Uncover the missing pieces and fit them together in your mind. Make all your decisions informed and calculated in this way.

STEP 5: Relish Your Freedom

True freedom is just a short mind-step away! It's as simple as closing our eyes and letting our dreams call the tune for a while. Normally, at the time we are trying to start or build a business, there is very little true freedom we can experience. It is a time when we are likely to be working long hours on our plans and ideas, experiencing stress and constantly trying to get other people – customers, employees, financiers and loved ones – to support our plans.

So, at a time when freedom is a real luxury, how magnificent that we can create our own freedom in a few spare minutes, simply by daydreaming. We really can escape to a place that can help us move forward. Imagination not only strengthens your creative abilities, it helps bring peace and escapism to a hectic existence.

Our imagination is a haven where we can shake off everything that's holding us back in the 'real' world and evaluate things from a perspective all of our own making. It's a place you can set your mind free from constraints and perceptions based on reality. Daydreaming helps you to let your imagination soar. Daydreams nourish the imagination. Daydreams are a combination of memory, intuition and imagination that take us on adventures, help us to find solutions and create fresh ideas.

> **TYCOON TIP:** Take time to reflect, to drift. Make space to daydream in your life and ignore anyone who mocks you. They will not be mocking when you are at the top of your game.

J. K. Rowling sat daydreaming on a stationary train between Manchester and London. 'All of a sudden, the idea for Harry just appeared in my mind's eye,' recalls Rowling. 'I have never been so excited by an idea.'

That seed of an idea sewn by her imagination has made her millions and has made the Harry Potter series of books the most successful children's book series ever.

We all daydream. Ninety-six per cent of us do it, according to research. For many, however, daydreams simply occur when thinking about something else. People get lost in their own little world, before something snaps them back to reality and they carry on with whatever they were doing. Their daydream, which gave them the freedom to escape life for a few moments, ironically remains trapped in their mind, extinguished by the lack of attention, or the lack of time to dream.

The Tycoon Mindset has instead learned to keep hold of those moments and capitalise on them. They consider what they were just thinking about and tap into those thoughts, both conscious and unconscious, to provide a rich source of imagery and ideas, fresh perspectives and connections.

What's more, the great thing about daydreams is that, unlike night dreams, they are controllable. They can be played, paused and replayed like mini movies or show reels; they can be built upon and developed. It is how you respond to your daydreams that is important.

Free thinking is vital in business. Daydreaming is good. Ideas are the seedlings of reality, which need to be sown and nurtured into real, living, breathing enterprises. The great thing about our imagination is that normal rules do not apply, so an idea can be sown, nurtured and reach full-grown maturity within seconds. This is real freedom to let your idea 'breathe'.

Imagination helps you to open doors of discovery and find fulfilment as a result.

STEP 6: Embrace Change and Learning

Tycoons exceed expectations and continuously think outside of the box. They don't just accept that this is how it is; they originate change. They are leaders rather than followers, and this allows them to innovate, to conceive alternatives.

We meet change constantly in every aspect of our lives, at home and at work. Yes, we can attempt to avoid it or pretend that it's not there, but these actions simply delay an inevitable process. Indeed, change is something to be vigorously embraced because it is a catalyst for success. And by the same token, those who readily accept change in business and go with it are likely to be more successful.

Welcoming change is all about having an open mind, and an open mind is key to using your imagination effectively to consider the possibilities that change can bring. So how does this relate to the entrepreneur? Well, it is the entrepreneur who makes change happen.

Low-cost airlines, for example, were certainly a great business idea involving change. There are many brands operating in this field now, but it took an entrepreneur's imagination – that of Stelios – to seize the moment and offer no-frills cheap flights to a variety of popular destinations and challenge the norms of conventional air travel.

And how about coffee shops? They've been around for years, but it took someone with a finger on the pulse of popular culture and an eye for an opportunity to create a global brand and chain of outlets like Starbucks. Anita Roddick changed the face of the cosmetics industry and helped blow the whistle on animal testing.

Sir Richard Branson has turned many industries on their head by challenging the status quo and improving on it. Evidently, Tycoons not only embrace change; they create and build it.

The era of the Internet and the dot-com boom has certainly helped accelerate this. The Internet has changed the way we work, shop, locate and present information. In the process, it has given people a whole new power, especially those with an eye for a business idea.

For example, ideas as simple as Amazon and eBay are shining examples of what can be done by entrepreneurs embracing and spearheading change. The founders of Amazon imagined a virtual world where people could buy books online. They pictured those customers being able to see similar books, search by subject or author, upload their own comments and even 'search inside' books before they bought them. They imagined changing the book industry and they made it happen. All it takes is a willingness to use your imagination, and a willingness to embrace change.

So how do you embrace change? Well, the more you learn, the more flexible and adaptable you become, so learning is core to this change-embracing mindset. Tycoons are resilient, curious, imaginative and motivated. But above all they love to learn.

The more we input through listening, learning and adapting, the more we are able to output through creativity, action and survival. This impact that learning has on the Mindset of a Tycoon is actually scientifically proven. Neuro-scientists have discovered that the human brain changes while it is learning, something they define as 'plasticity'. This means that new neural pathways are created by our brain every time we learn something new, and those neural pathways enable us to make connections we have not made before.

So, in learning, we are helping ourselves find new ways to make things happen. Learning makes that process easier; it opens up new possibilities and is therefore a crucial tool in embracing and creating change.

TYCOON TIP: Change can only come about if you are prepared to question everything. Get out there, observe and start asking questions. Be inquisitive. Allow yourself time to dream, question and learn.

STEP 7: Give Your Idea Substance

The new economy of knowledge has ideas as its currency. Intellectual property has become more valuable than physical property. But all great and valuable ideas need substance.

In our mind's eye, we can start to construct our idea to see exactly what the possibilities are, so that our idea becomes something we can see, touch, feel and interact with. Later, I will show you how we can take this up a level to create a simulator using our imagination, but first we need to build the actual physical idea in our heads.

Immerse yourself in your idea. Create an engaging vision and give it substance. Consider the following:

- Does your idea have energy? Does it have its own driving force to push it forward and pick up pace?
- Are you passionate about your idea? Explain why this is so to yourself. Imagine yourself telling others about your idea. What adjectives and verbs would you use to describe it?
- Have you visualised the possible, the probable, rather than the improbable?
- What is the purpose of your idea? What are the benefits to the end-user?

You just need to find an opening in your idea for your imagination to get in, so that you can breathe some virtual life into it and give it some shape, mass, presence and make it tangible. If the use of colour doesn't work for you, then try this exercise.

Imagine you are the head of sales in a pretend company and are about to present the idea to the sales team. There you are with your PowerPoint presentation at the ready, standing before your top 50 national salespeople. They are hungry to earn more commission, and they are desperate for you to unveil this grand new idea for them to sell, which will make them the most successful salespeople on the planet. Start your imaginary pitch . . .

Imagine all those faces. Put some personalities in there from real situations you have encountered in your past. Picture the most inquisitive person you know and place them in the audience. Give an imaginary pitch. Imagine that person standing up and asking a difficult question.

Feel your idea take shape as you explain it to them, overcoming objections as you go. 'Isn't there something similar on the market?' you imagine them asking. 'Well, actually, no, not like this because . . .' 'But why will customers buy this instead of xyz?' they ask. Imagine your answers. If you've given your idea substance, these will come relatively easy. If they don't, go and find out the answers.

Communicate why there's a need for your idea, what problems it solves and why. Talk about the brand, the personality of that brand, the overall vision and purpose. Uncover and answer all the difficult questions. Make it real in your mind's eye. Uncover the appeal of your idea. This appeal factor will become the catalyst for creating interest within the marketplace, so it must exist, and your imagination can help you uncover the strengths and weaknesses of your idea.

TYCOON TIP: Don't become disheartened if you don't instantly find the key to unlock your imagination. It is there; you just have to keep looking. Objections and obstacles are challenges and are there to be overcome. Tackle each objection your imagination brings out, and, in doing so, your idea will become more realistic.

STEP 8: Feel the Power

Remember we looked earlier at the importance of analysing SWOT (strengths, weaknesses, opportunities and threats) when using your imagination to make a decision? Well, this applies to launch forth with your ideas, because until you are prepared, you can't feel the real optimum power of your idea. Only once strengths have been polished and weaknesses have been smoothed over can you embrace the full power of your idea and drive it forward.

I use a gladiator analogy within my own company. I tell my people to imagine they are a gladiator and are about to walk out into the middle of a Coliseum-type arena in front of a baying and demanding crowd (the market) and face ferocious lions (the stiffest of competitors). You would not take those first steps into the arena until you are confident beyond measure in yourself and what you have to offer. You will make sure you have all the tools at your disposal, finely honed and crafted so that no matter what you face, you are as prepared as you can be. You are armoured to the hilt because you have done your homework and undertaken detailed planning. You have no Achilles heel because you have quantified and analysed the risks and have strategies to overcome them. You can feel the power of being well equipped.

Imagine winning. That is the Tycoon Mindset. If you can imagine this and believe deep down that you are ready to be a winner and that you can win, then you will have greatness. You have the greatness that is needed to take on the world and be the best in your class. Simply taking this journey into your imagination and putting yourself in this position will help you decide if you are ready to take on anyone and anything. It will make you see if you have the greatness you need, and if not, you will see your weaknesses and identify the areas where you need to strengthen your idea or plans to make them winning ones.

Adequate preparation is vital to turn your creative thoughts into workable ideas. That feeling of being prepared is an integral part of a Tycoon's Mindset.

Once you have confidence in your idea, you will not let your imagination work against you. What I mean by that is this: if you have not been successful in the past or have fears or concerns that develop in your mind, your imagination could lead to you living in the past and dwelling on it. This negativity may then make you imagine all the worst-case scenarios possible and create a negative perception of what might happen in your mind. Tycoons choose to learn from the past, rather than dwell on it. This means that Tycoons can feel the power of their ideas and enjoy working in the present towards the future.

Ultimately, you need to have faith in your idea in order to feel the power of it. And to really sense the strength of your idea, you need to prepare well and imagine being triumphant.

TYCOON TIP: Preparation is everything. Leave no stone unturned, then imagine winning. Now you have put yourself in a position of power.

STEP 9: Use Your Imagination to Inspire Others

A vivid imagination can be incredibly motivating. Listening to someone talk through an idea in detail with passion and enthusiasm is engaging, captivating and very infectious. Using your imagination to take those around you – employees, investors, customers, business partners – on a journey can have magical effects. Your imagination acts as a catalyst for other people's imaginations. By bringing your own imagination to the forefront, you actively encourage others to use theirs too. And a whole team tapping into their own imaginations is a very powerful tool.

Bill Gates knows this. 'Microsoft is a company that manages imagination,' great words from the second richest man in the world.

Proceed with caution, though. Using your vivid imagination as the basis of your 'pitch' to win over those around you can be dangerous – especially if you cross the thin but crucial line between 'fantasy' and 'imagination', which we discussed earlier in this chapter. There is nothing more off-putting than someone who has crossed that line and is preaching about something that is clearly not plausible. You've seen the collective head-shaking of the dragons in the den. Talking fantasy is a sure-fire way to lose credibility instantly, hence the importance of proof. In order to inspire others, engage them and encourage them to see and share your vision, you need solid and believable facts to back up your imagination-fuelled pitch.

So you need to make your idea coherent. Give it a storyline. Give it a beginning, a middle and an end. The result will become your vision, created by your imagination. This is the story of your future.

Cast your mind back. Try to remember being read a bedtime story, or being read a story by a teacher at school. Remember how you pictured the characters then, the situations described. You still use your imagination when you read a book, but your imagination was at its strongest then. You used your imagination and the story acted as the stimulus that propelled your imagination into action. That's why storytelling is so important in business. Anita Roddick engaged the media and the public with her stories of tribeswomen using various concoctions to keep their skin glowing. What's your story?

To succeed in business, you must win over the hearts and minds of people that will matter to you and your business. Openly discuss your imaginative and visionary plans with your people, partners and potential investors. Talk with conviction, but only if you can support that vision with evidence of why it will work. If your idea is pure fantasy, making people believe in your fantasy ideas puts you on a par with a confidence-trickster – with all the chatter and conviction to make others believe, but the deliverer of nothing but disappointment.

To me, imagination is like 'the Force' in George Lucas's fantastic *Star Wars* movies. It's something you have inside that you need to nurture and ultimately control in order to use it for the greater good of defending and furthering what you believe in. Just as Luke Skywalker needed guidance to rein in his powerful force when it became too strong to prevail, Tycoons know when to rein in their ideas and play devil's advocate.

By having the skill and polishing the Tycoon's tool of imagination, your vision will become a force that will engage others. It will allow you to transfer your thinking and ideas in a way that encourages those working with you to actively adopt your thinking and build on it with their own imaginative ideas. The subsequent results from creative thought and free thinking across a company can be quite exceptional.

TYCOON TIP: Do tell stories to inspire others. Don't tell tall tales. Be inspiring by not exaggerating.

STEP 10: Take It on a Test Run

The beauty of imagination is that we can simulate reality. Once we've questioned the ideas our imagination has created, once we've padded out our ideas with facts and figures, we can take those ideas on a test flight. Simulate your idea using your imagination. Just as a computerised virtual-reality flight simulator creates an incredibly realistic scenario, imaginations have the power to do the same with an idea. Your imagination gives you the power to take any idea on a test flight, to try it for size in your mind.

So, let's all be pilots! It is time to get into a flight simulator. This is the closest way a trainee pilot can experience flying an aircraft without ever leaving the ground. These days, flight simulators are elaborate electronic affairs, with an unbelievable amount of detail built in so that the pilot and flight crew obtain the best possible learning experience in the most realistic environment possible. In fact, I was told recently that these can be so realistic nowadays that one trainee pilot who'd had a particularly stressful and difficult ordeal at the controls of a simulator became so wrapped up in the exercise that, for a split second, he believed he was actually flying a real passenger aircraft. When he eventually brought the plane to a 'standstill' after several aborted simulated emergency landings, he promptly burst into tears. This is the power of suggestion and simulation when tapped into the imagination.

Great news for budding Tycoons is that we all possess an even more realistic simulator, and it's not just for flying; ours can be used for pretty much anything. Our simulator is our imagination, so the extent to which we use our simulators is limited only by our own imagination. We can create any environment we like, decorate it how we like, populate it how we like and add any amount of effects or scenarios to serve any purpose we like. So much can be explored, tested, checked and discovered with imagination.

This is a very powerful tool and, like a flight simulator, is perfect for putting our idea through a 'dry run' to see if it stands up to whatever we want to throw at it in our imaginary play-rooms. Does your idea stand up to whatever you throw at it in your imaginary playroom? Put your ideas to the test and seek out strengths and weaknesses. In doing so, you'll 'see' things you didn't even consider before. For example, testing an idea in this way may lead to the realisation that your packaging needs to be a certain way, or that a certain market would have more potential than another, or that your offer needs to be simplified, or that your idea will cost you a lot more than you envisaged.

The fact is, simulation creates realisations. And these realisations mould our decisions to optimise results.

When we close our eyes and relax into our imagination simulators, we are more open to prompts and information that come into play from our subconscious minds. This rich stream of internal data can take our simulation exercises to new levels and open up doors that can lead us to exciting discoveries and opportunities. By testing ideas within our imagination, those ideas can be shaped and grown to maximise their likelihood of success. We can uncover new opportunities and make new connections. We can immerse ourselves and see things differently, then build momentum.

TYCOON TIP: Try it. Close the door, turn off your mobile phone and take a few moments to take a test flight. You might be surprised by what you discover along the way. Fill out a logbook after your test flight, noting your key findings.

SUMMARY

You should now have an understanding of the rules that go to make up a true Tycoon and realise that your imagination is your starting point to creating your big idea. I have summarised below the key points for you to remember in the hope that those creative juices will start flowing.

TYCOON TIPS FOR SUCCESS
How to Put Your Imagination to Work

1. **Fire up your imagination.** You've done it before. Remember being ten? Let your antennae respond to stimuli, both conscious and unconscious.
2. **Create your vision.** Paint a picture of your ultimate destination in your mind's eye. Your vision will compel you to take action.
3. **Understand the difference between imagination and fantasy.** Substantiate your idea with real facts and figures. Question everything. Then hunt down the answers. Give your idea merit.
4. **Find the missing pieces.** Seek out what is needed to provide the right links in the chain and to turn weaknesses and threats into strengths and opportunities.
5. **Relish your freedom.** Make time to daydream in your life. See your imagination as your own private creative utopia, unhooked from reality. Find your flow, tap into it and get creative.
6. **Embrace change and learning** – they are both catalysts for success. Keep an open mind to consider the possibilities that change can bring.
7. **Give your idea substance.** Flesh it out, examine it fully. Make sure your research can prove its credibility. Describe your idea. Get involved in it.
8. **Feel the power.** Make sure you have all the tools and knowledge at your disposal to go out there and make your idea work. Feel the power and let your idea take shape.

9. **Use your imagination to inspire others.** Tell stories and encourage creative thought amongst your team.

10. **Take it on a test run.** Try your idea out for size by harnessing the power of your very own flight simulator – your imagination.

IMAGINATION + VISION + ACTION = RESULTS

3

WHAT'S THE BIG IDEA?

So, you've been putting your imagination to work to create and expand on your idea. You may have had more than one business idea. But how do you know whether your idea is a big idea or actually a rather small, feeble one? How do you know if your idea is strong enough to propel you towards success?

Well, before you do anything else, you need to take your idea on a workout: a rigorous, demanding, strenuous mental workout. If your idea falls along the way, then you must be brutal and discard it. However, if your idea makes it through all eight exercises, congratulations, because you really do have a big idea on your hands.

Ultimately, a successful business is born from many variables that work together to create success. The 'light-bulb moment' is merely the first step. Once an idea has been formed and a vision crystallised, the test flight your imagination took your idea on needs expanding upon. Strengths need building upon, weaknesses need to be improved upon, and evidence needs to be uncovered to substantiate the idea. It needs backing up.

This is where many of the budding entrepreneurs who put their ideas to the test on BBC's *Dragons' Den* fail. In fact, 95 per cent of people who encounter the dragons on the programme leave with nothing but advice. Generally, I have found that many people fail to get investment because of a number of key variables:

1. Some have a good idea but aren't the right person to take the idea forward. What they have in passion they lack in business acumen and resources.

2. Others have fantastic business ideas, but the opportunity or market is too small to warrant an investment. In this instance, their claims may also be overinflated.
3. Others fail to attract the interest of the dragons because the risk-reward ratio doesn't stack up. The concept is either not viable as a genuine business opportunity or the figures are too optimistic and the valuation unjustifiable.

Viability of your idea is vital, both to be able to convince yourself it will work and to convince others, such as investors, partners, bankers and even potential customers.

Of course, you may believe there are people crying out for your fantastic new product or service. Indeed, you may even be right. Your idea might be the next big thing with a huge untapped demand. But you need to prove it, either through your existing sales figures or, if still in concept phase, through evidence that supports your claims.

TYCOON TIP: Zoom in on your idea. Put it under the spotlight. Does it shine, or does it flicker?

One young entrepreneur I invested in on *Dragons' Den* was Huw Gwyther and his *Wonderland* magazine idea. The magazine market is fiercely competitive and high risk, and this was enough to put the other dragons off. But Huw had both experience and evidence. He had proof. His real strength was that he'd been an editor of *V* magazine in New York, so he had experience of being there and doing it. He also came in with very good statistics and good market research because he'd worked in the industry and knew the market really well. Huw knew exactly what he was doing and why. He got my interest and my first ever investment on *Dragons' Den*. Most magazines fail in the first year, but *Wonderland* has gone from strength to strength. It even featured Sienna Miller on the cover in February 2007.

In *Dragons' Den* and in life, investors will be convinced to part with their money by an entrepreneur with an idea that has impressive evidence, contracts in place or a vision for how sales will be forthcoming and a good presentation of the opportunity. However, unless the proof stacks up, the deal will fall through after the cameras stop rolling. Or the investor has completed his due dilligence.

For example, in the first series, Charles Ejogo came up with the idea for dispensing umbrellas at London Underground stations. He implied he had a contract with London Underground for 15 years giving him exclusive rights across the network. He presented peak-travel figures and, having found published passenger demographic statistics, outlined which stations were the busiest. This was a fantastic concept and I suggested we could go to the mobile network Orange and dispense branded orange umbrellas. The marketing message could be 'The future's bright . . . even when it's raining' to give them a good extension of the brand. Put a screen in the vending machine and it could play a rolling video message about their mobile phones and services. It was a great idea with clear demand and a sizeable opportunity, was backed up with evidence.

However, all was not as it seemed. As it turned out, when we started to inspect things more closely and wanted evidence of the contracts, the contract with London Underground wasn't there. Charles had an old, out-of-date sublicence with Cadbury. And, to even have that sublicence, he'd have to pay nearly £1 million if he wanted to take it up and install his machines in all Underground stations. When we put the evidence under the microscope, it didn't back up what we'd been told, so the investment didn't happen.

THE IDEA WORKOUT

Evidently, to evaluate whether your idea is blue-sky thinking or pie in the sky, realistic or romantic, you need to give your idea a reality check, a workout. What are the potential problems? Are there any nagging doubts you've been pushing to the back of your mind because they're not what you want to hear? Not to heed those doubts would be a very bad move. So think of the weak areas – is the idea too time-consuming, or impractical for another reason? Are you worried your projected targets might be a bit too optimistic? What do you know about the market, and what evidence can you gather to build on that and support your belief in your idea? Can you secure a contract or purchase order? If so, is it a proper contract that will stack up under due diligence (the examination of operations and verification of key contracts and material facts)? Note your queries and get the answers.

So it's time for you to question, delve and ultimately decide. The decisions made will involve using all the data you'll collect from the following exercises of your idea workout.

EXERCISE 1: Is It Innovative? Has It Been Done Before?

'Innovation' is a word that is used a lot in business. In my opinion, it is overused. True innovation is actually quite a rare thing. Many good ideas are simply an adaptation of something that's been successful before. This is what I call 'catalytic creativity'. I define this as one idea that precipitates another idea, which then evolves into an 'innovative' product, service or business. That's the alternative to a unique, one-of-a-kind idea. The secret is to take an existing product, service or concept and then take it up a level, by applying your own vision and creativity.

When we think of a great idea, one of the first questions we should ask ourselves is 'Has it been done before?' Usually, it will have in some way, but this doesn't mean we shouldn't continue with it. It just means we need to find a way that the idea can be made better. Your idea doesn't have to be totally new and original. Most businesses come from the modification of other successful companies, but the successful ones have clear differentiating factors that heighten their appeal over their competitors.

In a nutshell, being innovative is about creating new ideas, but those new ideas could be fresh perspectives on an existing concept. If you can differentiate your idea from the rest and you can justify, validate and protect your idea, you could be on to a winner.

For example, in any shopping centre there are likely to be many clothes shops. Some will be successful; others will be heading for failure. At first glance, they might look similar, but they are all different. The successful shops have features about them that create success. It could be their location, the quality or style of the clothes themselves, the friendly and helpful people working in the shop, the look of the aisles, the management, their suppliers, their profit margins (i.e. the percentage of each sale that is profit), the reasonable prices or a combination of all these things – a variety of factors have been differently handled to make them succeed when another clothes shop fails. But they are different, and that's why they coexist: different brands, different types of ethos, different products, different levels of customer service. I don't say, 'It's out there so I won't do it.' As long as the market is big enough for a differentiated and innovative version, then I will pursue it.

It is crucial that you research your idea by comparing others that are similar. Always look at the competition. And if you do have a truly new idea that has never been done before anywhere in the world (which is rare), consider where your likely competition will come from, because if there is no competition now, there will be soon, believe me. If you are a true pioneer of a service or product, people will look at your idea and try to adapt it. Some will try to copy it exactly and fail, but some may come up with something that differentiates their idea from yours, and then you've got real competition. Either way, you need to examine what is out there already. Look at failures as well as the successes and try and work out what factors have made them fail or succeed. Source problems, question everything, be resourceful. If you believe, after research, that you have something that hasn't been created or done before, protect your idea. Patent it.

TYCOON TIP: The more knowledge you have about how others have implemented ideas, the more chance you have to make yours successful.

Evidently, some of the best business ideas are a different take on an existing idea, but modified, changed, improved upon. Remember in Chapter 2 I talked about how Tycoons are often the architects of change? Change differentiates the Tycoon; it separates him or her from the rest of the pack, so go against the grain. Challenge current available choices. Unravel a fresh take on an existing business idea.

Many Tycoons start their businesses because of their constant dissatisfaction with the status quo in a certain market. That in itself provides enough energy to create change. If you think, 'Why can't it be done this way?' or, 'Why can't I do this?' and create something that does, there will probably be a good market for your idea, especially if you happen to be solving a common problem or providing a product or service that isn't being sold well.

Just as Roger Bannister forced us to change our perception of what was possible when he ran the four-minute mile, great Tycoons have changed people's perception of what is possible by launching successful businesses based on a unique and exceptional idea that changed other people's perception of what is possible. When Sir Richard Branson launched his own airline and his own financial services company, those types of company existed, but his were different. He had the imagination to create a truly innovative and groundbreaking business idea by challenging the status quo, challenging existing options and alternatives.

My Mindset

One day, in 1998, I was sitting in my lounge at the house I rented in Dorney, Berkshire, staring out of the window. It was cheap to rent because the house was right on the motorway, 100 metres from the M4. I could see and hear the cars going past, and it was then that I had my idea.

It was the idea to set up my telecoms business. I already had previous experience of working in the technology sector and truly believed I had a great idea that was different enough from the pack to succeed. Mobile-

94

phone distribution had been done before, but, up until then, most distributors sold all products, as is usual for a distribution company. To break into the market, I decided to break the mould, to go against the grain and focus solely on one manufacturer, so that my company would be recognised as a specialist in their products. As I said in Chapter 1, I called this 'single-brand distribution'. My company was then able to build a reputation as the experts in this manufacturer's products.

As a result, within 12 months we became the manufacturer's number-one partner and the Phones International Group dream was on its way to becoming a reality. I then replicated the concept with other manufacturers, which enabled the business to grow faster than the competition and be recognised as a partner that added real value.

It wasn't truly innovative, but it was groundbreaking in my own industry. I knew that sales organisations often had specialist teams focused on selling certain products before. But I knew if I focused on this single-brand-distribution concept in the early stages, I'd build a very quick reputation with my partner because they'd be getting dedicated focus and resources. It soon became apparent that because we became product champions, nobody in the market knew the manufacturer's product ranges better than us, so we were able to give a fantastic level of customer service to an extent where people truly believed for at least a year that we were the sales department of the actual manufacturer.

We quickly built immense credibility and became the number-one partner in the country almost overnight. Focusing on that one brand gave our partners and customers a better alternative, by challenging what was already out there. By taking a service that had been done before but doing it differently, we created rapid growth and smashed our targets year upon year. We found our winning strategy.

Tycoons are original thinkers and innovate frequently, but often our focus is on doing something in a new way, doing something better, giving the customer a better option. As a budding Tycoon, if you can break the market mould and dare to be different, you are on to a winner.

Think of ways your business idea can introduce some form of

innovation in the services, products or style that it offers. For example, your customer service or demonstrations could be carried out in a very different way, your designs could be different, your approach to selling or servicing your customers could challenge the industry norms, or you might target a market not tapped into before.

Does your idea meet demands not currently being met by existing providers? Could your idea shake up an entire industry? Use your imagination again. Are there gaps in the market that your idea could fill? What are people always complaining about? What problems could you solve? What can you do quicker, better, safer, cheaper than anyone else?

TYCOON TIP: Go against the grain. Break the mould. Be original, be different and be bold.

Sometimes, people go to other countries to find and import ideas that aren't yet around in their own country. The ability to think laterally, spot a gap in the market and fill it by importing a product or recreating a service you've seen abroad is something that many successful Tycoons do.

Alternatively, seeing how something is done elsewhere can inspire you to put a different twist on it, to change or refine it. I'm always interested in products and services I've not seen before when I travel abroad.

EXERCISE 2: What's the Degree of Difficulty?

Before giving up the security of a job, all entrepreneurs need to know how difficult, time-consuming and costly their idea is going to be to put into action. Implementation of an idea needs careful planning and consideration. You need to work out what needs to be done in order to get your idea off the ground and make it happen. This is vital because you need to know what your idea entails, to uncover whether it really is doable or not. The more work you can do now evaluating whether your idea is simple or complex, the more time you will save later on.

Seek out press stories about problems your idea solves or opportunities being created in your market. Really set to work fleshing out your idea's strengths and weaknesses to evaluate its viability. Assess the idea from all angles. Can you honestly implement the idea?

Pad out the idea. What needs to be done to get it off the ground and make it happen? Is it still possible? If so, why? If not, why not? Evaluate hard. If an idea is not researched properly before it is turned into a business, then it is likely to end in failure. I should know: this was the main reason why one of my businesses failed. So question everything. Then hunt down the answers. Give your idea merit.

> **TYCOON TIP:** Do your homework! If an idea is not researched properly before it is turned into a business, then it is likely to end in failure.

In my early days of being an entrepreneur, I set up a computer business, a support services company and a bar and restaurant. These businesses failed for different reasons, but they still failed. Sometimes it was because I gave credit to companies I shouldn't have; sometimes it was because I employed the wrong people. The bottom line: many mistakes were made – and I made them. If I'd spent more time researching, planning and understanding the threats surrounding the businesses I probably wouldn't have failed.

Had I looked into the potential risks for service companies, had a better understanding of the computer market and had prepared for the complexities involved in the restaurant business, I'd have stood a better chance. If I'd been more focused on putting in good management to run and operate that bar and restaurant, instead of trying to do everything myself with little experience, it would've worked. I set up a bar and restaurant that was cash-intensive when I didn't have the money, a bad time to start a business.

Now I put everything I learned from those mistakes into practice to assess the degree of difficulty of an idea. I always research the market and assess the idea from a variety of angles. I research and I plan.

From the day I started my telecoms group in 1998, we've always created an annual operating plan. That is a complete overview of the business, the sector and the market end to end. So that first year, we carried out a SWOT (strengths, weaknesses, opportunities and threats) analysis of ourselves and of our competition. We reviewed what our competition was doing in considerable detail. We included details on areas we were planning to develop and how we were planning to develop those areas. It was a 50- to 100-page annual operating plan, not a business plan, but an absolutely focused piece of work, with research, analysis, objectives and targets. We had then undertaken research amongst local companies, found out what they were doing, what our competitors were up to, what the market was saying. We spoke to the networks, obtained some of there own strategy documents in order to assess where they were going, looked to see how we could help them to meet their own objectives and searched for ways we could add real value. We did quite a lot of work; it didn't just happen without researching the market. We spent a lot of time planning and thinking about it, and have done the same every year since.

If an idea is too complex and likely to produce little return, we take the decision not to act, or devote the appropriate time and resources to deal with it. The degree of difficulty and the stages you need to go through to make your idea work needs analysis. This should go alongside a detailed analysis and plan of the business, sector and market.

Only then can you focus on the next exercise in your idea workout by uncovering the appeal of your idea.

EXERCISE 3: Have You Got the Right Balance of Feedback?

What is the first thing we do when we have an idea about something? We tell someone else about it, usually a friend, work colleague or family member. That's fine, if they are enthusiastic and encouraging about your idea and willing to discuss and talk it through with you. But what if they dismiss your idea and immediately tell you that it is rubbish? Or that you're 'mad to waste your time thinking of ideas', or you should 'get real' or 'come back down to earth'? What if they declare that you are 'too young', 'too old' or 'too inexperienced' to make your idea work? Then what do you do? Well, my advice is this: if you think there could be merit in your idea, then give it a chance to breathe and show off its true colours before you come to the conclusion that it isn't viable.

Certainly, your idea might indeed be hopeless, or very high risk, but don't discard it just because your friend didn't think much of it, because that is just one perspective, and possibly not a very informed one. However, if a whole host of experts and investors don't think much of your idea and substantiating it is proving difficult, it may be time to move on to the next idea. But if you believe it *will* work and can prove it, there's every chance that you'll be right. It all comes down to how you handle criticism and feedback.

One potential pitfall that many entrepreneurs fall into is to either:

- Be so wowed by their own idea that they ignore all constructive criticism, feedback, advice, even instincts and concerns, and decide to launch ahead regardless, without questioning those doubts or giving them any credence, or
- Self-criticise their own idea so harshly in the early stages and be so sensitive to other people's criticism that they take everything personally, subsequently fear it won't be possible, lose confidence and shelve it. What they should do is explore the idea further to uncover and work on those weaknesses and threats, and develop the idea into a more viable one.

Both pitfalls blight the success of an idea that could have worked. The first example leads to overconfidence, uncalculated risk and complacency – three things that the Tycoon avoids. The latter example results in the entrepreneur giving up before they've even taken flight – not very Tycoon-like either.

So, the Tycoon's Mindset needs to hold the right balance when juggling feedback. Remember, Tycoons don't assume. I will always balance the pros and cons and turn the cons into opportunities or figure out ways to overcome obstacles and reduce weak areas of the idea. I will modify and fine-tune the idea in my mind and on paper.

This characteristic of the Tycoon Mindset is known by psychologists as 'attribution theory'. It makes you aware of shortcomings in yourself and your idea and therefore keen to make worthy changes to make your idea the best it can be.

Entrepreneurs need to give the critic or the person giving the feedback the benefit of the doubt, even just for a while. You can then question potentially problematic areas and improve them. And should you find there was no valid reason for the criticism (e.g. 'you're too old', 'it won't work' – with no valid explanation why), you'll be able to prove them wrong and yourself right. And that confirmation will give you a healthy helping of self-belief to push forward. Conversely, if your critic is proved right and you are proved wrong, you'll have discovered a weakness you can correct, or be able to make a more informed decision about whether your idea is worth continuing with.

The key is to evaluate the idea from fresh perspectives, through the eyes of potential or actual customers, through the eyes of investors or partners, employees or work colleagues, and through your own internal critical eye – standing back from the idea and detaching from it. This gives you the freedom to be able to critique it honestly and accept constructive criticism from both yourself and others.

TYCOON TIP: Get feedback so you know how your idea is received from different target audiences. Write it all down. Collate as much data as you can. Include proof to prove or dispel opinions from the mix.

The best way to get feedback that's worth taking on board (i.e. constructive feedback that has a reason behind it) is to ask the right people at the right time. Seek out people who you respect, who you know have knowledge or expertise in a certain field or have an interesting but informed view on life. Ask most likely potential customers who fit into the market you intend to target; ask people who are passionate about the market you are entering. In addition, you should ask those people at the right time: when your idea has substance and evidence to back it up, when it has been developed and researched and doesn't need their own imaginations to go into overdrive to envisage it working. It needs to have appeal, but more on that in Exercise 4.

TYCOON TIP: Find people who are passionate about your idea. If your idea is within the musical-instrument market, go and speak to people who are passionate about playing the guitar. What are their needs and problems? How do they respond to your idea? What features would they prefer or change? What are their objections or concerns?

Of course, even when you've got a great idea, evidence, drive and passion, you may still face critical feedback. But you'll know which criticism to take on board and act on, and which criticism holds no value.

Walt Disney ignored those who told him his new theme-park idea wouldn't work because of their own limited perception about the existing theme-park market (and the problems of costly maintenance and seasonal profits). However, Disney knew other-wise because he had done his homework and intended to do things differently. I knew differently when I pursued my

American Inventor television-show idea, even after two top TV executives had expressed their doubts about the concept. And I continued with my Generation Telecom business even after my financial director suggested it wouldn't work. Each time, because I've validated my plans I knew they would work, and they did.

That's what J. K. Rowling did, as well as Steve Jobs and James Dyson. When they were dealt criticism and rejection, they responded to that criticism by bolstering their self-belief and increasing their determination to succeed because they knew otherwise. And they went on to prove themselves right – very right! Sometimes when you receive criticism, you may know otherwise, because you have the belief, the evidence and the drive. You've ticked all the boxes, and that gives you the courage of your convictions.

Ever since I set up my own tennis academy, aged 17, right up to the present day, I've always told people about my ideas. Not everyone I've told has seen my vision. Every Tycoon has faced disapproval by someone. Back then, people said I was 'too young'. In whose eyes? Certainly not mine. I forged ahead with my tennis academy while I took my A levels because I'd set targets and knew I could make it work. That decision and belief in my idea paid off.

Of course, sometimes it can be worth shelving an idea if it doesn't make the grade or prove its viability. But you need to find the right balance to appreciate criticism and feedback and use it to your advantage, to improve your idea and thus have even more confidence in it.

Seek out frank feedback, clarify criticism and you'll gain fresh ground on your idea and learn how to best serve your customers with the best version of it.

TYCOON TIP: Engage with criticism from others and yourself. Critique your idea. Flex your inner critical eye. Ask yourself what works and what doesn't. What is appealing, and what is less appealing? Confront issues that arise and iron out the creases.

Apart from providing very useful information on how to modify your idea to increase its attraction, feedback, if handled correctly, can have a springboard effect on a business. For example, when people, customers or potential investors provide feedback via advice, criticism or a complaint, if you handle that communication correctly, you can create the perfect relationship. If you act on their communication, you'll find that the people who gave the criticism in the first place become loyal and even champion your cause.

The fact is, through involving people in what you are doing, you attract their interest, and if you show them you have listened to their advice and done something about it, they are more likely to tell others about what you are doing. When people tell other people about you, you sell more. Word of mouth is a truly wonderful thing, and something that all Tycoons hope for.

TYCOON TIP: Listen to the needs of people you'll be working with: investors, customers, partners, employees. Listen, fix what needs to be fixed and present your offer again. They'll appreciate it and will reward you with their loyalty.

EXERCISE 4: What's Its Appeal?

By now you should have thoroughly assessed your strengths, weaknesses, opportunities and threats. You've spent time considering your qualities and creative ideas, listening to feedback and digesting constructive criticism. But in order to really prove your idea is going to work, you need to uncover demand and verify its appeal. Figure out why people will want your product or service, who they are and why they'll choose your idea over others. Consider what's in it for them if they choose to spend their hard-earned cash.

From the market research you've done so far you'll have gained some insight into the likely demand for your idea. But this should be ongoing. Find out what the best-selling products and services are in your market, read trade magazines and financial papers, review statistics, contact trade associations and use the Internet to see if there are a growing number of buyers entering the market your idea fits into.

Do all you can to uncover the size of the market, refer to your notes compiled when asking potential customers to provide you with feedback, test your idea and find out about the demand for a product or service like yours.

A good idea will attract your interest, but a great idea will hold and keep your interest and that of others too. Knowing which kind of idea you have can spell the difference between success and failure, because the wider its appeal, the bigger the potential success.

Question what is appealing about a particular idea. This is what I call 'sense-checking'. For an idea to work, it has to appeal not only to its creator, but also to those likely to invest in it, buy or use it.

TYCOON TIP: Work out exactly what it is about your idea that appeals to you. That will give you vital clues about how it might appeal to others.

Uncovering the appeal of your idea will help you to create its unique selling points (USPs), the differentiating factors that make it appealing over other products or services, and the purpose and mission statement of your business. These tools will help a great deal when you evaluate the likely reasons that people will support and buy into your idea.

Have you thoroughly considered the customer and the benefit your idea will bring? How does your product or service fulfil the needs of your customers? What are those needs? So, for example, you might make storage products, but what needs are you filling? You're not just filling a desire from the customer to buy a box. They need a certain kind of storage box to solve their storage problems and it probably needs to fulfil certain criteria around size, stability and appearance. OK, so who has storage problems? Which groups of society? Which consumers and which businesses? Why do they have those problems, and where do they use products such as yours? In what application (e.g. in their bathroom, garage, workspace or factory)? What do they usually or currently use to solve that problem, and why? What are the disadvantages of what they currently use? Uncover the advantages of your product or service over others, along with any flaws in the existing alternatives. What are the specific advantages of your product or service over others already on the market? These core benefits are what will get your idea out in the marketplace and selling, as long as you haven't plucked them from nowhere, as long as they are based on proof.

Your mission statement and USPs should capture the purpose and personality of your brand and bring clarity to your overall vision. This will help you consider those additional important questions going forward: who will your customers be? Why will they buy? What kind of people will you hire? Who could supply you? Who could advise you?

Business is about connecting with people. You can only connect with people by communicating with them in some way. Therefore, if you can define your expertise, your purpose and your USPs in just one phrase or strapline, the connection will be stronger, the understanding will be empowered, and your idea will be more magnetic, pulling custom towards it.

Having a purpose, a mission and some USPs (and communicating them) are vital. These are your competitive advantage points and they define who you are and what you do; they sum up your brand persona.

For example:

- Microsoft's mission is 'to help businesses and people to realise their potential'.
- Stelios's easyGroup has a strapline that captures its USP, mission and purpose in one easy statement: 'More value for less.'
- Phones International Group's mission is to 'be recognised as a group of highly skilled, determined individuals operating an ethical benchmark company at world level'.
- Sir Richard Branson's Virgin Group's 'brand values' are 'value for money, good quality, brilliant customer service, innovative,

competitively challenging and fun'. These principles were set out by Branson in the 1970s and still define what Virgin is about.

- Red Letter Days' mission statement is 'Unforgettable gifts. First-class service.'

Create some brand values of your own. Come up with your mission. What is it that you do, and why? What do you stand for? What are you about? What unique selling points do you offer?

TYCOON TIP: Create your own thumbprint to personalise your brand. Create a mission statement.

My Mindset

Across my telecoms group of companies, my mission statement has always been the same. "To be recognised as a group of highly skilled, determined individuals operating an ethical benchmark company at world level." This is just a way of saying that I want to bring in the best people (highly skilled). I want them to be determined and focused individuals. I want them to offer the optimum ethical service to our customers, because that builds loyalty, and I want us to be a benchmark company. If we are a benchmark company on a world level, it means we are the number-one player, so other people are benchmarking to us. This means I'm setting the standard, based around my people, the service we offer and the position I want us to be in the market, and summarising that in one sentence.

Differentiating unique selling points are vital, as is having a strong brand mission. All Tycoons know this.

With *Wonderland* magazine, the quality of the magazine is unmatched. It costs us more than any other publication to put together. The quality spreads to the people who are in there, from Sienna Miller and Ewan McGregor on the cover to Mario Testino taking photographs. It's the quality of the output that differenti-ates *Wonderland* in a highly competitive market.

Good knowledge of the appeal of your idea from your custo-mers' point of view helps identify the best markets to target; it unravels your potentially most lucrative sectors and gives you the confidence to launch forth. It clarifies who you are, what you do and why.

To uncover your USPs and mission statement, you need to find out what separates you from the rest. Can you offer added value and better customer service than anyone else? Do you have a strategic benefit (such as our strategy to train people in-store who are selling products for us)? Can you help simplify your customers' lives? Do something faster, better, safer than your competitors? Can you help them to be more effective in what they do? Can you save them money or help to make them more money? Can you help them get more from their hobby? Can you help them stay in touch with people more effectively or save them time? Can you help them to combat a problem? Can you help educate them or make them perform a task more effectively? Find clarity to uncover the unique benefits that your idea offers to potential buyers that will drive them to take action and make an enquiry or buy. Think about what's in it for the person buying your product or service.

If you can convey one or two unique benefits that summarise in just one sentence what you do and why, you'll have a powerful mission statement that will communicate what is necessary. This is sometimes referred to as an 'elevator pitch' because it is short enough to deliver if you were riding in an elevator with an influential person. Having a strong USP and elevator pitch will help your message stand out from the crowd and will help you be prepared at all times – armed with a clear definition of what you do and why you do it.

When I have been on BBC2's *Dragons' Den*, the people who have obtained investment from me are the ones who have put forward their idea clearly and concisely. Remember, for your idea to get backing, you need to sell its appeal, create interest for the potential investor and leave them believing wholeheartedly in why it will be a success. I have invested my own money many times on *Dragons' Den* and each time it is the clarity and appeal of the idea, as well as the person behind the idea that has engaged and enticed me.

Some people entering the 'den' have a decent idea, an innovative product and even interest from retailers. However, if there is little clarity but plenty of confusion in the pitch, they'll not find the investment they came for. They may have sold a few hundred of their product and have a patent pending. Their idea might be innovative and they might come across as likeable. However, if there are any areas of confusion or concern about the opportunity and potential return on investment (ROI), nobody will invest. Confusion results in unqualified and uncalculated risk, and Tycoons only take risks where there is no confusion.

For me, appeal and a great product are just half the battle. You need to bring clarity to your figures and your vision to clearly reveal the opportunity. The best way to do that is to know what you stand for, know what your mission is, know your financial figures and your unique selling points. This will bring clarity to your messages to customers, buyers, investors, employees and partners.

EXERCISE 5: How Big Is the Opportunity?

In order to succeed in business, you need to create demand for your product or service. But you'll only generate a good rate of custom if the opportunity is to make it big.

Opportunity is not just about demand, but about market share, growth, accessibility of that market and your own intended position within it. There might be huge demand but you could have miscalculated entry cost. You might have failed to identify the fact that your biggest competitor has a 70 per cent market share and very loyal customers who won't be easily persuaded to move. You may have uncovered a gap in the market, but is there a market in that gap? Is there enough demand and a big enough opportunity to profit from that gap by filling it? If so, is the opportunity sustainable in the long term?

Roll up your sleeves; it's time to embark on a fact-finding mission, to explore and equip yourself with all you need to put your idea into action.

Find out how far you have to go. And then dig deeper. Find out from suppliers of similar products about the demand for those products. Is demand climbing or falling? See if there are any external influences that could threaten your business. Is there scope to scale your business and grow it significantly? Your idea needs to inspire confidence, so you need to root out the facts relating to demand and opportunity.

When an investor invests, they focus on the opportunity and the size of it. They need to understand the likely return on investment, how long it will take for them to receive that return and what the factors in the market are like. They'll need to know if the market is growing, static or declining.

Therefore you need to ascertain the level of demand to establish the potential size of the market and your potential share of it. You'll also need to figure out how long it is likely to be before you can get your idea to market and when you can start to turn a profit. Look at trends, location, the market and the size of that market. Review your customers and the competition in as much detail as you can.

TYCOON TIP: Find the gap in the market and the market in that gap.

If you can find an idea within a growth market, where there are plenty of new buyers, this will set you in good stead. It's far easier to get new customers than ones loyal to another brand who need persuading to switch. Being able to piggyback on the growth of a market can be hugely helpful. I started my telecoms businesses when the wireless communications and data industries were growing. They still are. I bought a company called Wireless Logic, a company that provides wireless data connectivity services and solutions to SME and corporate customers. I did this while data and connectivity services were new growing opportunities. They still are now.

Seek out markets where there has been year-on-year growth.

Gather statistics, contact trade associations, get an insight into the growth – is it rapidly rising, or has it peaked? Has the market been growing rapidly for a few years but is now saturated with too many new entrants all juggling for the same spend?

On *Dragons' Den*, there are many examples of entrepreneurs who've missed the boat. They've found a market that is growing but are choosing to enter that market at the wrong time, when it is already getting to the point of saturation and growth is slowing, from those entering the aromatherapy market to those pursuing a business in the natural-juice industry or skincare market.

Let's summarise: if your idea fits into one of the following areas, you may find there is ample opportunity and room for you to gain a strong position within a given market.

Growth Markets

A strong idea within a growth market with low to medium risk is likely to appeal to investors and other financiers. Risks and vulnerabilities must be fully understood when entering a fast growth sector, including a firm grasp of what the competition is doing and a plan for how to exploit the growth in the market to your advantage. Static or declining markets are less attractive to investors because they produce lower returns, unless you can own most of the market. Whether you have outside investment in your idea or not, pay attention to the market-growth factor.

Specialists

Can you become a specialist in one product area? I did just that when I set up my telecoms group in 1998. We went against the grain to become recognised as a specialist in a specific product with our 'single-brand-distribution' concept. This added-value strategy became our specialism and is the key ingredient of our rapid growth.

Finding a Niche

Can you target a specific niche market with your idea that nobody else is focusing on? That's what I did with Generation Telecom by

110

focusing on the rail sector. I devoted all my energies to cracking that market and ended up with over 50 per cent of it. Tycoons are always able to find the niche and work out where they fit within it.

However, Tycoons also know the importance of assessing the size of a niche-market opportunity. For example, a few years into running my telecoms business, in order to grow faster than my competitors, I decided to raise money and bring in a venture capital (VC) partner. This would help us to fund the growth and acquisition of customers. I had accrued enough knowledge about the market, dynamics and opportunity to know its potential and was able to find a VC partner. Subsequently, we grew, made acquisitions and the VC made a return in excess of 20 per cent. Win-win – we were all happy.

Longevity

The market might be growing now, but for how long? You need a plan B, or to be able to prove you can expand on your idea to keep the momentum going over the long term. If the market isn't growing, how confident are you that your business can grow by taking market share away from your competitors? Question how you might get repeat custom by cross-selling to your customers. What additional products or services could you sell to your existing customers in the future? Repeat custom is worth focusing on and this is something that Tycoons will always do. They know it costs far less to keep existing customers than it does to attract and secure new ones.

Is your idea licensable or franchisable? Sometimes a great idea might require too much effort and investment to turn a decent profit, so it might be worthwhile licensing the idea to a manufacturer who could easily create and distribute the product on your behalf. You'd then earn a licence fee and royalty, which you could use to fund a new idea or save up enough to manufacture and distribute your own product.

Understanding how big the opportunity for your idea is can also be determined by looking at the practical aspects of the business.

Ask yourself whether you can put a tick beside the following boxes:

- **Clear financial plans:** have you worked out how much money you will need to start the business, enter the market, generate an income and cover costs? Have you uncovered market-research information such as data from partners, suppliers and distributors that will help you to estimate sales?
- **Market research:** do you know who your customers will be? Why will they buy? And what do they need? Have you proved your idea will work in the marketplace? Can you substantiate your claims?
- **Competitor analysis:** so you know who the biggest threat is, but how are you going to deal with this threat? If there is no competition now, how will you handle competition when it does arrive, because it certainly will?
- **Intellectual property (IP) rights:** have you protected your idea? We'll cover that part of the idea workout in the next exercise.
- **Experience or knowledge of the marketplace:** what skills, contacts and knowledge do you have about the market you are entering? How do you intend to gain more resources in these areas?
- **People:** do you know what key skills and roles you will need within your team? Do you have a management team or, at the very least, know which members of a management team you will need to find?

It's important to understand each area, each building block, to make your idea happen and not only happen but actually work, giving you and your investors a return on the investment.

EXERCISE 6: Have You Protected Your Idea?

Once you have assessed the appeal, opportunity, difficulty and viability of your idea, and are sure your idea is worth pursuing, you need to protect it. Tycoons have the insight to unlock the value of their creativity by effectively managing their intellectual property. They know that if they don't protect their creations, an obstacle could come between them and their vision.

As an entrepreneur, you must always file a patent or apply to register a trademark or registered design rights *before*:

- exhibiting your work
- approaching investors
- sharing your idea.

If you've applied for a patent against your specific idea and have put something together that allows you to have the intellectual property rights, even though you may not have had confirmation, you are already protected. This is called 'patent pending'. The point and date of patent application is vital to ensure this protection. Be aware, though – applying for a patent (patent pending) means exactly that your IP rights are pending. Do not assume full protection until you get back a registered patent.

Similarly, if you use your brand name, you acquire the rights to use it as an unregistered trademark ^{TM}. But to secure a registered trademark, you need to apply for trademark registration and use the date of application as your date of protection. If you are granted a registered trademark, you will be able to use the ® symbol and nobody will be able to use the same brand name as you in the classes in which you register your trademark. However, if your trademark is deemed by the Intellectual Property Office as 'too descriptive' or 'not distinctive', you could find that your application is rejected. This will mean that you can continue to use your unregistered trademark but are not fully protected from others using the same name, unless you can prove prior rights, in which instance you might be able to get protection. You will be reassured that others won't be able to register the trademark, as their applications would be rejected on the same grounds as yours (if they are applying for the same word). However, the only real way to protect your brand or product name is to be granted a registered trademark. You can protect designs and products by applying for a patent.

TYCOON TIP: Take time to protect your business name and brand names, product designs and Web address. It is worth the effort and cost to avoid somebody else beating you to it.

One frequent mistake that entrepreneurs make is to create some fantastic ideas but protect just the one idea, or just part of an idea. Think of the bigger picture before you walk in to see investors.

When the idea was pitched to me on *Dragons' Den*, *Wonderland* had secured the trademark to use the name, so no other magazine or product in the publishing sector can launch with the same name. In fact, each of the businesses I've invested in has protected their intellectual property, where we have deemed it important to do so. It isn't always vital.

TYCOON TIPS FOR SUCCESS
Idea Protection Do's and Don'ts

- Do check that nobody else has got there before you via www.patent.gov.uk. Is your idea genuinely novel?
- Do ensure you've included any changes to patents or your next submission against patent to reflect any additional components, those uncovered while gathering feedback.
- Do make sure you are entirely satisfied with your prototype or finished product.
- Do register or apply to register the company name with Companies House and secure your domain name to safeguard your brand.
- Do get everything in writing with partners, manufacturers and suppliers.
- Do catalogue everything, including, notes, sketches, diagrams, contracts, letters and emails.
- Do mark the copyright symbol, the name of the copyright owner and year of creation on all written, literary or artistic work.
- Do look into licensing your rights wholly or in parts to generate income from your IP assets.
- Do ensure you've fully researched competitors and new market

entrants. Are you paying attention to new trademarks being
advertised? (It is once advertised that entrepreneurs can
contest any trademarks that are infringing their own.)

- Don't enter an investor's office until you've filed your patent or
  trademark and also researched the market, spoken to people
  and tested the idea in the real world first (once applications
  have been filed).
- Don't start negotiations until you've asked potential
  manufacturers to sign a simple confidentiality agreement and
  have applied for a trademark or patent.
- Don't forget to renew your domain name.

EXERCISE 7: Does It Have International Appeal?

You've already assessed the size of the opportunity that your idea
presents, so does that opportunity extend globally? Does your
idea have international appeal?

Some products or services, if serving a market well in the UK,
can have the potential to do very well in other markets. For
example, on *Dragons' Den*, when I invested in *Wonderland*
magazine, I was looking at the bigger picture and the potential
international appeal. The magazine can often be seen in Australia,
Italy and France, as well as here in the UK.

When we look at international appeal, we are really looking at
the potential for a business or product to be replicated in as many
markets globally as possible, rather than just one. This gives a
business the biggest possible opportunity for success and growth,
without over-reliance on one or a few territories. However, it is
important to remember to think globally but to act locally. That
means that an idea that is a success in one market may not
necessarily be an instant hit in another. You need to get a feel
for the local market dynamics and adapt your business accordingly
for it to be a success in other territories on a global level. A strong
international appeal is increasingly important to investors, and is
something that separates a really outstanding idea from a good one.

Tycoons will always consider the global possibilities. So ask yourself whether your idea can be replicated globally. If entering global territories and assessing whether it is viable to do so, entrepreneurs need to get a grasp of the market dynamics at a local level and adapt accordingly.

Fully investigate international markets, but make sure you understand:

- **Competitive pressures:** for example, there may be more competition in one territory than another.
- **Cultural differences:** for example, in one territory your product design may come across as a luxury; in another it may appear cheap; or you may find that people in a certain culture place more or less importance on getting a certain benefit that your idea provides.
- **Economic pressures:** for example, one territory may have more of a reliance on a certain product or may not be able to afford a certain price range.
- **Management capabilities:** managing a business locally is one thing; managing over several companies is even more difficult. You need the right people.

To create your global plan and strategy:

1. Think about your idea. Picture your product or service in your mind's eye. Think about other countries that may experience similar problems to the ones your product or service solves. Use the Internet to research how your idea might work and what differences or problems you may face.
2. Which countries would you focus on? List them on a piece of paper and next to each write down your findings on any competitors already in that location.
3. Write down your findings on any cultural differences and economic pressures. Use the Internet, but also use your contacts. You may find posting on online forums with a global userbase is useful in order to ask questions about these areas

and communicate with people who actually live there. Could be very useful feedback.

TYCOON TIP: Creating a business that works well in one country means absolutely nothing when evaluating how it would work in others. Study global markets on a local level.

My Mindset

When I started Phones International Group, you can tell by the name that I had already thought about my own company's positioning. The group now owns three companies that distribute, operate and service telecoms equipment in the UK. The name was just the start, but it was a very good start. Positioning what your company does and including it in the name is a good idea in its own right.

Since then, the group has been voted one of Europe's fastest-growing enterprises, according to UK FastTrack. The whole team – several hundred employees based across several operating centres in the UK and one abroad – is focused on the long-term objectives of the group, which includes international presence, because there are major benefits and economies of scale in entering a particular overseas market. We opened an office in Romania, due to a high skill level for IT developers. This continues to perform well for us and the team is managed from the UK, reporting into our Director of IT services.

Seven years on, partner companies include Nokia and Vodafone, and we count Vodafone, Carphone Warehouse, Asda, Sainsbury's and Argos among our customers. Despite the recent difficulties in the telecoms market, we've managed to grow our sales each year from £13.9 million in 1999 to £180 million in 2006. Our future now will either be expanding in the other markets ourselves or merging with, acquiring or selling out to another global player who already has global market share. The point is that our global positioning and strategies for expanding into Europe were set out from the beginning. We will also look at ways to increase our overall margin, even if that means a reducing revenue line. Revenue is vanity, profit is sanity.

Evidently, setting clear positioning of your company and long-term objectives throughout an entire workforce are stepping stones to becoming a truly international business.

EXERCISE 8: What's Your Gut Instinct?

You've taken your idea on a rigorous workout, test flight and reality check. You're nearly there. But the other part of assessing an opportunity is about the stuff you can't see. It is something that you feel.

Do you instinctively think your idea has the strength and the power to become big? Well, that is just as valid as your practical assessments (although you shouldn't launch forth on instinct alone: you need to go through all the exercises to really ensure your idea makes the right impact).

It's time to use one of my Ten Golden Rules: intuition. Does it feel *right*? Does your instinct tell you this idea ticks all the boxes? If you are in tune with your vision, and your intuition is saying, 'Yes!' you will make decisions based on a strong purpose and vision – a critical differentiating factor between companies that grow fast and those that don't. Heed your intuition and respect your gut feeling. Intuition is a Tycoon's own built-in radar system.

Even after all the practical elements have been completed, there should still be something deep inside that says to you, 'This will work.' You need to listen to your gut instinct and attempt to un-ravel why the feeling exists. Be like a detective and go back over your work in minute detail, looking for the clues that are making you feel this way. Then examine the various elements of your idea or business plan. If you do not believe 100 per cent in the sheer and utter brilliance of your business idea, then you might as well give up now, or at least stop, question and turn round. Trying to turn an idea into a real business will involve sacrifice and dedication, and if you are not completely committed and don't strongly believe in yourself and your idea, then there is no point in continuing.

> **TYCOON TIP:** Sometimes a business that has all the right ticks in the boxes can still feel wrong. Stop and trust your gut instinct. Find out why your stomach is saying, 'No.' When you find the missing piece of the jigsaw, you will know instinctively.

My Mindset

When I decided to open my own bar and restaurant in Windsor, I had all the confidence and excitement that anyone could wish for in a new venture. My idea was going to be exciting and successful. Unfortunately, I completely failed to listen to my gut instinct, that small but insistent voice inside me that asked if it was really sensible to go into an area of business that I knew absolutely nothing about.

I shut it off and ignored it, because it was saying things I didn't want to hear. But, as I said earlier, after two years my bar and restaurant failed and I realised that the voice inside had been right. If I had listened to my gut instinct, I would have stuck to what I knew. And I wouldn't have lost a huge pile of money.

Since the doors closed on the bar and restaurant, the lesson I learned about heeding my instinct has served me well on numerous occasions. For example, I listened to my gut instinct saying, 'Yes,' when I persisted with both Generation Telecom and *American Inventor*. I listened to my gut instinct saying, 'No,' on numerous occasions during the filming of both *Dragons' Den* and reviewing investment opportunities that come via my website.

I'm not the only entrepreneur to launch a restaurant and fail. It's one of the business markets with the highest failure rate. Anita Roddick's restaurant Paddingtons (set up years before the Body Shop) failed because 'It was the wrong kind of restaurant in the wrong street, in the wrong town, launched at the wrong time.'

Since then, Dame Roddick has gone on to listen to her intuition to make good decisions and follow a path she believes in passionately. Once you've learned to use your intuition and go with your gut instinct, and you've asked yourself if the idea feels right, you are ready to put your idea into practice. But only once you've answered one more question:

Does your idea fill you with passion?

Because passion is what you will need to drive your vision and take your idea to fruition and beyond.

SUMMARY

So now you should have started to accumulate the building blocks of the Mindset of a Tycoon. You've read the Ten Golden Rules, have started your imagination and given it the freedom to run wild, and you've drilled down and focused on your idea and raised key questions about its viability.

Here's a summary of the exercises that make up the Tycoon's viability workout. And once the reality check is complete and you've completed each exercise in your idea workout, you can start figuring out the finance required and start knocking on the relevant doors.

EXERCISE 1: Is it innovative? Has it been done before?
EXERCISE 2: What's the degree of difficulty?
EXERCISE 3: Have you got the right balance of feedback?
EXERCISE 4: What's its appeal?
EXERCISE 5: How big is the opportunity?
EXERCISE 6: Have you protected your idea?
EXERCISE 7: Does it have international appeal?
EXERCISE 8: What's your gut instinct?

4

PLANNING AND PITCHING

With a sound business idea on the table, the next stage of your journey is likely to be to find the money to get your idea off the ground or find an investor. And this is when the real work begins. How well you do at this stage will ultimately determine whether your business idea ever gets up and running. Unfortunately, as I discovered while being an investor on *Dragons' Den*, this is also the stage where people are most likely to make costly mistakes.

The most common trap people fall into is thinking that they can just show up on the day and wing it, with minimal preparation and a surprising lack of evidence. Some people don't even bother changing out of their scruffy jeans and trainers! In order to attract investment, entrepreneurs need to tick a number of boxes.

Personally, if I am thinking of investing in an idea, I like to see:

- an engaging pitch to attract my interest
- an impressive, innovative idea, product or service (either entirely unique or a different take on something already out there)
- a convincing command of numbers, projections and forecasts. What is the likely reward going to be for me as an investor? What is the likely return on investment (ROI)? What contribution to profit is each part of the business going to be responsible for?
- proven business acumen and ability to sell and market the idea, product or service, and a likeable and workable individual with enough experience to see the idea through and deliver on targets
- a clear definition of the market opportunity and summary of the size and potential of a chosen market. This includes market

research from credible sources that underpin statements about the shape, size and potential of the sector.

- a clear plan of intended results and how those targets are going to be met with clear actions and timescales. If a business is planning to attack certain markets and attract targeted customer groups, I like to see, in some detail, what actions are going to be taken and what the timescales are. It is all very well stating that you are going to win customer X, but I will want to see a plan of the individual steps and milestones that are going to be taken to win customer X and achieve Y. I want to see a definition of how you are going to achieve your goals via the actions you intend to take. This doesn't have to be a huge document, because I like things concise. The point here is, it will help you gain a wider understanding of how you are going to achieve your goals and will give me an insight into what needs to be done to get there.
- a visible understanding of the potential risks, the competition, the threats they pose and how to deal with them. This includes a SWOT (stengths, weaknesses, opportunities and threats) analysis and competitor analysis, backed up with a selection of company information from sources such as Companies House or trade journals.
- a clear comprehension of the potential rewards
- a firm grasp of the product or service benefits. What does this idea have over any other idea already in existence? Does it stand out? Is it different? Does it serve a purpose? What problem is it solving? Is it solving a problem that doesn't exist or something we can all relate to and buy in to?
- an evident commitment to devote time and resources to the business, grow a team and deliver on promises to fulfil expectations.

If I see all of this in a pitch for my investment, I'm engaged – you've automatically attracted my interest, enough for me to study the evidence you've provided and, should it all stack up, make you an offer. Investors are risking their hard-earned money. Would you invest in something that didn't tick all the boxes?

Clearly, finding an investor is not just a matter of asking someone for money and expecting them to put their hands in their pockets and say, 'yes'. In fact, finding an investor requires just as much time and commitment as you devoted to conceiving the idea in the first place.

There's plenty more work to be done. You need to figure out a number of factors *before* you write a business plan or plan your pitch. You'll need to:

- **STAGE 1: Amass supporting evidence** to back up the entire plan (and pitch) – market research, test data, feedback, focus-group assessments. There's little point putting time and effort into planning if you haven't already put time and effort into research, into collecting evidence to support your idea.
- **STAGE 2: Overcome the identified risks.** How will you tackle competitors, consumer trends or internal risks such as poor planning or management?
- **STAGE 3: Decide exactly how much investment you need to get started.** Be precise. Specify what you will spend it on and why. And consider where you'll get it from: friends and family, the bank, business angels, venture capitalists, investment fund managers or via a government grant or loan scheme.
- **STAGE 4: Work out the likely return on investment.** You need a firm understanding of what the ROI will be. This is what fuels an investor's interest and is what motivates them to invest in your idea.
- **STAGE 5: Write a business and financial plan.** Finally, once you've gone through each of the four stages above, you can collate your data and create a business and financial plan.

In order to give you the best chance of success, I've divided the process of planning your business and pitching for finance into ten stages. The first five stages, listed above, focus on planning.

The final five stages focus on pitching for investment. I promise that if you take the time to work through each of the stages in turn, you will be giving yourself the very best chance possible to turn your business idea into reality. First things first. . .

STAGE 1: Amass Supporting Evidence

In Chapter 3, I asked you to give your idea a workout to test-drive its viability. Now it's time to refer back to that research to collate the evidence you've accumulated. In amassing supportive evidence, you are arming yourself with crucial information so you can make informed decisions. This in itself could give you the competitive advantage over others. It also helps with credibility, as you'll be better prepared to forecast your approximate sales and expenditure accurately. It is this lack of clarity on the numbers and evidence that leads to many entrepreneurs coming unstuck in front of a potential investor – be it on *Dragons' Den* or otherwise.

Take a long, hard look at the evidence that supports the case for your business. I have looked at a number of business opportunities as a potential investor where, on the face of it, the idea has seemed good, but on deeper inspection – often referred to as due diligence – there is little or no substance to uphold the case for investing in the opportunity. As a result, I have just walked away.

Supporting evidence can vary from idea to idea, but the bulk of what is required is the same, regardless of the type of business. Much of the initial information required by an investor should be within a business plan. But what an investor is really looking for is the proof to back up what you say – the reference points that substantiate your claims.

Essentially, potential investors analyse the evidence in the same way a detective would. For a detective, this is the time to get forensics, to pull out the detail and really examine it under the microscope. Investors need evidence, but so do you. How are you going to back up your own belief in your idea without it?

So how do you uncover all this data? Where and how can you access this information to build up a good stock of evidence?

- **Customers:** look at your research – which groups of people or businesses are likely to be your best customers? Create a customer profile. Focus on spending and buying habits – how do customers like yours prefer to buy and why? Ask people already working in the industry. Look on the Internet for annual sales figures and market statistics. If you are opening a shop or eating establishment, look at the footfall outside your chosen location. Visit online forums. Network online. Constantly ask questions. Find those fitting your target-audience profile to test your products or services and give you honest feedback. How would they improve it? What do they like about it? Would they buy it?

- **Forecasts:** research prices. Find out about credit terms and minimum orders from potential suppliers. Try to figure out how long it will take you to get your product to market and how many units you are likely to sell at what price in week one, week two and beyond. Be cautious as you may only be able to estimate, and many businesses fail because they dramatically underestimate expenses and overestimate revenue. Get prices from suppliers and competitors; find out what your gross margin and net profit will be and how many of your product you will need to sell; find out what is selling and what isn't. Calculate website traffic. Request figures from statistics providers and research companies. Get cost estimates from utility companies and service providers based on similar enterprises locally. Find out about insurance and import-duty costs. Be as prepared as possible and you'll find it far easier to accurately forecast and stay cash-positive. Conduct your own 'business survey'. Target a small selection of your intended customers and ask questions that will give you an insight into their buying habits and allow you to give an informed view of potential sales.

- **The market/industry:** uncover forecasted market trends and market drivers. Hunt for headlines and search for stories. Is the market big enough to grab a piece of it? How much market share is needed to establish a healthy annual profit? Find the

125

pulse in your industry; look for market leaders and issues facing your industry as a whole. Who is setting the benchmark, and how can you improve on that? What are they doing? How are they doing it? When did they start? How did they start? Is the market growing? How big is the market? Do any gaps exist for a smaller player? What is missing in the market now?

- **The competition:** probe for information to uncover what your competitors do and don't offer. Visit competitors' websites, become their customer, make an enquiry. Place orders, evaluate packaging and delivery speed. Find out about returns policies and delivery options. Ask what's in stock, what is selling well, and don't be afraid to ask questions. If you're going into a retail venture, see how much floor space is being devoted to certain products in similar stores. Unearth the weaknesses of your competitors. These factors can be used as stepping stones to your own successful strategy. Make their weaknesses become your strengths. Assess who is underdelivering or overcharging in your industry. How can you exploit that for the customers' advantage to give you the competitive edge? Can you tackle a market sector that your competitors have ignored?

It is vital to understand which niche groups of consumers or businesses are likely to become your best customers. How can you tailor what you are offering to suit different niche groups? Which untapped sectors can you pursue?

Cobra Beer is a fantastic example of targeting a niche audience. Half of the £60 million of beer they sell every year is sold across a UK network of Indian restaurants. This is evidence of thinking of something that nobody else is doing. Other brewers hadn't considered targeting the Indian restaurant market specifically. Karan Bilamoria did, and became a successful Tycoon in the process.

TYCOON TIP: Don't skimp on the detail. The more hard facts you can provide, the more real the business will seem in a potential investor's mind.

STAGE 2: Overcome the Identified Risks

After assessing the evidence that you have put forward to support your business case, a potential investor will have identified a number of risks involved. He or she will want to know how you plan to deal with these. This is a time when you need to be very thorough. There needs to be real substance to your plan of how you intend to tackle the risks involved because most investors will balance risk against reward when evaluating an idea – and if the balance is not on the reward side of the equation, then a potential investor is likely to walk away.

For example, on *Dragons' Den*, I have found that risk was higher than reward on many occasions. In particular, I remember the lorry-wash idea at motorway service stations. I felt that the whole business model didn't stack up, on the basis of not being able to get the throughput of lorries needed to make a healthy return on an investment. I felt that most haulage companies have their own spraywash at their depots anyway, and the smaller independents might use it, but that wouldn't be enough to have the units booked out each hour throughout the day. I was surprised to see my fellow dragons invest, but, as it turns out, those investments didn't close anyway.

So what could be the potential risks to your idea and your business? Well, business risks can take on many guises. Some can be predicted and you can be proactive in your handling of them to protect your business, and some you can turn into opportunities. Some cannot be predicted. You won't be able to tell exactly who you'll be competing against in the future, or may be unable to predict some changes in the market. But if you keep your finger on the pulse, you'll know about threats and risks sooner and quickly enough to deal with them reactively when you need to.

What Are Your Risks?

External threats:
- the competition, both now and in the future

- changes in market dynamics
- fluctuating economic conditions
- shifts in consumer trends and behaviour.

Internal threats:
- over-reliance on key personnel
- poor succession planning
- poor reward and development planning to retain and attract high-calibre people
- poor management of company information and data
- no performance monitoring.

There are many other potential threats. What are your identified risks, and how will you deal with these? Write them down. Once the time comes to write your business plan, detail those risks and how you intend to deal with them. This is a tool to reassure investors with. Furthermore, if you can uncover ways to turn these threats into opportunities, you will be well on your way to developing the Mindset of a Tycoon. Turning threats into opportunities can become relatively habitual behaviour for Tycoons; it's what Tycoons thrive on. By noticing a shift in consumer behaviour towards a certain trend early enough, you could unleash a product or service that will capitalise on that advantage.

Whether you turn risks into opportunities or simply become more aware and prepared when it comes to dealing with threats to your business, you should observe and get as close to the issues as possible in order to fully understand them. That way, when an investor raises the question of risk with you, you will be confident about your ability to overcome these potential future issues and this constructive and proactive approach will shine through and reassure the investor. In fact, your confidence and belief in your ability to overcome the risks involved will be one of the most compelling factors in convincing an investor of your potential and that of your business.

SWOT analysis – create a one-page analysis of the strengths, weaknesses, opportunities and threats for your business. Outline how you intend to optimise strengths, smooth out weaknesses, make the most of opportunities and deal with threats.

- **Strengths:** do you have a fantastic product or service? How and why is it different? What advantages does it have over your competitors? Do you have a skilled team? Are you entering a growth market? Are you targeting an untapped market or doing something better than anyone else?
- **Weaknesses:** do you foresee problems hiring the right staff? Might gaining credibility in this market take a long time? Does the location cause problems? Do you have enough money? Do you have a lack of experience in the sector?
- **Opportunities:** have you spotted a gap in the market or a specific niche audience you can target? Has a large competitor gone out of business? How can you take advantage of this?
- **Threats:** has a new competitor entered the market with a credible backer? Has someone created an online version of what you plan to do? How will you deal with these and other threats?

TYCOON TIP: Be realistic about the risks your business faces and turn yourself into an expert on how to deal with them.

STAGE 3: Decide Exactly How Much Investment You Need to Get Started

If you have put together a financial forecast that includes a profit and loss account and a detailed cash-flow projection, then you should have a very good idea of how much investment you need to get your business off the ground. If this is something that scares you, or you just don't know how to put something like this together, don't worry. Keep things simple: work out what you predict you will sell each month for a year, and deduct all the costs you can think of that you will have to spend each month.

You will see very quickly if you are likely to have a business with profit potential.

At this stage, you should be considering a list of potential investors. Remember you are not just limited to high-street banks. Business angels, venture capitalists and investment fund managers are all out there looking for the right people and businesses to invest in. Finding them might be difficult and will take time and effort, but if becoming a Tycoon was meant to be easy, everyone would do it. Remember, no pain, no gain.

So what are the options? Well, if you need less than £50,000, friends and family should be the first port of call, as this is the cheapest way to borrow. (Family may be keen to invest in you and your future without charging you for late repayments or high interest, but be wary of risking relationships.) The next port of call should be banks and local enterprise organisations to enquire about grants and loans that may be available. For example, Business Links are a useful gateway to grants to subsidise the training of new staff, pay towards connecting to the Web or redeveloping your website or even to subsidise marketing costs. There are also various grant opportunities for those investing in making their businesses environmentally friendly or targeting specific export markets.

You might approach a business angel or angel investor who'd require less of an equity stake than a venture capitalist. Venture capitalists are looking for high returns in fast-growth markets and are worth approaching if you are prepared to sell more equity for your investment and need £500,000 to £1 million or more of investment. They also look for reassurance by way of strong management teams with proven track records.

For existing businesses looking to scale up, banks can provide working capital and various methods of finance, and a Department of Trade and Industry initative, the small firms loan guarantee (SFLG), is available for businesses that are up to five years old who need a guarantee against their borrowing. This type of loan helps provide lenders with a government guarantee for loans up to £250,000 against default in certain circumstances.

You may find that overdraft finance and a loan from your bank are the best port of call. But remember, banks do not take risks. They need evidence and, nearly always, some form of security, in the form of assets that you own (your house or commercial property, etc.).

No matter which avenue you take to finance your business at start-up and beyond, those lending you money or investing in you will need to either know or believe that the business will be able to pay them back and return at least their investment and, more often than not, give them a very healthy return.

Before you start to approach an investor or apply for grants or loans, you need to work out all the figures. You need to have a firm grounding of what you are likely to pay out and receive for the first year of trading. Direct costs, expenses, bank charges, costs to acquire sales, everything should be listed, along with targeted sales.

- Can the income cover outgoings?
- Will you need to buy assets, machinery or have a website designed?
- What are your staff and outsourcing costs likely to be?
- Can you obtain credit from suppliers?
- How much can you afford to repay each month if you are taking loan finance?
- Can you ensure you won't run out of cash?

Remember, you might have invoiced a customer for a large sum, perhaps a quarterly payment, but they could take 60 days to pay you. If that were to happen, would you have enough cash to pay wages and cover all expenses? Running out of cash is the most common reason for business failure. Many profitable businesses go out of business because of poor cash flow. I lost my computer business after running out of cash. Red Letter Days went into administration because it didn't look after the costs of running the business and ran out of cash, before Theo Paphitis and I rescued it. (See pages 160–163 to read the story of how we turned round Red Letter Days.)

Consider everything from the cost of computers, product development, stock and stationery to postage and packaging, marketing materials, tax payments, rent and parking. If you are providing a service, what is the time input involved? How much do you need to sell to recoup your start-up costs? How much do you need to make to break even? How long is your sales cycle? So how long will it take from first making contact with a potential customer to taking the order, sending the invoice and receiving payment? How much working capital do you need to pay expenses until sales develop? Question everything. The end result will be a firmer grasp of how much you need to get up and running and stay running.

> **TYCOON TIP:** Be precise about exactly how much money the business needs. This shows potential investors that you have properly evaluated and have a clear understanding of what the business needs in terms of investment and, most importantly, what you intend to do with that investment to make it grow.

STAGE 4: Work Out the Likely Return on Investment

An investor will always want to get an idea of the likely return they will achieve from getting involved in a business. It is one of the key factors that fuels their interest in a project. Most people fail badly in this area of their business planning by not taking the time and effort to build up a solid picture of what the business is capable of and what the rewards are realistically likely to be.

You should examine and express your projections in three ways – the likely case, the best-case and the worst-case scenario. Draw up a detailed chart showing planned sales week by week, and a plan revealing how these sales and growth will be achieved.

For example:

The Likely Scenario Planned Sales	How We'll Achieve Them
Wk1 Wk2	
The Best-Case Scenario Planned Sales	How We'll Achieve Them
Wk1 Wk2	
The Worst-Case Scenario Planned Sales	How We'll Achieve Them
Wk1 Wk2	

In my early years of running a business, I hadn't appreciated the importance of clarifying the precise return on investment for a backer. I spent more time talking and getting excited about the idea that needed investment than I did putting solid financial plans together and demonstrating the actual return on investment, and left out the monetary reward they'd get from working with and investing in me. This left me with no alternative but to go cap in hand to the bank. As a result, I ended up having to give away so much more than I would have had to with an investor on board, including eventually the keys to my house and my car, because banks lend money and, for that, they want security. An investor invests in you and your business. Since then, the importance of ROI has been a focal factor in my success.

For Tycoons, the return on an investment is always a focal point, whether they are investing in someone, making an acquisition or preparing their own business for investment, sale or merger. Many will have learned the lesson of prioritising ROI the hard way when they ran out of cash.

So you must develop an understanding of the importance of ROI before you proceed. This will also help you to measure ROI across your business on every investment made, not just the ROI for your investor but the business ROI. Essentially, ROI measures how effectively a business uses its capital to generate profit: the higher the ROI, the better, from your marketing or ad campaign spend and your launch costs to telesales or website sales. For example, calculate what you have spent on your website, then total the actual sales that have come from your website. It may take time to get a return on your investment, but you need to measure and assess which expenditure has accrued value over time. So, if over two years your investment in your website has been £25,000 and in that time you've generated £70,000 profit through sales, it has been a worthwhile investment, with a good return. You can then invest more in the areas of your business that have seen a good return on investment in order to increase the business and boost profits.

Clearly, it is vital to know the return on an investor's potential investment *and* to know the return on investment for your own capital injection. Is what you spend on certain areas of your business making money? Is it enough to justify that spend? In knowing the answers to these questions and having a good grip on ROI within your business, you will enhance your business's value, not just because you are all on top of the numbers, but because you are focusing on the areas in your business that produce the best returns.

Remember, the reason an investor invests in your company is not to make a difference to your life and your lifestyle, but to make a return on the hard-earned cash of their own that he or she is placing in your capable hands.

It always amazes me when people pitching to me for investment aren't clear on their figures (their revenue, gross-profit and net-profit projections), or the real level of investment required, let alone having no idea on how to get a return on that investment.

TYCOON TIP: Get to know your figures inside out. Imprint them in your mind so you can explain them without referencing paperwork.

You will also add serious credibility to your business case if you are able to explain the seasonal peaks and troughs that will affect your business, as well as their impact on your working capital. If you can do this, it will demonstrate not only that you have a clear insight into the financial projections of the company, but that you are really on top of your game. The combined effect will give a potential investor or lender an important level of comfort that they are not about to throw their money into a black hole. And that will bring you one step closer to getting them on board.

TYCOON TIP: Don't ever believe that someone would invest in your idea for a business without knowing how much they will make in return.

STAGE 5: Write a Business and Financial Plan

A business plan is vital not only to attract an investor, but also for yourself. It helps you know where the company is going and how it is going to get there. Planning your business reinforces your passion about it. Having a map towards your vision reinforces your drive and boosts your confidence. It is also a key ingredient in attracting an investor.

To succeed in business and successfully get investment to help finance it, you need to know what you aim to achieve. Where do you want your business to be in one year's time, in three years' time and five years' time? How do you intend to achieve those goals and grow your business to achieve the market share you are striving for?

Do you plan to grow organically, by reinvesting all profits back into the business to avoid outside funding? Or do you plan rapid expansion with the help of outside investors? Which will be the best route for you and your business? Make these decisions now, before you set out your business and financial plans.

A business plan is a crucial tool for budding Tycoons to:

- Guide you in the right direction.
- Provide a benchmarking tool to focus on tangible and specific results.
- Help prioritise tasks and manage your goals more effectively.
- Attract investment or bank finance.
- Reach your endgame, which could mean selling the business in year three or floating the company.

And now that you have done all the groundwork that the previous four stages cover, you are ready to filter that information into your business and financial plans.

Your business plan should include:

- **Background:** what have you done so far? What experience do you have? How much time and money have you already invested? What have you sacrificed, and what are you prepared to do to achieve your vision?
- **Snapshot** of how the business will operate and what it actually does, including product or service benefits. What is your USP (Unique Selling Point)?
- **Market analysis:** is the market growing, declining or static? How do you intend to position your business in the market and achieve market share? Use statistics to reveal the size of the opportunity and reveal your timescales for entering specific markets. Who will your main customers be? Include your SWOT analysis of the position of your business within the market. Outline your expectations and elaborate with evidence.
- **Competitor analysis:** explain who the competition is and how you are differentiating your business. Detail how you intend to win customers from competitors.
- **Supporting evidence:** include bullet points from all the evidence you've collated to substantiate your claims and reassure yourself and your potential investor.
- **Marketing and sales:** briefly explain how you intend to reach your target market and communicate your messages to them, plus how

you intend to get your product to market and continue selling.

- **Detailed financial forecasts** for your business with a profit and loss account and a cash-flow analysis.
- **Action plan:** end with a 30-day plan. Specify everything you intend to do and why in your first 30 days.

If all this sounds completely daunting, don't panic. You can find a Business Plan Wizard on my website, **www.peterjones.tv**, and there are various start-up guides and software available to buy that will really help in planning your business effectively.

During my time in business, and notably more so since I've started investing in other companies, I have cast my eyes over a great many business plans. I've noted what grabs my attention and what turns my attention away. So here are my key rules for creating an effective and useful business plan:

1. **Keep it clear and concise.** This is crucial. Don't be tempted to stretch it out to dozens of pages, because the longer it is, the more laborious it will be for a potential investor to read. Think about it – is someone really going to sit down and trawl through 40 pages? Investors have a very short attention span because of their limited available time, so give them the headlines and the vital, salient points. If your business plan doesn't excite them in the first two minutes, they are not going to continue reading; it's as simple as that. In fact, I believe a compelling business plan can be written in three pages. That provides enough space for background, a quick snapshot about the business, its financial figures and forecasts, plus something about the market that the business is in.
2. **Include hard facts.** Think maximum impact and minimum fluff. Excite the reader. Give them something real and viable to believe in and invest in. Use evidence, statistics, feedback and market data from reliable sources.
3. **Reveal your passion, drive and determination.** Clearly illustrate your belief, summarise your vision and reveal what you've done so far.

4. **Know your market, your financial figures and forecasts and the risks involved.** Be aware of competition and be able to provide evidence to support your claims. Know your figures and return on investment. This is key not only when it comes to attracting investment, but also for your own peace of mind. Know your start-up costs and how much is coming in and going out of the business at any given time.

> **TYCOON TIP:** Keep your business plan clear, concise and compelling. Map out the direction you plan to take, have already taken and include enough evidence, facts and data to back up your future vision for the business.

All Tycoons know that planning for your success is as important as achieving it. You need to know exactly how you got there, what you did specifically to achieve your vision.

STAGE 6: Walk the Talk – How to Pitch

My five-year-old daughter, Natalia, watches *Dragons' Den* and sometimes she'll turn round and say, 'Daddy, that guy's silly. He doesn't have a very good idea at all.' Now, I know you're not pitching to get a five-year-old's interest, and five-year-olds may not be your target market, but if Natalia can see flaws in an idea, you can be sure a seasoned investor will in a heart beat.

So how can you stand out from the rest and get an investor's interest when you pitch? I've seen countless pitches and the majority would be far more successful in reaching a deal if they abided by the following Tycoon Tips on pitching:

1. **Dress appropriately.** That first impression is crucial. You wouldn't ask your bank manager for a loan dressed in jeans and a T-shirt, and you shouldn't expect me to invest in you if you don't know what is appropriate to wear in a given situation. Dress according to the request you are making.
2. **Be confident.** Have faith in yourself and your idea. Often I look

to invest in an individual as much as in their concept, so show what you can do! You get few opportunities to pitch directly to investors, so make the most of them. Even if they choose not to invest in you, it is a great opportunity to get some feedback from experienced businesspeople, and a confident pitch is more likely to generate either a deal or incredibly valuable feedback.

3. **Be honest** about your company and your forecasts. There is nothing more embarrassing than seeing someone who is pitching crumble when their figures are questioned and picked apart by savvy investors. Do not overestimate your capability: it will not inspire investors with enthusiasm or confidence in you. Some investments that are made on *Dragons' Den* fall through because pitchers exaggerate their past sales and business contracts, or are misleading about their contacts and their progress so far. In other instances, some clearly haven't thought their idea through well enough.

4. **Practise your pitch** in front of a mirror until you know it by heart and it is word perfect. Ideally, then practise it in front of your mum, your partner, your best friend – in fact, anyone you can rely on to give you honest feedback. Of course, when you're in a very small company, it can be difficult to know if your pitch will be effective. You're the person coming up with these ideas, but how do you know that somebody is going to buy it? Presenting your idea is crucial, and when I was building my business, we would have many meetings where my team would present to us. Whether it was a new sales division or marketing idea, we would all sit in a room and present our concept or idea. That enabled us to brainstorm. Would I buy it? Do I like the idea? Would I like that type of approach or not? What approach might be more effective? What are the risks? What's the opportunity? Occasionally, some members of my team would call me and try to sell the product to me. I would then critique the pitch, talk to them about it and give them feedback. It's very important to critique your pitch, to

fine-tune it and get it right, so that everybody is comfortable with it before you go out and use it to gain your objectives.

There's nothing better than sitting round a table and pitching your ideas to each other, because then you get to refine it. You look at specifics and ask yourself why you would want to buy that product or service. Why do I like that idea? Why am I interested? Why would I pay that amount of money? Why do I need it? I've always found that answering those 'why's can be very useful.

> **TYCOON TIP:** Eat, sleep and breathe your financial forecasts and the main points in your pitch. This will make the difference between success and failure when trying to secure an investment deal.

STAGE 7: Tell the Investor What You Have Been Through to Get to This Point

When talking to a potential investor, it is really important to be able to demonstrate the time and activity you have already put into your idea to get it to where it is now. Explain clearly what you have done, how you have done it and what you intend to do from here.

Half-baked doesn't cut it with me: I need to be able to see what has gone into an idea to get it to the point where it is ready for investment in order to grow and unleash its potential.

The more experience you have and the more clarity you can bring to your idea, the more impact it will have, both in the investor's office and in the marketplace, and therefore the more attractive an investment it is for an investor. This is the time to show the investor what you have given up, what you are prepared to do and what experience you have gained, to get across the passion, drive and determination you have for the business.

You may have sold your house, spent years building up solid foundations and contacts, and worked on testing the idea in the marketplace without paying yourself a salary. You might have given up a high-paid career to pursue your life-long dream, or spent a long time perfecting and honing your idea. Whatever commitment you've made thus far, you need to reveal this to any potential investor.

They're backing you, so you must convince investors that you don't intend to give up. Welcome them into your vision, share it with them.

'People buy from people' is a sales mantra that really means products are only half the battle. When it comes to selling a product, the person selling the product or the vision they create about that product is just as key.

Personality is critical, and so are first impressions. As an investor, you want to surround yourself and work with people that you believe you can get on with. Having said that, I'm not saying that I always invest in people who I like – there are some fantastic ideas I have seen from people I don't instantly warm to. If I think I can find a way to get on with an individual, I will still invest. I'm not looking for a new friend; I'm looking for another great business idea. There are people in my businesses who I wouldn't choose to go out for a drink with, but they do very well for the company. So I'm very open and I don't just dismiss people because I don't see them as people to socialise with.

If a business idea is very solid, then sometimes I'll invest in a person I don't particularly like or in someone who has qualities that I don't particularly like, as long as I know it's something I can work with and mould, because in time people change. The thing is, it takes all different kinds of people from all different walks of life to make a great business and it's ultimately success that matters. I would still invest if the idea interested me enough. However, if a person has a great idea but I know I definitely can't work with them, I'd rather walk away. Personality, passion and first impressions count for a lot when prising investment from a Tycoon.

TYCOON TIP: Investors invest as much in a person as in an idea. If you can really demonstrate your passion and commitment, then you are already halfway there.

STAGE 8: Decide Whether the Investor Is Right for You

So you have found someone who is willing to give you the money you need to start your business. This is great news, isn't it? Well, that depends. If your potential investor is not the right person for your business, you might be about to make the biggest mistake of your life. As desperate as you may be for the money, you really need to take time to get to know the person behind the investment before you sign on the dotted line and commit. Would you give someone you didn't know the keys to your car? Or your house? Thought not. You should therefore exercise the same amount of caution when choosing an investor.

Don't forget, you are going to be joined at the hip with that person until he or she is able to obtain a solid return on their investment, which could be many years. You don't have to like them, but you do need to get on with them and value their judgement and opinions.

It's like going out and finding somebody off the street to become a member of your family and then realising that you don't get on with them. There's a lot of risk when you take that on. It's like taking someone into your family who then feels that they're in control: they want to tell you what to do, when to wash the dishes, when to make the beds, when to get up and when to go to bed. And that's not necessarily a good thing. I, for one, couldn't stand it.

When I was looking for investment in Generation Telecom, we were lucky because I liked the individual and the investment directors that we met. Subsequently, I worked with a fantastic guy who came on board from their team and actually worked *with* us, and he wasn't overbearing. He saw and bought into the strategy, and they got a good return on their investment when the business was sold.

Ideally, choose an investor who will add value to the business, such as access to relevant people and businesses as well as cold, hard cash. This will really help to boost the success of the business by increasing the opportunity.

Sometimes entrepreneurs entering the Dragons' Den will be made an offer. Yet on occasions the entrepreneur opts out of the deal because they don't want to give away as much equity as they are being asked to hand over. In some instances, they might be right to do this, but not very often in my experience. They have not regarded the extreme added value that the investor would bring to the table.

In my opinion, it is far better to have a small slice of something huge than a huge slice of something tiny. With their investment of money, time, knowledge and contacts, the dragons offer many benefits and can help make a far larger business far more quickly than an entrepreneur might be able to do on their own.

> **TYCOON TIP:** Be discerning. You could end up spending more time with your investor than you do with your family.

STAGE 9: Decide on the First Thing You Will Do If You Get the Investment

Entrepreneurs commonly make one big mistake: when someone secures the investment money they wanted to fund a new start-up business, they think that the job has been done. In fact, getting the money you need is just the beginning. While the details of where the investment is going will have been spelled out in the business plan, keeping your investor informed about what you are doing with their money, when and why is a vital part of building up a solid working relationship between the two of you. If there are any surprises at this stage, on either side, then the relationship can become strained, and that could be hugely detrimental to the business. You must be open and honest in all your dealings at all times. Remember, they want the best for you and the business, so don't exclude them from being able to help. They will also have a wide network of contacts who might be very useful.

When we received the venture-capital funding for the group, we chose to invest in a business I named Generation Telecom. There were some months it didn't go well for us and we didn't hit targets, but there were always good reasons for that, and we were always moving in the right direction. Our communication channels with our investor were very strong. I never avoided them, and we always had an open-door policy. I think that is vital. There's nothing worse than silence.

You've got to respect the fact that your investor has put thousands, and in my case millions, into your business and therefore has to protect his or her investment. Even when things aren't going well and you want to hide and bury your head in the sand, it's best not to. It's far better to be open with your investors and financial partners. If you can forecast things are not going to go well, it's better to let them know, tell them what you're doing about it and where you think it's going. A lot of people bury their heads and wait for the big bang to happen; then the big bang comes and there's even more pressure.

In the case of Generation Telecom, I think the way we handled the relationship with our investor was one of the main reasons why it worked so well. And that's why I handle every relationship like that. You will work far better as a team if you deal with your issues and problems together than if you say, 'I didn't tell you about it because I thought we'd just get through it.' That's not good. You've got to have that transparency. At the end of the day, they're investing money, they're backing you and they're backing you for a reason, so you must convince investors that you don't intend to give up. Explain exactly what you are doing, welcome them into your vision, share it with them. Get their buy-in and believe in the team approach.

You also need to keep your suppliers, bankers or other financiers in the loop. Spending time developing key relationships with people – like bankers, customers and suppliers – is absolutely crucial, as you will give them a better understanding of your business. By keeping them regularly updated, you actually give them confidence in what you're doing.

A lot of people make this mistake. They borrow money and the next time they speak to a bank or a lender is when something's happened or gone wrong. Keeping them updated is vital. No one likes surprises, least of all when it's their money on the line. If they have confidence in you, they'll support you even further, so share information and take action.

It's a good idea to consider all the different stakeholders in your business and have a strategy for communicating with each of them. This also means that if you have times when growth gets a little bit out of control, especially when it grows very fast, you can pick up the phone and have a meeting quickly and explain what has happened. It's unusual for a business to experience explosive growth out of nowhere, unless you get a major order, but if you've already got a relationship with these people, they can see the business moving in the right direction and they will have the confidence to support you, then that's exactly what they will do.

Another benefit of building a great relationship with your investors and bankers is that when you need more money or additional help and resources, that line is open. Relationships are absolutely fundamental and key to success. Some entrepreneurs are loners and don't develop such relationships – not many of them go on to become Tycoons.

TYCOON TIP: Never lose sight of the fact that getting the money is the beginning of your journey, not the end. Develop an open-door policy with your backers from the outset and you'll help them to help you.

STAGE 10: Dealing With Rejection

So you didn't get the money. Rejection can be harsh. But as the saying goes, 'What doesn't kill you will make you stronger.' Dealing with rejection is all about passion and conviction and never giving up. If you get 99 people saying, 'No' to you, you have to believe that the 100th person will say, 'Yes' Looking at how you deal with rejection will help you understand what sort of person you are, and, more importantly, it will show those who observe you what kind of character you have.

How do you respond to what you're confronted with? Do you recoil, or beat yourself up about it, or do you learn from it and bounce back? How resilient are you?

Yes, you can dwell on rejection, and it is certainly worth

learning from a situation in which you have been rejected, but you need to stay focused on your goal and take the next step on your path towards your ultimate vision.

Don't be disheartened if you do visit the banks and find them not interested. The majority of Tycoons have had their requests for financial help turned down by banks. The notable factor is, this did not dissuade them from their efforts; it simply made them more determined to get what they wanted.

TYCOON TIP: Take rejection in your stride. Tell yourself it is their loss. Learn from any useful feedback and continue on your way.

SUMMARY: TYCOON PLANNING AND PITCHING CHECKLIST

- Have you generated honest appraisals for your idea?
- Have you taken your idea for a test flight?
- Have you substantiated your idea with real facts and figures to give your idea merit, and have you answered potential questions and objections?
- Have you assessed the viability of your idea? Is it different, better? Is it specialist or niche? Can it go global? Does it feel right?
- Do you believe in the idea and have the confidence to take it forward?
- Have you protected your idea?
- Have you pitched your idea to your team and others? Have you practised and polished your pitch?
- Does your pitch clearly and concisely reveal the opportunity, the return on investment and substantiate your claims?
- Have you bought your suit or got appropriate clothes to wear that look presentable and smart?

If so, you are ready to go out there, secure the investment you need and make it happen!

5

IGNITION! MAKING IT HAPPEN

The title of this chapter has been carefully chosen to try to capture the true spirit of the moment you have just reached on the path to becoming a Tycoon . . . Ignition! If you have ever purchased a new car, you will have appreciated that perfect moment when you drove your new vehicle for the first time. There it is at the dealership, gleaming, radiant and inviting . . . Once inside, there's that unmistakable new-car smell. You take a glimpse at the interior, taking in any extras you may have purchased, and glance at the dashboard and instruments, and then the moment comes when you turn the key and start the engine for the first time . . . A few gentle revs on the accelerator, some seat and mirror adjustment, and, tentatively, you're off. Once out of sight of the salesman, you will very likely proceed to the nearest stretch of straight, fast road to see what she's got. It's a magic moment, and it doesn't matter how many times you buy a new car, that first drive is always exciting.

The reason there is such a parallel for me between the moment that you kick-start your business into action and that of roaring off the forecourt in a new car is because that moment of ignition is the end of one very intense process and the beginning of another. Like your business development and planning process, a great deal of creative thought, design and market analysis went into the manufacture of the car before you bought it, and what happens to it after you turn the ignition key for the first time is purely down to you . . . because you are in the driving seat. As with driving, so with starting a business. There is potentially great enjoyment and satisfaction ahead, but also pitfalls and dangers – especially if you get overconfident behind the wheel of your embryonic business.

And, as a serial entrepreneur, I can tell you that it doesn't matter how many times you ignite a new business into being, it's always a magical and exhilarating moment.

This is where your journey begins. You could be at one of two destination points. Firstly, you may not have raised the money you need to start your business but have decided to press on regardless because you believe you can make a success of it by starting small and growing gradually. This is hard to do, but if you are following my methods, you will have certainly done all the planning and research to give yourself a better chance than most to be successful. You still need to make it happen, and this chapter will help you bring your business dream to reality. The second destination point could be that you've got the money for your cracking business idea. In that case, you are definitely 100 per cent ready to start making it happen. I'd like to say, 'Congratulations!' because you've come a long way.

Whichever position you are in, you now need to take a deep breath, as this is where the real fun begins. From now on, the stakes (and the potential rewards) are a lot higher, so you really need to remain focused if you want to stay on track towards your vision. There are a lot of distractions and diversions out there that can trip you up at any point; never forget you are on a mission to succeed. And you *can* do it. Just follow my 'highway code' checklist of how to proceed from ignition towards your success. It's divided into six mission steps, and it starts by getting you into the right frame of mind for the next stage of the journey.

MISSION 1: *Prepare, Focus, Commit – the Real Journey Begins Here*

'A successful, focused entrepreneur is a Tycoon'
ANONYMOUS

You might want to relax after all the hard work you've done in creating and validating your idea, especially if you have managed to obtain investment; this is a mistake that a Tycoon wouldn't make. If you think that all the hard work is behind you, it isn't. The truth is, this is when the hard work and pressure really begin. Yes, you've done the legwork to justify why your business will be a success, and you've also inspired interest and backing in your idea. Now it's time to step up to the plate and show you really have what it takes to make your vision a tangible entity, to make your dreams palpable.

Often when people come on *Dragons' Den* with a slick pitch and a great idea and secure the investment they wanted, they act like they have won a competition. You can see them breathe a sigh of relief and think, 'That's it now – I don't have to do any more. I've got my money sorted. I am going to succeed.' But they need to understand that this is just the beginning. In fact, if this was a race, they'd only just be approaching the starting block. The good news is, provided you remain focused and complete the missions laid out in this chapter, your hard work and preparation are highly likely to pay off.

If you look closely at the way an Olympic athlete operates, you will see that they do an enormous amount of preparation before they actually get on the track to start a race, before it's time to shine and seize their moment. They focus intently and put their preparation into practice in order to win. They commit. From the first visualisation they have of themselves winning to sitting down to their high-protein breakfast, to their six-hour daily practice regime, to the journey toward the starting block and the running of the actual race, all of this time they are continually and relentlessly focused. They start focusing as soon as they create the vision of their destination (the finishing line), and they don't stop focusing until they cross that finishing line and reach that objective.

Are you ready to win the race and maintain a strong focus, no matter what comes your way? That's a Tycoon's way of thinking. You'll need this focus, grit and determination to reach the top of your game.

TYCOON TIP: Stay focused. A person who aims at nothing is sure to hit it. Fix your aim and begin; focus your energies on the journey ahead and on reaching your chosen destination.

Of course, it's not just about what an athlete does and how they commit *before* a race; what they do on the track is equally important and ultimately determines whether they will win or not. If they don't prepare, they won't perform well, but preparation without performance counts for nothing. So, just as rushing out into the marketplace with an incredible product and little preparation will dampen an entrepreneur's chances of success, plenty of preparation without action or results will equally doom an idea to the reject bin.

Tycoons have a shared quality: they don't just prepare, they perform. They commit to action; they focus on goals. They get things done. It's the reason that Tycoons are so effective and quick at making decisions. Commitment is the bridge between deciding to do something and actually doing it, between decision and action.

The decision and commitment to take action in order to get the results you want, that's the *ignition* to make things happen! Commitment to act is a motivating force. It's empowering because it enables momentum to build. It helps you turn the key and get on with your journey. That's why commitment is one of my Ten Golden Rules for Tycoonism.

And what's great is that by completing the tasks, stages and missions outlined in this book – from crystallising your vision and researching your idea to planning your business and securing finance for it – you've already committed to your goal. You've done it. You have taken the first steps towards realising your goals and making your dreams a reality.

I have always committed to act – from the day I printed my first tennis-academy flyer to the present day. I commit from the moment I leave the house to the moment I return and beyond.

I work an average of 70 hours a week, and generally always

have. Tycoons work hard; that's part of their Mindset and one of the key factors in a Tycoon's success – effort, commitment, action. I always have weekends off, unless there's a deadline, in which case I will work from home. Saturday and Sunday, I'm at home and go out with friends in the evenings. On Sundays, we go for walks and have Sunday lunch with friends and the children, so I do manage to maintain some work-life balance. If I didn't, I wouldn't have the energy to maintain momentum and do all the things I have to do.

Indeed, I find myself busier than ever now because of TV and radio appearances. I can often be up before 6 a.m. and out of the house into London by 7 a.m. And then, from the media world, I come to work at 9 a.m., in the business world.

I'm committed to my businesses. A typical day for two or three days of my week would involve looking at what's happening on the TV side of the business, then reviewing the investment side of the business with my investment team. I'm then on the phone to co-directors of my other companies, which takes me through to a working lunch: talking about opportunities and what we're trying to achieve. In the afternoon, I'll look at deal memos, talk about contracts and go through areas of strategy, updating everyone on 'where we are now'. Then I'm out meeting with people, socialising and having business meetings in the evenings. Three days a week, I'll get home anytime between 10 p.m. and midnight. Fortunately, though, the other two days I'll be at home at 7 p.m., so I can help Tara put the children to bed and read them a story. I spend the whole weekend with them (which is very important to me and hopefully to them too!).

When I started my computer business, I would often be in the office at 7.15 a.m. and would literally focus on one business, but I had a bit more of a week-night social life at the time. And that's the difference. Back then, I was trying to do one thing right. Now, I'm trying to do a multitude of different things well. Evidently, to be a Tycoon, you need to commit time, effort and energy to your business – whether you are focusing on running one company or multiple companies, a focused, committed attitude is imperative. What's more, if you're not committed to your business, why should your staff, your suppliers or your customers be?

Right, let's commit right now. Go on, focus, take action. COMMIT. Commit to your vision right *now* by completing this exercise. You should, having read Chapters 1 to 4, be ready to fill in the gaps and commit your dreams to paper. So, let's do it!

My business idea is _____

_____

The business will provide _____ to _____

who needs this product or service because _____

_____

They will buy from me because _____

_____

_____

The product/service my business provides will be better than the competition

because I bring the following skills, experience and contacts to the table

_____

_____

My business will be called _____

Great things about my business are _____

Knowledge and skills missing includes _____

_____

The strengths and opportunities of my business are _____

_____

Key weaknesses and risks are

_____

_____

These will be managed/overcome by

_____

The business will succeed/I believe in this idea because

_____

In two years' time, the business will be

_____

In five years' time, the business will be

_____

I will make this happen, signed

Once you've committed to your business by conducting research, getting an understanding of the market, the potential customer-base and what's already out there, and have committed to writing a business plan and sourcing finance, you've made a vital commitment by preparing for the journey ahead and have started to take the action needed to get you to where you want to be.

But the real journey begins here! You've done the groundwork to validate your idea, you've committed to that idea, but you've only just begun.

Tycoons need to prepare adequately. And just as what an athlete does on the track determines whether they succeed or fail, the same is true in business. It's what you do once you've started the business that will create its outcome. Prepare adequately, but then act effectively.

TYCOON TIP: Preparation without performance counts for nothing. Prepare and make sure you've done the groundwork to validate your idea, but then commit to take action to make it happen.

MISSION 2: *Devise an Exit Strategy and Set Up Your Business*

Now, the title of this mission might surprise you. Why on earth would you start your business and consider how to end that business at the same time? The answer is simple: just as your vision is vital to provide a destination to plan a route to take, an ending is needed to complete your story. You need to know how you intend to get out before you get in. This is something that Tycoons often learn after they've lost a business or have run one or two businesses, and is not a lesson usually realised by a novice entrepreneur.

However, knowing the ideal ending is vital. Consider your business as a story, with an introduction, a beginning, a middle and an end. The introduction is the idea formulation – the research, the planning and the securing of investment; the beginning is the business launch – when you turn the ignition, get out there and make it happen; the middle is the part during which you flourish and grow, take on staff, build relationships with partners, invest, diversify, acquire, and the time when 'the plot thickens'. And the ending? Well, the ending is up to you. You want a happy ending, so write it down, plan it out, commit to making it happen. This is called your exit strategy, and you will often have people asking you what yours is, as you progress with your business.

An exit strategy is quite simply what you intend to do with the business after it is up and running and achieving your goals, usually between two and seven years after you started it. You'll need to consider whether you want to:

- Sell the business (either entirely or in part).
- Float it on the stock market.
- Merge it with another company.

- Build up enough profits to buy a key competitor.
- Simply make money and run the business for the cash it generates.

It may sound crazy to be talking about selling a business you haven't even started yet, but you really do need to think very carefully about where you are heading long before you get there. Potential investors are understandably keen to know all about your exit strategy because if they invest in your company, they want to know when they'll be able to get their money out and get a return on their investment.

If you do not intend to sell your business, then you need to work out how you intend to repay the investor; from profits? From a bank loan further down the road? Either way, you need to think about your future plans now.

Tycoons always keep in mind how they intend to get out before they get in. They think carefully about where they are heading long before they get there.

TYCOON TIP: Devise an exit strategy so you know whether you intend to sell, float or merge your business and when you intend to do so.

Tycoons also make sure that they exit in the most tax-efficient way. The best way to do this is to make sure you own the share capital in the business for at least two to three years, and it's an individual company, not part of a group. (Share capital is the main portion of a corporation's equity, which can be retained or obtained from issuing shares in return for investment.) If you own a group and put companies into that group, you'll need to sell the group to benefit from tax relief, because selling one company within a group generates a higher tax liability. Selling a business that you have owned for at least two years means you qualify for 'taper relief' and will only pay 10 per cent of the sales proceeds on tax.

My advice is to:

- Keep your companies individually as limited businesses for at least two to three years. Then, when you sell all your shares, you get taper relief. (So you pay only 10 per cent tax instead of potentially 25 per cent or more.)
- Work out exactly who you're going to sell to: who the likely buyers are and who the big players are.
- Find out who's invested in those big players. There are a lot of private equity groups who've invested in big players. Not many people consider private equity groups, but they might invest in you if they've invested in the big players already. They often want to grow the companies they have invested in and are very keen on acquisition. It grows their business and takes a competitor out at the same time.

My Mindset

In 2002, I set up a company called Generation Telecom, which provided mobile phones as well as airtime to businesses operating in the rail sector. These types of companies often employ large numbers of people spread across a wide geographic area, all of whom need to communicate effectively because they rely on quick transfer of information, be it voice calls or use of data services (such as email on the move). Mobile communication is therefore a key industry requirement.

My strategy for this business was very clear to me: our best approach for the business was that we would not dramatically grow the customer base, unless we could acquire customers cost effectively. Instead, we would get more out of our existing customers. In other words, we would dedicate more time and resources to understanding the actual communications needs of our existing customers and deliver targeted products and services to meet those needs. In short, we would maximise and increase revenue from each individual customer, rather than spending money to acquire new customers.

We wanted to build it into a very niche and profitable business that would tie the customers into long-term contracts to create long-term business value. My medium-term strategy was that within two to three years I wanted to sell the business. I even knew who the most likely buyer was. You see, we weren't growing for growth's sake, because I realised we could never dominate the marketplace by becoming the biggest player; we were growing to make the business the best possible acquisition target for a company who wanted to have dominance in a particular niche market area.

The exit strategy happened just as I'd planned from the outset. Within two years we sold the business to a large UK mobile-phone network, Vodafone, for millions of pounds – the strategy had worked.

I knew the endgame from the outset. Because of preparation, research, knowledge and understanding the market, I knew who the potential buyer of the business would be and why they would buy the company. The exit strategy and how we intended to get there was mapped out from the start.

It can't always happen as straightforwardly as this, and it certainly wasn't as simple as it sounds, but this is a very real example of how a Tycoon's mind works – sometimes, identifying the killer business idea isn't enough; it's also about having enough awareness and under-standing to know how investment in the business can be realised quickly through a sequence of smart, considered moves.

Interestingly, people often wonder why large corporate entities choose to acquire small, niche businesses rather than just putting a team in place to grow that segment or market themselves. It brings me back to return on investment (ROI). Sometimes, for a large company that is, say, quoted on a stock market and hence is focused on creating shareholder value, investment in a slow-burn opportunity that may not reap rewards quickly doesn't cut it with the analysts - unless they can really see a huge pay-off looming for all the effort. However, a quick acquisition that immediately delivers increased shareholder value, or consolidates a particular area of the market, thus increasing the bigger player's foothold, should deliver a very healthy ROI, especially if the business being acquired is profitable and adds great value immediately.

It's worth looking closely at how large corporations operate, and what their drivers and pressures are. You never know, this kind of knowledge could provide a very valuable exit route for your own business one day.

Set Up Your Business

As I said, you need to keep in mind how you are going to get out before you get in. So, once you know the planned ending, you need to create your beginning. And that starts with informing the relevant authorities.

If you want to be a lifestyle entrepreneur and earn enough revenue to cover your personal bills and costs, it is deemed more tax-efficient to take sole-trader status, as sole traders retain all profit after tax and record-keeping is less complex. The personal risk to sole traders is, however, higher. If the business fails, a sole trader is liable to pay for business failure from their own pocket.

You can become a limited company after being self-employed or set one up from the outset. However, if you want to be a Tycoon and grow a business or group of businesses, you will generally need to be running a limited company, unless you are starting a law firm or a firm of accountants, for example.

Setting up a limited company from the outset gives entrepreneurs a shareholding director position within the company. Despite increased paperwork and corporation-tax liability (a director pays income tax as an employee of the company; the company pays corporation tax on its net profit), you and your business are viewed as separate entities, so the liability for business debts is reduced. It can be easier to borrow money as a director of a limited company, and entrepreneurs can establish improved credibility within their marketplace by operating as a company.

If setting up a limited company, you need to register the company with Companies House and pay a registration fee. You must also notify the Inland Revenue. You can use www.peterjones.tv and www.tycoon.com for all your information needs, from giving you real examples of how to set up a company to contact information and resources to create a new business.

A partnership is another option and can be set up with one or two other people, giving each partner a percentage of the return of the business, depending on how much time and money they've invested. Partners are classed as self-employed, though, so each partner is liable personally for debts incurred by the business. Partners share the profits, but also the burden and risks, so if one partner incurs business debts, other partners are liable for them as well.

Once you know the status your business will assume, it's time to file the relevant paperwork, notify the authorities and take the next step by creating a strategic action plan.

MISSION 3: *Develop a Strategy and Plan of Action*

strategy

● noun. **1** a plan designed to achieve a particular long-term aim; **2** the art of planning and directing military activity in a war or battle.

Tycoons are strategists and tacticians. Every business needs a core strategy. Your business plan details where you want your business to go and how you want it to get there. A strategy is essentially a game plan: a long-term action plan for achieving a goal. And tactics are the actions planned to achieve that specific end goal.

The word 'strategy' originates from the Greek word '*strategia*', which means 'generalship'. Certainly, you need to lead your team via strategic guidelines and give them tactics to employ, just as a general might, but without the brute force.

Strategy is important because unless you are able to explain your company's goals and aspirations, strategy and tactics to the people who work with you, it will be very difficult to achieve the vision of the future you are trying to create. You also need to monitor your strategy at regular intervals to check that you are still on track and still moving in the right direction.

For that reason, a strategy needs to have a realistic timeframe. If a business is going to take years to plan, then you could find that by the time you have put a strategy together, someone else has already beaten you to it. If an opportunity comes your way, you need to get moving on it straightaway – in other words, days and weeks, not months and years. Working out your long-term strategy quickly enables you to get on and deploy it earlier thatn the competition. Speed is a key part of strategy.

For example, viewers of *Dragons' Den* may remember the pair of entrepreneurs who paid a visit to the den twice with their Baby Dream Machine. The first time they pitched their innovative portable pushchair rocker, they turned down an offer of investment. The dragons advised them that somebody else would beat them to it, and, sure enough, when the pair turned up for the following series, there were similar products on the market and they also wanted to raise nearly £100k more than the last time, which resulted in the dragons not being interested enough to invest.

However fast you act, it's important to have a clear strategy to help you meet your objectives.

My Mindset

Sometimes Tycoons need to employ tactics and strategies to turn around businesses they invest in. For example, the gift-experience company Red Letter Days ran into trouble and went into administration. Fellow entrepreneur Theo Paphitis and myself decided, after considering the opportunities and risks, to step in and save the business. After acquiring the business from the administrator, we set about creating a strategy to completely overhaul the business and return it to its number-one position in the marketplace.

Sounds easy, doesn't it? But it was one of the highest-profile company administrations in recent years, which attracted a considerable amount of press and media attention over a sustained period of time. It wasn't just the fact that two high-profile TV entrepreneurs had stepped in to save the day – it was more that millions of people were sitting on vouchers for experiences they hadn't yet claimed, and the company going into administration effectively made these vouchers worthless. It was a turnaround that was right in the public spotlight from day one.

The day we took ownership of the assets of the business, we effectively had a house that had fallen down, so we had to clear the rubble, while keeping the foundations in place. Rebuilding the house without doing damage to the foundations was the core goal that underpinned every action. From that core objective, we created a strategic action plan with the tactics we'd need to use to meet our objectives and head in the right direction. This plan included assessing the existing activities and looking at the existing suppliers to make informed decisions going forward. However, a priority was to restore public faith in the business and the brand – one of the business's main assets.

The first decision we had to make was whether to honour the majority of vouchers that were out in the market. The money for those vouchers had been taken by the old Red Letter Days, so we knew we weren't going to receive any money back if we did. In fact, we would lose millions, since we had to pay the suppliers in order for our customers to receive their Red Letter Day experiences. Both Theo and I agreed wholeheartedly that honouring those vouchers was the right decision: we believed our customers would appreciate it and we'd not only maintain the brand's credibility but build huge loyalty among customers and suppliers alike. Theo and I worked tirelessly in those first few weeks, meeting suppliers and deploying our turnaround strategy. We did this together and nine times out of ten we held face-to-face meetings with the suppliers whose own businesses were affected by the problems of Red Letter Days. This action alone meant a lot to the people we were talking to, who had their own livelihoods at risk. We felt it was an important part of our job to communicate our strategy to as many people as possible - as we needed support and understanding to restore the business and get it back on track.

It didn't take long for Theo and myself to get under the skin of the old business and look at how we could make a huge difference very quickly. Key to this was the need to ensure we could have margin control (i.e. control over how much profit would be made). We needed to know what our margin was going to be and couldn't rely on non-redemption of vouchers, which the business had been reliant upon up to that point. Maintaining margin control became the first strategy within the overall goal of rebuilding the company.

We took the bold decision to pull Red Letter Days vouchers out of retail channels because it took a large percentage of the margin away from the business – a big decision, but key. We now go direct to the public so we are able to give them not just a better service, but more of a selection, a far improved choice. Rather than just buying a driving day from Red Letter Days for £99 or a choice of one or two other experiences that a store might offer, you can choose from hundreds of experiences on the website, www.redletterdays.co.uk, or over the phone. This clever tweak of steering away from retail sales toward direct sales has been successful. We are considering working with retail in the future, but will only allow that to happen if the margin isn't greatly affected, and we can keep our level of service at an exceptional level.

We also looked at operational strategy to ensure the money being spent on wages and services was the best use of the available funds. This led to us downsizing the business in certain areas. In our operational action plan, we listed tasks such as outsourcing the call centre for a period of time, until we got our internal call centre right, then closing that outsourced service down to bring it in-house. We also needed to take tough decisions in terms of staff numbers, as it was clear the business we had inherited could not support the number of people it employed, which was in hindsight one of the key factors that led to its demise.

The next step was to put a very effective management team in place by recruiting some of the best people for the roles required. Bill Alexander, a turnaround specialist and qualified accountant, took over the managing director role after Theo and myself had steadied the ship, and is still there today. He has been instrumental in turning around Red Letter Days and returning it to its position as the UK's leading experience provider.

We also brought in Zach Soreff, who was previously the head of marketing for the Hard Rock Café chain, and tasked him to use his creative talents to inject new life into the brand and the marketing activities of the business. The marketing strategy was about optimising quality and focusing on generating cash and loyalty. The strategic action steps included working closely with the suppliers to honour most of the vouchers that were out there when the company went bust. It was a case of spending wisely to generate the right reward and achieve the right objective.

Now, Red Letter Days is back. It's managing its own upward growth, which is very good. We've done all of that within 18 months. But we couldn't have done it without a clear goal, a clear strategy and an action plan to get us there. This project has seen Theo and I working together, and it's been enjoyable to have a different perspective. One month I'm chairman, and the next month he's chairman. We're making it work by implementing clear strategies of spending wisely and maintaining margin control, plus focusing on customer choice and building a team of people who are regarded as the best in the industry.

In Chapter 4, we looked at the importance of having a plan of intended targets with clear actions and timescales, along with completing your business and financial plans and drawing up a 30-day action plan. Well, at this stage, you should create a 100-day strategic action plan, outlining the key tasks to complete in order to achieve certain results by taking on a certain strategy, so turn your 30-day plan into a 100-day plan. You will be amazed how far you can see, and it will, without doubt, bring out elements you hadn't actually thought about before.

So many people say, 'Right, I've got my business, I've got my office, I've got my telephone lines, these are the people I'm going to contact, so let's just get on with it.' Well, that's not strategic. It's not good enough to do that. You need a 100-day plan that details everything you need to do.

> **TYCOON TIP:** Create a strategic action plan. Expand a 30-day plan into 100 days to uncover all the areas you need to tackle to reach your objectives.

Ask yourself, 'What do I want from this business?' Before you step on the path, outline in clear and concise detail everything you intend to do in the first 100 days of your business's existence. This gives you a picture in your mind of what you're trying to create and what you need to do. It gives you instant milestones to work for and focus on. I am not saying you should work in rigid 100 day chunks and ignore things you haven't planned for, things you need to just get on and do, but I promise you that you will find it quite amazing when you detail everything you need to do and it will really keep you focused.

The more resources and research you put into your idea, the better. Detail everything from organising stationery and contact with the bankers to VAT and planning your website . . . all the things you have to do. You need to work out how you'll gain and retain custom and what actions need to be taken in order to do that. Then link your strategic action plan back to your business plan and monitor it, ticking off your milestones and actions as you go.

Remember, action and results are two of my Ten Golden Rules for achieving the Mindset of a Tycoon.

By focusing on results-oriented tasks and strategies, you can create a blueprint for your long-term business success. Strategy is crucial.

Sometimes entrepreneurs have appeared on *Dragons' Den* with something that in principle stacks up and could work. It might be timely and solve an issue that has received a lot of media attention or public support. The entrepreneur may have sufficient evidence to substantiate their claims. They might even have valid proof that a consumer segment is motivated by the benefits their product offers. However, they might not have spent enough time on working out their strategy and tactics to achieve the goals they put forward in their pitch. Their idea could still be flawed. For example, there might be a huge target market of 30 million potential customers and a loyalty scheme may be pitched as the key revenue driver and strength of the proposition. They might even use supermarket loyalty schemes as a benchmark for their own planned scheme.

However, most loyalty schemes are born out of an activity that already has a lot of users, subscribers or customers – in other words, a captive market. The business seeking investment has no such database and no direct relationship with any of the 30 million potential customers. The plan might involve attracting them to a website, but that would cost a lot of investment in driving traffic to the site and raising awareness. If an investor or backer uncovers flaws in your idea or thinks you are over-estimating the opportunity and underestimating the cost and resources it will take to realise that opportunity, you won't secure investment. And if you can't clearly define a strategy to overcome that flaw, your business may not work out as you had hoped.

Having a clear direction is one thing, but the strategy needs to be workable. Creating an action plan is a great way to find out where refinements need to be made. Use plausible benchmarks and you'll find out which strategies to pursue and which tactics to take.

TYCOON TIP: Failing to plan is planning to fail. Use your action plan to dig down to uncover potential flaws in a strategy and adapt accordingly.

My Mindset

We use the 100-day plan even today, in our established businesses, especially when we are planning group IT projects. This is simply a list of everything we need to do in the first 100 days following the launch to make our IT implementations happen. When starting a new venture we create a plan and it can have as many points on it as I need to cover everything – it could be a list from one to 3,000, if that is what is required. This 100-day plan will cover everything from buying a desk, opening up a bank account and setting up a website through to speaking to customers. Absolutely everything you can think of should be on it, and it is also good to divide the plan into sections, such as finance, marketing and so on. It's the same concept as writing a to-do list. This is a business to-do list with a strategy.

MISSION 4: *Get the Logistics Right*

Logistics is another word to describe your delivery mechanism. If you are delivering a service or product to customers, then you need to carefully consider how you are going to get it to them – this doesn't just mean the costs and methods of postage, but every operation from order to dispatch to delivery, follow-up or return.

The simplest way of thinking about your logistics is by drawing a flow chart. At one end, draw a picture of your product or service, and at the other end, draw a picture of the customer. Now write down each of the stages the product takes to get to the customer. This could include taking the order, packing the product at the warehouse, delivering it to the shop, training the salesperson and so on. Whatever the stages are, the secret is to write it all down and visualise the complete process from beginning to end.

Logistics sits right at the heart of your business, so you need to invest time to ensure you have the capacity to deliver on your promises and goals, and have the ability to expand and scale your business as it grows.

166

A very experienced MD I once employed taught me a valuable, yet unusual lesson. He explained a great method of getting a better understanding of logistics. You might find this a bit strange, but remember what I said in Chapter 1 about imagination? Well, I have been known to pretend to be the product myself. Yes, that's right, the actual product. If I was delivering a mobile phone, or repairing one, I would pretend to be that phone. I would turn up in reception (being delivered from the supplier) and then get my team to handle and deal with me in the same way they would if I was a phone. They would take me to the 'booking-in' area (I would get to see how long I was there for), they would label me, store me or, if I was being repaired, take me to the test bench and so on until the end of the process. I can tell you, it is the fastest and most effective way to test your logistics! Try it yourself – you might be amazed at the results.

Many people fail in business because they keep so much information in their head that they forget to do things or become so stressed they become ineffective and do the wrong things. Then when they start to build a business and take on staff, the problem is compounded, because no one really knows what is going on. It's not written down or documented. There are no procedures, processes or operation manuals. If you are disorganised and not thinking clearly because you haven't documented anything, then you will end up creating a company that acts in the same way: it will be disorganised and ineffective. In fact, it will be even worse, because the people you employ will not have the same level of passion and drive and enthusiasm as you do for your company, as they won't know the strategies or vision, so won't buy into it. As such, they will not have your mindset. Logistics and operations need lots of thought.

For me, building a business is like building a house. If you want to build a house that is going to stand up to the weather, then you need to build it correctly. Don't skimp on the foundations, because in five years' time you are going to have problems with subsidence. Don't put the wrong roof on the house, because it is going to leak. Putting the right framework and foundations in place for your business is vital. Cracks will inevitably begin to show if your foundations, logistics and procedures are not solid.

To stick with the house analogy, the four corners for the foundations of a strong business are:

1. **Leadership:** the personality traits have to embody determination, passion, drive, enthusiasm, creativity, imagination, a 'never give up' attitude – those Ten Golden Rules that make up a Tycoon's Mindset that we looked at in Chapter 1. You have to have those personality traits as the first foundation.
2. **People:** you have to understand that business is about 'team' and not about 'I'. Tycoons must have that team-building emphasis and be able to develop a team but work *with* a team, not just employ people. Understand why you're employing people and the job you want them to do, then give them clear and focused objectives. A solid team ethos is a vital foundation and building block to success.
3. **Structure and operations:** next, look at the foundations and the layer cake of what it takes to operate a business. Make sure you have the right infrastructure in place, the right funding, the right IT systems and everything else in position before you go down a long, dark hole.
4. **Planning:** the planning and the research that goes into that business – that's the brick, that's the square – a vital foundation to turn an idea into a winning enterprise. Without planning, your business may topple.

With these four 'corners' in place, selling the 'house' becomes easy. Relate this to the business and a successful company will result.

'But what about spontaneity and acting on sudden creative impulses?' I hear you say. 'Won't structures, flow charts and foundations hamper that zest for creativity? How do you ensure that there is a structure in place so that everyone in the company feels confident that they know exactly what they are doing, yet people can still act on instinct and make decisions very quickly?' The answer is to put in place the right kind of structure that will underpin rather than dictate the flow of the business. As you and your team gain experience of running the business, you will find certain structure-based actions become instinctive over time. It becomes second nature to do something a certain way. Please don't sacrifice creativity for planning and structure. Build a framework, but allow change. In fact, welcome change – especially when it has occurred as a result of creative ideas and solutions.

That ethos spreads down into the team, individuals within it and the actions they take. And that creates a structured, effective and organised operation in itself with tight procedures *and* creativity. This filters into everything, from creating new proposal ideas, down to answering the phone. When someone first joins a company, they will be given a script telling them what to say when they answer the phone. After a few days, they are not going to need a script any more, because they will remember what to say. They will pick up the phone and just do it – it becomes natural.

> **TYCOON TIP:** Putting the right framework in place is fundamental to the success of a business. Get the four corners in position, ensure operations and logistics are documented, and create a transparent ethos where everyone knows the right way to do things.

MISSION 5: *Kick-Start Your Sales and Marketing*

So, you've created a strategic action plan to help you achieve your objectives and targets, from setting up your IT system and contacting suppliers to securing your first customers. Of course, in order to attract those customers in the first place, marketing the business will be a priority action on that plan. And in order to persuade them to buy, sales will be another key action. Yes, it's time to get practical, to get out into the marketplace and get active with marketing and sales.

Sales don't just happen. They need to be actively fought for and won. All too often new entrepreneurs leave sales and marketing to the last minute in the belief that they will be fairly straightforward to get going. Unfortunately, they forget that without sales and marketing, and clear plans to drive these activities, their business will not deliver revenue. No custom, no sales, no profit, only operating losses, which means it won't be going anywhere fast. All that serves to do is put unnecessary pressure on you and your business before you've even started.

Therefore your sales plan should be a fundamental part of your business plan. That means you need to have a good idea of where the business is looking to generate its revenue and how this will be delivered. For example, are you planning to have dedicated employees who will be solely focused on getting sales? Or will you focus on developing e-commerce sales via your website?

When you think about sales, you must think about marketing. You need a marketing plan. In order to generate custom, you need to make people aware of your existence, and there are many ways to do so from getting known as an expert in your field by writing articles for publication in targeted publications and websites to TV and radio interviews, or getting your press release in trade and local press, running seasonal promotions and deals, networking at business events or direct marketing activity to a targeted audience. Harness the power of your imagination again to brainstorm ideas that will have an impact on your target audience, enough to persuade them to buy from you. You need to start thinking about the branding and identity of your business and draw up a calendar of marketing events you plan to hold throughout the next year – not forgetting how much they are going to cost you and how much revenue you hope they will bring in. All ideas need effective marketing and sales strategies to make them work.

Unfortunately, some people who have pitched for my investment have let a good idea cloud their judgement on the business basics. For example, their website might have little information about the product or the business, with no assurances and USPs (unique selling points) about the product available, or they haven't had a sales or marketing strategy for attracting attention in the marketplace and getting big retail partners on board. You need to tick the sales and marketing box in order to make your business operate effectively.

Marketing is about attracting attention, inciting action. It's about keeping customers and prospects informed, letting people know about what you have to sell and doing so in a way that stands out from your competitors.

Fortunately, Tycoons are creative types. As such, they have many impressive marketing ideas. You might not have the cash to put all of your ideas into action. The good news is, word of mouth costs nothing. This means that if your product or service is outstanding, your customer service is exceptional and you deliver on your promises, your customers will do some of your marketing for you. They'll do this by recommending you to others, and referrals are by far the best kind of custom. Not only that, they don't cost a thing.

Word of mouth is a key ingredient of a successful marketing strategy. Naturally, there is much else to consider, from creating a strong brand identity, mission statement and marketing messages with impact to uncovering the right audience, defining marketing objectives and strategies and using the right promotional tools and tactics to achieve them. The best product in the world won't sell if you don't market it and make people aware that it is available. If people don't buy it, word of mouth becomes irrelevant. And no customers equates to no business. In getting out there and taking an idea to the marketplace, Tycoons know they must communicate what they're offering in a clear, compelling and concise manner, and that can take practice.

We spoke in Chapter 4 about presenting your pitch for investment to others and asking questions to refine it. Well, you should use the same approach to marketing and selling. If testing the market by phoning people to gauge interest, use *all* feedback. It doesn't get you anywhere to make 1,000 calls and not get one result; it's what you do with the feedback provided by those who say, 'No.' If someone says they're not interested, go one stage further: ask them why they're not interested. This feedback is vital. It will enable you to overcome objections at sales stage, enhance your sales pitch, tailor your marketing messages and even shift your focus towards new target audiences. Marketing messages must be memorable. Always keep in mind 'What's in it for them?' Listen to all the feedback you generate.

To succeed in business, you need to think about action-oriented marketing and sales literature that has enough impact to encourage the reader to act. Tycoons take action very seriously themselves in order to get them to where they want to be, but they also encourage action from their customers. They want customers to pick up the phone, visit their website and place an order. For that reason, marketing material must tell the reader exactly what they should do next. Make it compelling. Ask yourself, 'Would I call and order it?'

With consumers and businesses being bombarded with so many marketing messages on a daily basis, you need to be different and slice through the noise to grab attention.

TYCOON TIP: Make it clear why buying from you is a far better choice than buying from anyone else. Magnetise your messages so your customers are drawn to you.

The good news is, because you have completed Chapter 3, you'll have researched enough to uncover the key benefits of your product or service, which will give you the right words for your sales pitch, marketing messages and literature, so you should already have what you need to create messages and materials with maximum impact.

Once you've attracted attention with your marketing, you need to sell. And in order to sell effectively, you need to add value. So dig deep. How can you add value to beat the competition? How can you use your competitive advantage to really make it happen? How can you stay one step ahead and smash your sales targets? Think tactically.

I'm often asked how my telecoms business achieved sales of £13.9 million in our first year of trading. After all, it's widely reported that the majority of new businesses make a loss or minimal profit in the first year or two.

Well, I'm letting you into my mindset, so let me explain:

My Mindset

We started to look at the product set that the manufacturer, Ericsson, had. They had created a range of about five types of products. So we looked at each of those products and rather than just trying to sell them all, we looked specifically at who would buy the individual models, using Ericsson's new product-development information and our own thinking to try and take it on a step in terms of targeting potential customers.

Our plan was to buy carefully selected media advertisements where we knew the audience best matched the target customer of the product concerned. We then placed specific targeted adverts in trade press, national press and even in the *Sunday Times*, focusing on the key products. For instance, the PDA MC218 mini computer device, we put into the *Sunday Times* supplement magazine and sold it off the page; we sold a lot. Conversely, with one of the simpler mobile-phone products, we went to small dealers and sold it in the local shops. So we looked at the product set and asked, 'Who's going to buy that?' Through continued expansion of this approach, we eventually developed new channels across a range of market segments that Ericsson had previously seen as just one. We didn't see it as one; we split it up and that increased sales exponentially.

We then decided to increase the number of partners we had and the number of retailers selling those products, to scale up our already effective strategy. We set up an authorisation programme to get people in local stores trained so they could talk in a more informed manner to potential customers in-store. So when someone came in to ask for a mobile phone, the salesperson could suggest that the customer choose an Ericsson phone or PDA device, because it had certain features, a particular battery life and so on.

We believed if we had those people well trained, they'd sell an Ericsson because they knew all about it. At that time in the mobile phone market, staff training and product knowledge was generally quite poor. They didn't know about the Nokia or the Motorola or the Samsung, because they weren't given detailed training and information. We were one step ahead by equipping them with the knowledge to sell more of the phones we wanted them to sell. We were tactical about it, and it just exploded.

Once that was all in place, we focused on certain handsets. For example, we saw the flip phone come out, the T28. And I said to my team, 'That is going to be a best-selling handset; people are going to love the "Beam Me Up, Scotty" flip phone.' It hadn't come out before, and there'd been a big push with James Bond around that time, so we decided to do a promotional marketing campaign among all of our customers to go and push this flip phone to the end user. We ended up selling thousands and thousands of this model by using a focused strategy. In fact, we sold £3 million more of this product in six to eight weeks than we planned to sell, smashing our targets.

Of course, our success wasn't all about the strategy I deployed. Ericsson obviously played a major part, by spending a lot of money on marketing and activities themselves to drive consumer awareness, and that obviously helped us massively. But we maximised on the opportunity by being focused and introducing innovative ways to sell their products. We used their umbrella awareness and branding activity to support our niche marketing approach.

Every time we bought products, we made sure we paid Ericsson as promptly as possible. We were selling the product almost as quickly as we were getting it in because of our activities, so we were cash-generative.

- We harnessed the right marketing and sales strategies to win custom from the competition.
- We set clear targets; we focused on the customer profile, target audience and their needs.
- We focused on training and equipping operatives with specific knowledge to arm them adequately with the tools they needed. (See the advice about the gladiator approach on page 82.)
- We scaled up and out via developing partnerships with other manufacturers.

We later grew our business by developing partnerships with other manufacturers but though adapting the same sales philosophy. Something I called, as you know, single brand distribution.

The Marketing Mix and Plan

Over 40 years ago, the four Ps of the **Marketing Mix** were identified by marketer and author J. McCarthy. These are:

- **Product:** what it is about your product or service that meets customers' needs? What are those needs and wants? What problems does it solve? What are its unique or noteworthy characteristics? With my telecoms business, we figured out where to distribute and who would buy after answering these questions. We honed in on individual products when others didn't.
- **Price:** how much will you charge for your product or service? What will the cost be to the customer? How can you add value to what you offer?
- **Promotion:** what marketing and promotional tools will you use to communicate your core marketing messages? Via PR, classified or newspaper advertising, in-store promotions, networking, telemarketing, incentive schemes, online, via customer newsletters, TV, radio or direct mail?
- **Place (or route of distribution):** which location will you operate from? Where will your customerbase be located?

How convenient will buying from you be? What will your position within the marketplace be?

I would add an additional P to the mix: People! Relationships with people, both customers and partners, are crucial in creating an effective marketing and sales strategy and meeting marketing objectives. It is these relationships that help entrepreneurs to grow a business effectively, to spread the word about their brand and use their influence, one of my Ten Golden Rules for being a Tycoon.

Influence should be used to create win-win results. Relationships in business are king, especially if these relationships, or partnerships, are with leading brands. That is one of the keys to our success with Data Select, our telecom distribution business; we focus on building strong relationships, create win-win situations and think about our customers' customers.

The advantage of partnering with leading brands is that they continue to spend on their own brand awareness, which feeds your own. Working hard alongside them and finding ways that you can be an extension to their arm bring huge opportunities to your own company. Think about how you can help your partners and customers to reach their objectives and create win-win opportunities.

Developing relationships with customers and getting to know them as best you can is vital, as is gaining as much information about customers and prospective customers as possible. This enables you to segment a market, focus on a niche area, uncover the genuine needs, interests and problems of that audience and be better placed to provide the perfect solution.

TYCOON TIP: Knowledge is power. Gain knowledge about your customers, partners and competitors. Arm yourself and give your business the competitive advantage to win customers.

The Importance of PR

PR is one of the most cost-effective marketing strategies available to businesses of all sizes. By gaining coverage across a variety of media, from newspapers and relevant magazines to TV, radio and the Web, entrepreneurs can raise brand awareness to a large audience with minimal outlay. Press coverage also makes it feel like there is a buzz around your product or business, and there is the implied endorsement that comes with getting a positive mention within editorial as opposed to paid-for advertising.

In the early stages, to spread the word about our company, we did everything on a shoestring. We used a local newspaper photographer to come into our company and help us create pictures that would be interesting for the media to use, and from here we would identify stories about the business and write it up in a way that would make the reporter's job easier and hopefully improve our chances of getting a good mention. We employed a small one-man PR company, run by a former national-news journalist, to help with this when we felt there was a more strategic approach that could be taken through a media PR campaign. He took our raw ingredients and created one core news announcement for us at a very key time in the business's development, which resulted in a considerable amount of interest in the business on the City pages of many of the UK's leading national newspapers, including the *Financial Times*, the *Telegraph*, *The Times*, the *Express*, the *Daily Mail* and many other news outlets. It was great for our business. We brought him in for a very reasonable fee and he put the release out using his key contacts and the Press Association's Newswire, which feeds news and pictures to every major print and broadcast news outlet in the country. That relationship developed, he was good at his job, and I ended up employing him as our group marketing director. In fact, after seven years of working together, he's now the MD of Peter Jones TV. Another good example of the importance of relationships, but the point is, we focused on very localised and targeted PR, and we still do today.

PR has always been handled internally. Of course, when I went on *Dragons' Den*, I was advised to find a newspaper-savvy PR who was clued up on the way TV and media work. I was given Max Clifford's name because he looked after some key big-name celebrities, such as Simon Cowell. I thought he'd be a good person to talk to, and, as a result, we use his company for our media and TV coverage. From a business perspective, we've always done PR ourselves via interviews, although, on a few occasions Max's team has set up profile interviews for the business media. That spreads the word about our business. We use the local press that's pursuant to our particular business and the trade magazines because marketing is about getting the right message to the right target audience at the right time.

How to Harness the Power of PR

- Identify the media you want coverage from. Discover what your target audience reads, watches, browses and listens to.
- Send your products, or explain the service your company offers, to leading targeted magazine editors, inviting them to try your product or service with no catch. Subsequent coverage can evoke interest from retailers, other media and potential partners, as well as customers, and the momentum can build exponentially.
- Use your expertise. Get quoted as an expert in a target publication or write and send articles including your name and Web address. As well as raising awareness, this helps establish credibility within an industry.

Persuasion and Successful Selling

Selling isn't purely about closing the deal. Selling is a process that goes through four key stages:

1. Attracting prospects, leads and referrals.
2. Getting and keeping the prospects' interest.

3. Closing a deal by convincing them to buy.
4. Providing the product or service and providing after-sales service and follow-up.

Once the deal is done (i.e. the customer has been persuaded to buy), the product or service needs to be provided, the contact followed up, and the cycle begins again: gathering referrals and leads, attracting prospects and so on.

In sales, there are many variables that will need fine-tuning to optimise results and reach targets. You need the right:

- team
- product or service (solution)
- tools and training for your people
- effective customer service
- audience.

Each depends on each other. A great product may not sell well if the sales staff are poorly trained. Equally, a great sales team may struggle to sell a poor product with few unique selling points.

So how do you make sure you get each variable right to optimise sales?

How to Increase Sales

1. Focus on clear targets, objectives and rewards to deliver more than the competition. One of the biggest reasons for the success my own company enjoys is that we deliver more than our competition per capita head. We've got a very small sales team, but we focus on that team going out to the market under a specific plan of attack with a specific strategy. We know at the start of the year exactly what we want to achieve and how we're going to achieve it. Every month staff are set very clear objectives which they're rewarded upon delivering. Because we're so focused, we can deliver far more than if we instructed our salesforce to sell 'as much as they can', or if we gave them a

basic commission plan. Our staff-incentive plans are based on financial targets, goal objectives and group-wide results, not just focused on profit and sales.

2. Prepare your sales team. Take the gladiator approach. Gladiators were successful because they were very well trained, well honed and were given the right tools and strategies for the job in hand. When a gladiator stepped into the ring, they delivered 99 times out of 100. Make your sales team the gladiators. Give them clear objectives, the tools to deliver the job and the training that's required to be more effective than your competition. Match that with a portfolio of products and solutions, and a clear understanding of the strategy behind the business, and your sales staff will maximise sales and reach targets.

3. Encourage communication between the sales team and your customers. People buy from people they like and respect.

4. Get feedback. Use positive feedback to generate repeat business. Also use it as customer testimonials on your sales literature. Ask for referrals from happy customers. Use less positive feedback to fine-tune your offering.

5. Deliver on your promises to customers. Go the extra mile where necessary.

TYCOON TIP: Make getting sales your number-one priority. Your business is going nowhere without them.

MISSION 6: *Make It Happen Tycoon Checklist*

So you're ready to launch your business. You've done all the groundwork of researching and verifying the idea, securing finance and planning the business, strategies, marketing and sales. You've committed to take action, and you have your logistics and foundations in place. You even know your endgame: your exit strategy.

But are you being as resourceful as you could be? Tycoons make the most of resources available to them. Indeed, many

Tycoons will also talk a lot about how they didn't have access to the help and free resources, or even the Internet, when they first started up in business. And they'd be right. So use the resources that *are* available for today's budding Tycoons.

Use the Web, local enterprise agencies, government resources and information, small-business forums and networking groups. Sign up to online forums to speak with like-minded people and those in the same position as yourself. Gather as much free information as you can from the Internet, and get leverage from the free and subsidised courses, workshops and advice services that the government and local council provide.

Finally, it's time to run through the Peter Jones Tycoon Checklist to make sure you really are ready to launch your business and become a Tycoon. This checklist covers everything we've been through in the book so far to make your business happen.

1. Do you have a name for your business? Have you registered the name with Companies House? Have you looked into applying for a trademark (or patent if necessary)?
2. Have you notified the relevant authorities about your intentions to start up your own business?
3. Have you decided the status your business will take?
4. Have you figured out your endgame? Planned your exit strategy?
5. Do you know exactly how much needs to be invested into the business to start and run it?
6. Have you worked out what you need to spend money on and what your sales figures are likely to be?
7. Have you done your financial forecast – profit and loss as well as cashflow?
8. Do you know the likely return on investment (be it your own or an investor's)?
9. Have you checked that your idea is different in some way?
10. Do you know the unique selling points of your idea?

11. Have you evaluated the market sector appropriate to your idea? Are you fully prepared in terms of research? Do you know enough about your competition, your market and your potential customers? Has potential market share realistically been identified? Has the level of demand been ascertained?

12. Have you evaluated who your competitors are?

13. Have you written a business plan and a strategic 100-day action plan?

14. Have you raised finance?

15. Have you gained the relevant experience and knowledge you need to launch forth?

16. Are you ready to commit to take action?

17. Do you believe in your business and yourself? Have you assessed the viability of your idea?

18. Are you sure you have no Achilles heel, because you have quantified and analysed the risks and have strategies to overcome them?

19. Have you assessed strengths, weaknesses, opportunities and threats and how you will improve strengths, iron out weaknesses, harness opportunities and reduce threats?

20. Have you assessed the timing of your business start-up? Considered the sacrifices involved? Ensured you can devote the time and effort required and have anticipated the changing needs of everyone involved?

21. Do you have the relevant health and safety requirements, operating licences, insurance and liability cover? Have you identified the risks and protected yourself as much as possible?

22. Are you open to learning and ready to learn from mistakes?

23. Are you feeling motivated? It can be a lonely road as an entrepreneur and you don't often get a pat on the back, motivation and encouragement. That comes from within. When things are great, being an entrepreneur is probably the best feeling in the world, but when things go wrong, it can be

a lonely and isolating world. Feel the power of being prepared. Feel the power of your commitment, of actioning your ideas, of achieving results.

24. Do you believe that revenue is vanity and profit is sanity? You should do. Running a business that doesn't generate profit means you won't generate much-needed cash to keep your business alive. Cash (and therefore profit) is king.

Now it's time to get out there and start making that dream a reality!

6

BUILDING YOUR FUTURE

*'Perseverance is not a long race; it is many short races one after
another'*

WALTER ELLIOTT (PRIEST AND MISSIONARY)

So, you've launched your business, got through any teething
problems and are officially up and running. You've taken
your business on a journey; from concept and idea validation to
raising finance and launching the business, you've made it happen. Now it's time to continue to make things happen as you drive
your business towards success. However, as many entrepreneurs
discover a few months into running the business, it can be all too
easy to get so caught up working 'in' the business that you have no
time left to work 'on' the business. And if you don't continually
work 'on' the business, you could come to a grinding halt or head
in the wrong direction. In building the future you've visualised,
and becoming a Tycoon, you need to take steps to protect that
dream future vision. So follow my steps to ensure you stay on top
of your business and avoid the pitfalls that can stunt its growth.

STEP 1: Act Like a Leader

Tycoons command respect, not through exerting power, but by
setting a good example, making good decisions, coming up with
good ideas and following them through. Tycoons strategise,
synchronise and harmonise. Taking the reins and steering your
business in the right direction need strong leadership. And leadership is not about domination; it's about direction.

For me, there are three core ways to behave like a leader. These
are:

1. **Synchronise** your team and conduct your 'orchestra' effectively – communicate your vision.
2. Make good **decisions**, worthy of respect – take action.
3. Show interest by being **creative** and follow the progress of your joint ideas with your team.

Let's tackle those one at a time.

Synchronise Your Team

Firstly, in order to act like an effective leader, you should see yourself as the conductor of a large symphony orchestra. As you stand in front of your team, everyone will look to you to follow your lead and direction. By calling the tune and setting the tempo, your team will follow. It is your job to use your position at the front to see what areas require more work and which areas are out of sync with the rest of the team. Then it is up to you to bring all the key aspects of your business, all the departments and individuals, together in harmony.

As the conductor, you should guide your orchestra towards the crescendo and the applause that the end of their performance heralds, towards the results and endgame that have been planned.

Effective synchronisation requires the creation of a harmonious culture within your company, a culture that instils a sense of purpose and belonging into each team member. Building this symphonic team culture will take time and effort. A strong team will not materialise out of nowhere. A team needs a leader, and a convincing one at that. The company has got to believe in you as the leader; your staff need to feel instinctively that you are their pilot, steering them in the right direction. Not only that, you have also got to see yourself as a leader and believe in your own abilities. You are taking your people into battle against the competition, so you need to stand up and be counted, lead by example and navigate your team through obstacles in your path.

To synchronise and conduct their team proficiently, Tycoons need to delegate effectively. If they don't, they'll run out of steam or lose their sense of direction. That's why Tycoons give power to those who work for them. Sir Richard Branson, Bill Gates, Steve Jobs, they all have a strong team ethos and are all highly respected as leaders within their companies. You need to be able to say to people, 'I empower you to do this; this is your job function; this is what I expect you to do in the business.' It's vital to lay those foundations, even if you go through a learning curve in the early stages.

When I'm asked questions by a member of my team, I throw things back immediately. For example, somebody might say to me, 'Look, I've got this opportunity, but I don't quite know what to do . . .' I will say, 'Well, what would you do?' And they'll say, 'I was thinking of doing this . . .' Nine times out of ten, I'll say, 'That's exactly what I think you should do.' That's essential, because it gives the power back to the individual; empowerment is motivational. The individual who feels motivated and empowered feels valued and will perform far better. And the better your staff perform, the better results they will achieve.

Because I deal with so many things, I could all too easily take on too much. In fact, I often do, even though I am very good at delegating. But I know that if I took on everything myself, I'd be completely demoralised and would have too much pressure and stress to be able to work efficiently. If I keep taking on more, much of it just won't get done.

Delegation and having the right people in place to do a job well are great stress-relievers. Because I empower people to do the job, I handle stress really well. I make sure I'm always passing back functions and tasks. Delegation does not mean lazily passing everything on to be done by someone else, with no input from you, while you swan off to do very little. It's about relieving the right amount of pressure while passing some power to your team. This gives you time to perform tasks that need your attention. Essentially, your time is freed up to focus on priority tasks that will help you to develop and build your company.

My Mindset

Of course, Tycoons don't find delegation that easy when they are Tycoons in training. Indeed, the transference from being a one-man band and doing everything yourself to delegating responsibility to somebody else is very difficult. It was for me. Doing everything myself made me a complete control freak: even when I had a telesales person in, I'd end up making the calls and the appointments myself, not just to show my competitive edge, but because I thought I'd be better at performing the task than my new employee. Even when we were delivering or building computers, I'd want to take pride in doing it, so I'd do that myself too. But I couldn't have continued to do that as the company grew. If I had done, key business development and other areas that needed my attention wouldn't have been given the adequate attention and direction they needed, and success would have taken a lot longer to achieve.

The transition from doing everything myself to delegating to others was very challenging. As a passionate budding Tycoon, I wanted to be all over everything. However, I soon learned that you can do that and delegate as well.

If you speak to my people today, I'm still all over everything, but it's more of a helicopter viewpoint. There aren't many things that happen in my business that I don't know about, and I take pride in that, because I'm right in the middle of it. You need to delegate, but you need to have that helicopter view, that conductor's view, so you can see everything that is happening rather than *do* everything yourself. You absolutely have to be in the thick of things, but you also need to know what to do yourself and what is no longer your responsibility. You need to co-operate with your team, so they can cooperate with you and deliver for you. That's why I utilise the teams in each individual area of my business as my sounding board.

We create a lot of time to brainstorm ideas relevant to key decisions and have regular creativity talks. From those meetings, I will absorb all the strengths and weaknesses of each project under discussion and put those two components together to create a solution and a plan. But the most important point for me is to take action. I never want to make decisions in a meeting or have discussions with my team and not do anything about the key points that are raised, otherwise you don't move forward. You stagnate or go round in circles if you don't have an action plan stemming from each discussion. You must agree on what needs to be done and take action.

Using your people as a sounding board and enabling them to bounce their ideas off you as well are crucial to keep progressing forward. For example, an afternoon for me in my business might include a discussion with my TV team about a product from a TV programme. Half an hour later, I'll be chatting with a member of another team about a strategy for our investment business and meeting somebody who could help us with that. There's always discussion between my people, a balance of delegation and participation.

I'm not an egotistical, overbearing boss; I am, however, a team player. Tycoons need to be. Tycoons have a strong sense of their individuality, but can also work in a team. That is essential in order to grow successfully.

Being a valued team member doesn't mean never using individual initiative. On the contrary, it strengthens the shared vision, optimises performance and also creates a proactive culture. You want to employ people who want to work for you and stay working for you; you need staff who see the bigger picture, are passionate about the vision and know exactly what is expected of them. That way, you can optimise performance, productivity and results and continue to build towards your dreams. You synchronise and conduct a team by empowering them, by delegating to them and by piloting them in the right direction, conducting them at the right tempo.

TYCOON TIP: Embrace a team ethos, utilise your team as your sounding board, participate in discussions that incite action and empower your team by delegating and allowing them to make decisions.

Decisions, Decisions

While synchronising and conducting your team, the next function of acting like a leader is learning how to make (and stick to) decisions. When you are in a position of leadership, you will have many tasks battling for your time and attention. Therefore it is vital that you don't sideline the decision-making process, as you'll end up not making a decision at all before moving on to the next thing.

Every decision made will always have an effect, a consequence that happens as a direct result of taking that decision. So before making any decision, it is crucial to measure the effect your decision is going to have in as much detail as time allows. If you don't know what effect your decision will have, don't make a decision until you have found out, because it could be a vital piece of information. Find out why you don't know, resolve the issue, *then* make the decision.

But don't just put off making a decision indefinitely. Get on and find out what you need to do to make an informed decision and take a step forward. Tycoons are, by nature, very quick and effective decision-makers. This doesn't mean every single conclusion Tycoons make is the right or the best decision. It does mean that Tycoons make more decisions than the average person – a large percentage of those judgements create a lot of wealth for Tycoons in the process.

Should you end up owning more than one company and steering more than one ship, you will need to retain focus on one topic when many others are vying for your attention. Giving equal attention but focusing on each decision is key to managing this well.

I do this by compartmentalising topics. I enjoy talking about everything I do, which makes it a lot easier for me to talk about different subjects at different times but almost simultaneously. For example, during meetings in which I'm talking about strategy, often the door will open and I'll be asked a question on a completely different topic about another business within the group. I can completely switch my focus to answer that question. I've certainly not had any mental training, but I'm very methodical with regard to compartmentalisation. I can switch easily and quickly between topics.

As a Tycoon, you need to be able to compartmentalise topics and switch between them, giving each business and department equal 'airtime' in your mind. Because they're concentrating on one topic, when asked a question about something else, some people can't focus. But to be a Tycoon, you must. I do, because I know how important that decision will be, so I focus my attention purely on the question that has been asked. I'm a good listener, but I'm very clear and give specific, direct answers; I don't mess around – there's no time to. You must have a sharp, focused attitude and attention to detail when it comes to making effective decisions quickly.

Creative Leadership

The final critical responsibility of acting like a leader is continually to have new ideas. That way, you will create a culture within your company of brainstorming and envisioning new ideas. This creativity will become the *modus operandi*, the norm. It's a Tycoon's job to be forever seeking out different ways to do things and to innovate. Remember, if you don't develop into that kind of leader, your employees are unlikely to start contemplating new ideas on your behalf. But if you can lead by example, then eventually your team will start thinking creatively all the time. Consequently, they will bring fantastic new ideas to you. You see, your business is like a child. It will grow in your likeness and act as you do. Don't shirk that responsibility. Lead with a creative force and motivating attitude. Be a good influence on those you work alongside. Be a worthy role model. But remember, business is about making money and having *fun*. Don't forget to have fun!

TYCOON TIP: Think of yourself as a general leading your troops into battle. You'll need to think creatively to forge new ideas that defeat the competition. In order to build and earn respect, you'll need to put your cadets, soldiers and sergeants into position with a clear strategy and direction and lead them by example. And you'll need to make decisions that will support and protect them in the field, rather than leave them vulnerable.

STEP 2: Harness People Power

By now, you'll have learned the importance I place on people when it comes to building a business. Influence and caring make up two of my Ten Golden Rules for becoming a Tycoon, and, crucially, to build your future, you need to harness the power of your people.

Yes, success in business always comes back to people. Employing and retaining the right people are key. But hiring the right people and keeping them is a considerable challenge for budding Tycoons, perhaps the most challenging of all the components of business success. A business is absolutely nothing without its people! It is the team that helps the Tycoon drive his or her vision forward. Ultimately, success is a team effort. Your people will represent your brand and help you achieve your objectives.

Entrepreneurs who take on the wrong staff or have low retention of staff face an uphill struggle to achieve success and the business will suffer. Hiring the wrong person wastes time and money. Mistakes in this area result in more time spent managing the individual to uncover where things are going wrong. The costs of retraining staff and recruiting replacements can create a huge dent in profits and time. Tycoons know that a strong team is a critical success factor in business and realise they can save time, money and increase productivity by hiring right first time round. It's worth maximising effort in the first instance to build the right team from the outset.

It's not just about hiring the right people; it's about *managing* them the right way to retain them and get the most out of them. Creating a team who will take your vision forward with you is about guiding, managing and leading those people in the right direction, giving them the right tools and the right dosage of motivation along the way.

When I first started up in business, my judgement about whether to hire people I interviewed would be based on their experience, but also on whether I liked them. That is the wrong hiring method, in my view. As I've climbed the ladder to become a Tycoon myself, I've learned that, in actual fact, I need people who are very different to me. Tycoons need to fill the gaps in their own skill set, their own areas of expertise, their own experience and persona.

Over many years of hiring (and occasionally firing) I've learned that only hiring people like me is an ineffective recruitment method. It's more important to hire someone who can deliver the skills I'm looking for, which are more likely to be skills that I don't have. I'm very analytical, but I may need someone less analytical and more aggressive for a sales role. You need the right mix of people to grow your business and build your future.

So how do you get your recruitment right the first time you hire? And, furthermore, once you've recruited, how do you build and motivate a strong team of valued, productive and loyal individuals?

The Right Recruitment

1. **Know what you want.** Analyse exactly what you want from each individual and match the role and responsibility.
   - What do you want to see in the individual?
   - What is the role, and what are the responsibilities?
   - How does the interviewee fit into the business?
2. **Be analytical.** Use psychometrics. Implement tests to evaluate what kind of person the interviewee is. Remember, some people expand the truth and tell you what you want to hear at interview stage. This is dangerous because you can fall into a false sense of security, hence the importance of matching roles and responsibilities clearly and being analytical to build a wider picture of the candidate.

   Within my group of companies, we use personality profiles to determine an individual's personality, figure out their character and gain an insight into their internal motivation

192

and management abilities. We use questionnaires for most of our positions. These consist of the individual interviewee choosing words that 'most describe them' and 'least describe them'. Their answers help us determine their personalities on a 'colour wheel', which gives us an insight into their key motivations and characteristics. This means we can easily identify areas of strength and weakness and probe during the second interview to expose and discuss those areas with them. We can also get an idea of how that person will fit into an existing team or business. Will their personality type upset the existing balance or be a benefit overall?

The words chosen by the candidate will help decide which 'colour' best defines their personality. For example:

- 'Red' people are extroverted, strong, dominant personalities who take action. They are generally driven by success and money and will strive for perfection. 'Red' people are generally good at selling.
- 'Yellow' people, like 'red' people, are extroverted and dominant, but they are also talkative, social, gregarious and love to be loved. They enjoy the limelight, but aren't so hot on detail, organisation and writing things down. 'Yellow' people enjoy public speaking and tend to be marketeers, trainers and consultants (and the life and soul of any party!).
- 'Green' people are more refined, reflective and introverted. They are more in touch with their emotions and feelings and are motivated by a sense of belonging and helping others. 'Green' people can make great managers.
- 'Blue' people, like 'green' people, are reflective and introverted, but they are also analytical. They question things and need time to reflect on decisions. They are well suited to financial, analytical or technical roles.

As well as our general questionnaires, we also use a 'sales personality' questionnaire to gain an insight into an individual's sales style: how they go about trying to sell, whether they are a hunter or a gatherer, whether they are good with paperwork or detail, whether they will like field sales and being on their own or whether an office-based sales environment is better for them. It also reveals their motivations to sell – is it money or recognition that drives them?

Questionnaires and 'colour reports' at second-interview stage bring alive the personality of the individual you are interviewing. You can uncover information that an ordinary line of questioning may not uncover, which gives you another dimension to the information you have gathered. This means you are able to gauge experience, ability and personality, all the areas that you want to uncover during the selection process.

3. **Make joint decisions.** Involve existing staff in the hiring process: a panel of more than one person to interview and make the decision to hire. Make sure people who will be managing or working with this person are involved in the decision-making process. A panel of objective views works far better than one individual making the decision.

In my business, we no longer rely upon one individual making a decision over recruitment. We bring in the manager of that department because that manager knows their existing staff and how that individual would fit. We bring in an independent individual, someone from HR to give an autonomous view of them. We also bring a head of the unit, the MD or director of the business, to actually give an overall appraisal. We don't rely on any one person's decision.

Even if you're a sole trader embarking on your first recruitment of staff, I advise bringing someone else into the interview, someone you've met as a business advisor, someone you trust to give an additional perspective. Objective views of others who know the needs of your business and core requirements of the role will help you to make a more rounded recruitment decision.

4. **Go into detail. Ask for specifics.** What experience specifically has the potential team member had? Can they give examples? Drill down to individual successes. What results did they

achieve? What motivated them to achieve those results? Why?

5. **Get a mix of different types of people across the company.** Diversity is crucial to optimise dynamics. Don't match every persona to yours. Ensure the talents and personalities of each individual you take on complements what's missing in others, including yourself. The strongest businesses have innovators, entrepreneurs, sales and finance specialists, analysts, operational specialists, creatives, technical experts . . . It's about getting in the right mix of strengths to dilute and diminish any weaknesses.

6. **Use your intuition.** This gives you a gut feeling whether you can work with a person, whether what they're saying stacks up and whether they have the skills, energy, drive and enthusiasm to perform well. First impressions do count. However, don't rely just on instinct. Trust it, listen to it, but use it alongside analytics and role and responsibility matching to make the right final judgement.

7. **Steer people in the right direction.** Once you have committed to employing someone, detail and define the roles, responsibilities and objectives clearly from the outset. Make sure people know what is expected of them, what the role entails and why. Help your people to help themselves and you.

8. **Get to know people as individuals first.** Find out what motivates them and what makes them tick at analytical-interview stage. The salary could be a motivator, but so could the opportunities, the vision, the team vibe of the business. Taking time to understand what gets each individual team member motivated will help further down the line to motivate and reward staff effectively in order to generate results and loyalty. You reap what you sow with business relationships. By providing meaningful and relevant opportunities and rewards, and something to believe in, you'll create a united team as well as a spirit of cooperation.

Once you really understand the key motivators for individuals, you can then put a team together in which everybody works together in harmony, in sync: from the person putting the product portfolio together to the person knocking on doors and selling. As long as your team enjoys what they do, there will be a heightened atmosphere of cooperation and increased productivity. And the more you get that solidarity, the better and faster the results will be, no matter how small your team is. Teamwork involves working toward a common goal, and, with it, ordinary people can achieve extraordinary things.

9. **Empower your team with decision-making responsibilities.** They will feel valued as a result. Sadly, many people are given a job purely as a function, with no power to deliver and make decisions on behalf of the company. I believe companies should live a bit by the sword and empower individuals to make decisions within a certain scope. Not only is this good for the customer (because there's a wider remit to go the extra mile and exceed expectations), it's great for the individual employee to know they're valued and can make some decisions without having to refer to others. This is one of the best ways I know to create a loyal and effective workforce in any business, whether big or home-based.

10. **Celebrate group successes together.** I am hugely motivated by seeing a whole team succeed, and so are others within my teams. Remember the feeling you used to get at school when your team won? Just being a spectator was exhilarating enough, but if you were actually involved and actively helped your team to win, there's no better feeling. And that feeling is multiplied by the fact that it's a shared experience. Winning together is vitally important. Sharing a common goal and celebrating team achievements are valid ways to increase loyalty and share the value of the experience with others in the business. This spurs you and everyone involved on, both those directly responsible and those not involved in that particular success. It's motivating to share achievements, engage in them and celebrate them together.

STEP 3: Manage Change

Once you have a winning team, it doesn't mean that everything will be plain sailing from now on. You will face challenges, from both internal and external forces, and you will need to stay on top of everything to stay ahead of the competition. To do that, you need to manage change effectively. So, although you should maintain a steady approach and retain procedures and initiatives that are working well for your business, this doesn't mean you should reach a certain level of success and never change. Inertia can be very damaging for companies, especially those looking to grow.

In order to be a Tycoon, you need to embrace change with open arms and not let change initiatives sink in a sea of complacency. Indeed, change is about challenging and questioning, rather than reinforcing the status quo.

Tycoons adapt quickly to the ever-changing business landscape around them. This was personally vital as my own business moved from start-up to blue chip in what felt like a nanosecond.

You should always push your business to improve the quality of products and services and the quality of the customer service provided. You should constantly seek out new opportunities for growth and ways to increase productivity. Those opportunities, methods and improvements that you uncover will need implementing, and that means something will have to change.

Innovation, change and experimentation are all vital to build steady growth and, ultimately, huge success.

TYCOON TIP: Embrace new initiatives and innovation, not inertia and the inevitable deflation.

Most people fear change because it takes them outside of their comfort zone. And when people get into a comfort zone, that's when they don't perform and will never exceed expectations in their job. They just do what's required and don't go the extra mile: there's no reason for them to. To fear change is to say you worry about your own ability to do something slightly differently, yet adapting is something that all humans are good at.

There is, of course, a right way and a wrong way to manage change within the workplace. The right way results in guiding people outside of their comfort level, to educate and empower a team of individuals to embrace change and see its benefits. The wrong way results in confused, defensive and demoralised staff who are left with no valid reason to bother accepting and accommodating change.

The *Wrong* Way to Embrace Change

Often, organisations making changes will say, 'Things aren't going right, so this is what you will do.' That's it. That's all they say. To say, 'This is what you will do,' means people's roles change. That is just poor management, because it completely destabilises the workforce, resulting in people performing roles that they weren't employed to do without explanation, validation or motivation. They won't embrace change, and why should they? They want to protect their own position and haven't been given a clear understanding of why change is for the better (both for them and the company as a whole).

The *Right* Way to Embrace Change

For me, change is about brainstorming, about think-tanks. Tycoons embrace change by utilising their senior management team (or business advisors) to:

- Consider everything that isn't being done: how to make things better, how to do things differently, how to put changes in place to maximise results, minimise problems and stay innovative.
- Evaluate why changes need to occur, whether there is a crisis to manage and why that has come about. Unearth the root of the problems or the reasons for further developments.
- Brainstorm and pinpoint areas that need to change in the business to avoid similar problems or to capitalise on similar successes.

- Explain to teams why you need to change, communicate the change and bring the teams in to discuss how to manage that change even further. As early in the brainstorming process as possible, slice through the 'us and them' approach to engage those who will be directly affected by changes.
- Implement change from a collective. Rather than one person saying, 'This is how we're doing things. This is why we're changing,' this actually says, 'You've made the change: you know why we're changing and have enhanced the business.' This gets buy-in from those involved, and change becomes a lot easier to deal with as a result.

I've heard that some business manuals and courses suggest entrepreneurs invoke a false crisis within their business to stimulate change and avoid inertia. I disagree with this method. That's non-productive. That's management from the top down using scare tactics and a lack of transparency. Instead, change decisions should come from the team, from the group, from the staff involved. Managing change effectively is about driving the team, getting their feedback and suggestions, and getting their full support. People who aren't on board have only one option – to jump ship!

That's why Tycoons always try and create a culture within their companies where innovation and change are welcomed rather than rejected, embraced rather than feared. These companies have strong leaders, passionate teams, and, together, united, they make decisions. They measure the effects their decisions will have. They uncover what they don't know and why, resolve issues, make decisions, together – teamwork! It's a powerful mechanism for success.

New ideas are a vital part of being a Tycoon, and new ideas involve some degree of change. By leading from the front within a culture that welcomes change and brainstorms new ideas, you are far more likely to succeed in the long term.

TYCOON TIP: Implement change from a collective. Brainstorm with your team. Empower group decision-making and help everyone to understand the reasons for change and the enhancements they'll be bringing to the business as a team, moving on up together.

STEP 4: Pursue and Accelerate Growth

At the start of this book, when we looked at the first Golden Rule of vision, I encouraged you to 'reach for the stars and reach your full potential'. Well, dreaming big is the embryonic stage of each business that a Tycoon runs. But it's the ability to accelerate that growth process and pursue that big dream that needs the most attention. The dreaming part is comparatively easy.

The bad news is, growth can kill. Growing too fast or not fast enough can destroy a business. The bottom line? If you don't get the balance right, and don't plan adequately for growth, your business is likely to face serious problems and a large uphill struggle will ensue.

Managing growth can be arduous, complex and demanding. If you find your business succeeding, you might find that overheads increase (with the need to hire and pay more staff to service your customers). Subsequently, you could end up operating under capacity or having too much business to be able to handle and over-trading. You might not have enough money to fund new business. Either way, getting the balance right is a critical factor, and this is far from easy.

It is easier to bring in additional resources and add to your business than it is to scale it back if forecasted results don't happen (or don't happen as quickly as you'd like). Before you scale up and expand your business, it is best to be bursting at the seams. That's a much safer way of growing than to predict you will double in size within the next year and so hire staff and get an office: if the business doesn't come in to meet those growth projections, you've had it.

This optimistic 'running before you can walk' scenario can result in overdue liabilities with unpaid suppliers, which leads to diminished credibility and reputation, a lack of working capital to pay bills, suppliers, staff or buy stock. Consequently, you will be overstocked due to slow movement of your inventory or under-stocked and unable to fulfil demand. Coupled with the potential inability to keep up with rent or finance payments, the conclusion is frequently the closure of the business.

Don't become a victim of your own success. Before heavily investing in or implementing marketing campaigns, make sure that you can fulfil orders and make your customers happy. You don't want to make customers unhappy because you can't deliver.

Smooth Out the Creases

Another risk factor when it comes to growth is compounding and duplicating mistakes made within the primary business model. Attention to detail is vital.

Evidently, the most important factor surrounding growth is actually planning for it effectively. In order to scale up in the best possible way at the right time with the right foundations and investments, you need to ensure there is enough working capital to finance growth, establish whether growth is necessary now (and if not, when) and understand when to invest and in which areas. There are so many people who say, 'But growth just happens.' Well, yes, growth can just happen, but you need to at least have a vision of what you want to achieve and act accordingly.

Growth, and the mismanagement of growth, is the potential sting in the tail that can knock even businesses with the highest turnover off their perch. But growth can be managed effectively, notably by planning for it well, using that helicopter view to see the bigger picture and taking the appropriate steps to grow in a steady manner.

Forecasting and planning for growth enable successful entre-preneurs to build the business without strangling it or running out of cash. And therein lies the key factor in effective growth management – cash! We'll examine exactly how to handle cash flow in more detail later in the chapter. For now, it is important to know that when it comes to the critical success factors for growth, effective growth always comes back to the amount of cash that you have available in the business. Scalability (i.e. the potential for a business to operate effectively as it increases in size) is often down to the amount of money that you have in the company to invest in that growth. How, when and what you invest your profits in are the core drivers of growth. With scalability, achieving balance is critical.

For example, a sales-generating business may have periods of exceptional growth. What's vital is how that upsurge is handled. Over-investing to cover development is a common mistake. Unfortunately, if a few lean months happen to follow that period of advancement, staff costs may need to be reduced. And what if you've taken on bigger premises to cope with the growth that you can no longer afford, now that level of business is not being sustained?

You might be overachieving your sales targets, but does that mean you now need to double the size of your business? No, it doesn't. Scaling a business up should be done in a piecemeal fashion (unless, of course, you have identified key opportunities to acquire another business and have managed to obtain financial support to do so). Implement a short-term small growth phase, even if you've had an upsurge in your business. Over-investment and over-committing financially can kill a growing business.

You should only consider an infrastructure rethink (more staff, more stock, bigger premises, increased costs, etc.) if you have a guaranteed income or your run rate is increasing and you believe this will continue. By 'run rate', I mean how your turnover would look if you were to base it on current results and spread that out over a certain period of time. For example, you may turnover £5,000 per month for a few months, so that monthly sales figure would be your run rate. The danger is, if you forecast your turnover based on a run rate that doesn't actually pan out (so your ongoing income is less than your run rate), you can end up facing financial problems. Only invest heavily in growth if your run rate is climbing rather than declining.

If you *don't* have a guaranteed contractual income or have a run rate that is consistent but isn't based on one-off orders or seasonal or temporary upsurges in profits, ensure that you:

1. Keep costs to a minimum.
2. Keep the profit.
3. *Then* reinvest when an opportunity to make more money arises.

Reinvesting profit smartly is of crucial importance when growing a business successfully. You need to know how best to reinvest in your vision, and only scale up when you have profits that are sustainable, ongoing or guaranteed in a contract.

Stable and solid growth comes back to the all-important forecasting model . . . and the question 'What are you doing with your cash and how are you reinvesting it?'

Think about this question constantly as your business grows. It is one of the most important questions any Tycoon can answer themselves. It's an integral part of a Tycoon's Mindset. Make sure your answer to this question is the right one. The answer will help you to decide whether to invest cash and when the best time is to do so.

My Mindset

Just as sometimes a business will invest too much in growth and be unable to scale back when that revenue is not sustained, other times businesses can invest too little early on and hinder the chance to make a larger return in the future.

As you know, within two years of starting and building Generation Telecom, we sold it to Vodafone. However, there were many learning curves along the way. Early on, especially after venture capital investment, we were in a strong enough financial position to have invested more money in generating more subscribers, but we decided not to because the cost of acquiring those customers would have been more than we believed they were actually worth had we decided to sell the company.

I always ensure that when I dream big, I plan well and do enough homework in order to invest shrewdly in the right areas at the right time. I have got it wrong, but eight times out of ten I make it work. The key is to make sure the couple of times you get it wrong doesn't outweigh the eight!

TYCOON FABLE *Remember the story of the tortoise and the hare? We all know what happened – the adrenaline-fuelled and overconfident hare raced off and, along the way, took one too many liberties. The slower yet well-paced tortoise remained steady and sure. The hare soon left the tortoise behind, but, overconfident about winning, he decided to take a nap. When he awoke he found his competitor, the tortoise, had already won the race, having crawled slowly but steadily across the finishing line first. The moral of this famous fable is that 'Slow and steady wins the race.' In business, you need to pace yourself to stay ahead of the competition; you need a steady approach to growth.*

Before racing off in a hurry with a complacent attitude, make sure you've paid enough attention to detail to avoid compounding mistakes or issues as you grow, and are progressing at a steady enough pace to invest at the right time in the right areas of your business. Organic, steady steps are more effective than manic, rushed, unplanned ones.

Scale Up

When a business is finding it relatively easy to achieve the numbers and the budget forecasted, this shows it's working. That's brilliant! (As long as you didn't set yourself easy targets in the first place! Tycoons set realistic yet challenging targets. If you smash targets, it's great for morale, but you should continue to raise the bar constantly.) The Tycoon won't stop there, however. This is the time to focus efforts on the areas that are working and outperforming others, while smoothing out any creases that do exist (because no business is perfect).

1. Ask yourself which area has particularly outperformed other areas of the business.

2. Focus on that area. Invest more in that area to push that growth even further and overachieve.
3. Accelerate! Turn your overachievement into long-term, sustainable success.

Effective growth lies in capitalising on the areas of the business that are excelling. The acceleration process is key. It's like driving at 50 miles per hour down a country road and then moving on to a motorway. Once you're on that motorway, you can put your foot down on the pedal a bit. You know it's safe and that you can do 70 miles per hour, so you accelerate.

Once you've got a good business model, it's operating well and you're delivering and maximising results, it's much easier to assess the incremental and percentage performance of each of those areas. You can then reinvest more in key areas to accelerate the growth, because it's a proven business model. That's a secret of a great many Tycoons' success – stable and steady growth based on the optimisation of areas of excellence.

STEP 5: Evaluate and Review Results Regularly

'People with goals succeed because they know where they are going . . . It's as simple as that'
EARL NIGHTINGALE (AUTHOR AND PHILOSOPHER)

Tycoons evaluate, monitor and review goals and results regularly in order to ensure that they pay appropriate attention to detail, avoid compounding mistakes and grow in the right direction at the right pace. It's part of the Tycoon psyche to evaluate and assess results consistently.

The evaluation process involves:

1. analysis: SWOT snapshot
2. regular reporting
3. reaching outside comfort zones.

I place huge importance on systematically and consistently reviewing company performance on a day-to-day basis.

Analysis: SWOT Snapshot

Evaluation is not just a one-off process that you do to test the viability of a potential business idea. Evaluation is something you need to do over and over again as your business evolves and grows to make sure you are still on track. You need to evaluate not only what your own business is doing; you need to continually review the market, the competition and the steps you will need to take to reach success. A good way of doing all this is to carry out a regular SWOT analysis.

In each segment of the below chart, list all the strengths, weaknesses, opportunities and threats to your business. The end result will give you a visual snapshot of where your business stands at any given point in time. We touched on this in Chapter 4, but it is worth remembering when you do this that 'strengths' and 'weaknesses' are always internal factors within your business (e.g. skilled people, warehouse space, IT systems, flexible working hours, price point, unique differentiation factors, limited cash resources, etc.), whereas 'opportunities' and 'threats' will be external to your business and are things over which you have limited control but need to focus on diligently in terms of changing or influencing them (e.g. niche areas in the market, aggressive competition, impending legislation, poor skills in local workforce, availability of government grants, growth or declining markets, etc.).

STRENGTHS	WEAKNESSES
OPPORTUNITIES	THREATS

By uncovering such threats and weaknesses, you can figure out exactly how to deal with them at any given time. For example, if there is a strong competitive threat, you might create a specific offer to retain and attract customers, or to overcome the lack of skilled people, you might look to set up your business in a location where there is a high population of people with the skills you need that aren't being tapped into or you might build a focused training programme that deals specifically with this issue. You might be able to make changes to your business processes that deal with impending legislation ahead of its impact, or you could map out a plan to raise finance if one of your weaknesses is the fact you have limited cash resources. This snapshot for each project you pursue is paramount.

Regular Reporting

It's vital to monitor your business goals. Each area of the business should have an operational plan with financial forecasts, regular measurements against targets and regular reporting to monitor whether those targets are being met or not.

Our businesses have challenges every single day, but we centralise reporting, which helps to overcome obstacles and know where we are at any given moment. For me, financial reporting on my business on a daily basis is vital. I get reports across my business every day before 11 a.m., based on the previous day's results and the month and year to date. The reason for that is, it's an indicative driver of where we are against target and budget, and where we're going by division and area. If you read your figures properly, you really can see into the future of your company. You can see what's doing well and, obviously, what isn't, allowing you time to find out why and take remedial action. I spend a lot of time away from my HQ, but, due to the reporting I get daily, it feels like I am in the office every day.

Each MD in my business holds regular Monday-morning briefing meetings, plus internal team meetings. Those briefings on a weekly basis are vital, as are impromptu team meetings. We abolished the old-school monthly team meeting, as they don't work, especially if you are meeting every week. The board then meets every month, and this meeting focuses more on strategy than day-to-day operations because they have already been dealt with. A combination of proactive and reactive meetings is required to stay on top of everything and deal with situations as they arise. We don't just have meetings for meetings' sake, where everyone leaves with nothing to action, none the wiser. We have meetings and discussions during which decisions are made and actions are laid out, so we step forward steadily. Never hold a meeting without agreeing the actions, so everyone understands what has been agreed and knows who has agreed to do what and by when. Make every meeting count and build a culture where meetings need a result at the end. Don't have a meeting without a specific purpose, it wastes precious time, the only commodity we can't influence and change. Time is key – don't waste it.

We hold proactive meetings to stay on top of the business, plan, strategise and brainstorm, and we have reactive meetings to deal with issues as they arise. If there's a problem, we won't ignore that problem until the Monday-morning briefing; our business can't work like that. For businesses of all sizes, that's an ethos that is destined for failure. If you have a situation that needs to be dealt with, it needs to be dealt with now. There's no point waiting. Discuss it immediately and resolve the issue.

Reaching Outside Comfort Zones

Instead of just reaching targets, Tycoons constantly focus on enhancing, improving and building upon what's working and fixing what isn't. Tycoons change both what is working *and* what isn't working for the better. By enhancing effective areas and improving less-productive areas, Tycoons win over the rest – this driving force towards changing, refining and perfecting enables the Tycoon to smash targets, continue to grow and build up core effective areas of the business far more quickly than they would take if they aimed for targets, hit them and changed nothing, ever.

For example, in my businesses, if all of our indicators are being hit, that's brilliant, but we don't get into a comfort zone. It is vital to then look at other areas, not necessarily new areas, but at how to enhance what we already have. With both Generation Telecom and Data Select, we built on our existing customer assets and built value by setting the benchmark and aiming to lead the marketplace.

> **TYCOON TIP:** Build intrinsic value into your business. Strive to become the number-one company in a niche marketplace. Get the edge over your competitors. If you have intrinsic value, you become a potential acquisition target.

It's also important to review areas that aren't working so well. Considering what you may have done differently, with the benefit of hindsight, is a great tool for growth and for learning. Take time to review this after all major milestones, deals and performance reviews. Give yourself feedback, put that feedback into action and grow faster to achieve greater value.

> **TYCOON TIP:** Take time to stop, think and reflect. How can you put right what isn't right and enhance and optimise what is?

How to Evaluate Results

- **Review performance.** Monitor the business, set out clear goals and have an area operator plan. Each area of the business must be properly planned to ensure the team knows the specific direction, targets and required results.
- **Be analytical.** Study, uncover strengths and innovate. Review the drivers in the market, do your research, understand the opportunity and study your competition through SWOT analysis. Find ways to be even more innovative. What are you doing right? Focus and add to those things to build incrementally and scale up those effective parts of the business.
- **Continue to focus on results.** Give everyone involved clear objectives and expectations. Match and track your perfor-

mance against the competition. Uncover what you're doing right. Communicate this with your team. Remember, results are one of the Ten Golden Rules to becoming a Tycoon, because being results-oriented brings clarity to the goal for everyone involved.

STEP 6: Stay on Top of Cash Flow

As I mentioned in Step 4, one of the key things to bear in mind when managing growth is to ensure your business doesn't grow at a faster rate than the cash resources that are available, otherwise success will be short-lived as you won't be able to fund the operation. For me, cash is king! Making sure you've got cash may sound like common sense, but it is a lot easier than you might think to run out of capital.

For example, you may provide services and invoice on a quarterly basis. However, the client may take 60 days to pay that invoice, or could even pay you late. Then what? You've got staff, developers and suppliers to pay, and you can't afford to develop further or buy in more stock until the client has paid you. In the meantime, you come grinding to a halt. If you haven't planned for the worst-case scenario when it comes to the flow of cash into the business (which isn't the same as the amount invoiced), you could find your business in serious problems. What's more, if you have an invoice outstanding, you can't assume that you can simply trot along to your bank, brandish your invoice and expect them to extend your overdraft or help you out. Sometimes even a purchase order won't persuade a bank to budge. There are solutions that banks do provide (such as invoice discounting and factoring), which we'll look at later in this section. However, if you can't access the cash you need before the vultures start to circle, you'll be falling into administration quicker than you can say, 'Cash is king.'

For businesses growing organically, generating enough profit to reinvest is a constant struggle. Not having enough cash to cultivate the company is a common hurdle for small and start-up enterprises. For that reason, managing your cash in a focused manner is more than just vital; it could be the difference between success and failure.

How to Improve Cash Flow

- Monitor profit and avoid over-commitment. One common mistake entrepreneurs make is that they see the run rate of their business and immediately start to incur costs. They'll rent an office, take on new lease commitments or buy a new car. These monthly payments can result in losing sight of the real cash that's generated through the business. Monitoring profit against commitments is a key component of managing cash flow. It is far better to take out a medium- to long-term loan at a low rate in the early stages than over-finance the business by taking on big commitments.
- Grow the business organically and keep costs down, especially if you can't access bank finance. Focus on keeping costs to a bare minimum. Forget the office: work from home. Forget the car: use public transport. Grow the business, grow a pot of cash and then invest in the business. Using that money to reinvest is vital to successful growth.
- Build relationships and trust with suppliers. In business, there are situations when you have to commit to buying more stock or commit more of your time. In order to reduce the risk of over-committing, it's vital to build strong relationships with your suppliers. That way, your suppliers get to see your focus and are more likely to support and trust you.
  - Align yourself with a key supplier and devote more time to selling their product set.
  - Ask for extended terms early on. Don't say on the day payment is due, 'By the way, I can't pay you for another three weeks.' Getting a bad reputation for payment is a disaster. Getting a reputation for being open and honest from the start will build stronger relationships.
  - Offer to pay a slightly bigger premium in exchange for

211

extended terms to spread payments over a given period. Being open and working out that cash-flow model from the outset is vital.

- Review financing options. Compare the cost of each. Consider the following options:
  - Bank overdrafts or loans: the cost of borrowing money from a bank isn't overbearing. Banks today will certainly lend against a good, strong order book. Figure out what it will cost to borrow from your bank.
  - Sales financing and factoring provide methods of getting cash into the business. These options enable you sell a product on credit to a customer one day and the bank will then pay you 80–85 per cent of your invoice value a couple of days later. The bank can also take the onus on collecting the money from the customer if you are prepared to pay a little extra. This is called factoring. If you take the onus on collecting the money yourself, the bank becomes a sales-financing vehicle. Ask your bank what sales financing or factoring will cost you.
  - Another option is early invoice discounting and involves having arrangements with your customers to incentivise them to pay you earlier than usual. They receive an incremental discount, while you generate cash within 30 days, seven days, immediately or even upfront. In this day and age, especially on commodity products, incentivising by giving an extra 2 or 3 per cent discount is very attractive to companies that don't have financial worries. Figure out what discounting early payers will cost you over a given period.
  - Extended credit terms. Paying interest or a premium in order to extend credit terms is a viable method of leaving more cash in the business over a given period. Figure out what the necessary interest or premium will cost you over time.
- Match the cost of each financing option to each other. Which option is the most cost-effective for your business model? An entrepreneur's borrowing ability is based around his or her

ability to repay the interest against that loan and the risk of the original capital being borrowed. That's what's critical. If profits generated more than cover the interest payments (by at least two to three times), a medium-term debt-funding option will be preferable over taking extended credit or giving larger discounts. Weigh up the costs of each financing option to see which is the most viable for your business and cash-flow situation. Review:
  - the cost of borrowing from the bank
  - the leverage and level of debt (i.e. how much you've taken on as debt and your ability to repay).
- Reinvest profits wisely. Firstly, understand what your start-up and ongoing costs are. Be realistic. It is better to overestimate expenditure and time and underestimate revenue than fall short of revenue and overspend. Secondly, be sure to evaluate and monitor profit continually. Finally, reinvest your profit. That way, you'll build the business faster than if you use the profit to rent another office building or buy a car. It's how you spend the profit that's important. Tycoons always spend profit on the business. They invest that profit on the right areas to maximise growth and enhance existing offerings.
- Forecast all costs and profits regularly. Focus on daily cash flow. The first challenge is to be aware of start-up costs, sales cycles, how long it will take from first customer contact to first payment, estimating time, equipment, packaging, tax and staff costs. The second challenge is knowing how much you need to earn in order to cover all outgoings, including salaries, stock, materials, other overheads and capital expenditure, plus how much you need to break even and turn a profit. But it is the flow of money, the balance of cash that flows in and out of a business on a daily basis, along with the way in which profit is invested, that can make or break a business.

Profitable businesses can still go under if they run out of cash at a critical moment or they simply run out of time finding finance, credit or a buyer. Forecasting is the most focused method of avoiding that obstacle. Many businesses with large turnovers go into administration because they focus on achieving a high turnover rather than a high profit.

My Mindset

In my telecoms business, we have looked at ways to increase profit, and if revenue drops, we are not concerned as long as it doesn't have a major impact on our profit. Last year, we generated £180 million in sales revenue, but a large amount of business was on fulfilment, generating small profit. (i.e. Delivering products and services for a low margin.) We changed that and started to fulfil based upon a fee per consignment with our client providing the equipment. They also then carry the inventory risk so it means we don't have any stock write-offs. This has given us lower revenue but a higher percentage margin. It also means our cash flow operates more effectively because we don't need as much to run the business at similar profit levels.

The result: a better business and a good demonstration again of my belief that revenue is vanity and profit is sanity.

Clearly, then, delivering high turnover is one thing, but it is the delivery of profit that is a critical success factor in becoming a Tycoon. When a business runs out of cash, it can be strangled, regardless of potential, size or stature within the industry. Big players often sink because of cash flow.

So please make sure you have solid financial reporting processes in place. This is vital. Making your money work for you is fundamental if you want to grow quickly and effectively and sustain that growth.

How to Stay on Top of Cash Flow

1. Have you committed only to what you can afford? Are you avoiding over-financing the business?
2. Are you monitoring profits against those commitments?

3. Are you keeping costs to a bare minimum if growing organically?
4. Are you reinvesting profits effectively? For example, when
you experience a high run rate or a seasonal upsurge, are you
focusing on keeping costs down, utilising the profits and
reinvesting without overstretching the business in less profitable periods? Or are you incurring new staff or premises costs
and scaling growth because you have guaranteed income
secured (via a contract)?
5. Have you focused on building relationships with bankers and
suppliers?
6. Have you reviewed each financing option available to find
out which is the most relevant and cost-effective to use?
7. Have you reviewed the cost of bank borrowing and the
leverage you have (your debts and your ability to repay them)?
8. Are you aware what is coming in and going out of the
business in terms of cash on a daily basis? Have you effective
forecasting tools in place?
9. Are you focusing on lead generation (i.e. generating leads:
finding potential customers with a qualified interest in what
you offer) and closing sales?
10. Have you increased your sales, kept costs to a minimum and
forecasted the effect on cash flow?

STEP 7: Build Relationships

Cash is certainly king, as I said earlier, but you won't be
generating any cash into your business without customers, suppliers and a good team in place supporting your endeavours. As
such, relationships with customers, staff, partners, suppliers and
financiers are the cornerstone of any successful business. Nurturing and building relationships is absolutely fundamental to successful growth.

Remember, one of my Ten Golden Rules is influence because
there are times when all Tycoons need others.

How to Build Relationships to Maximise Growth

1. Add value to your partnerships and relationships. When you look at your business partner or business customer, don't keep thinking what you can sell them or what service you can give them or get from them; think about *their* customers.
   - What are their customers looking for?
   - What can you give your client in terms of added value?
   - Which tools can you provide them with to do an even better job for their customers and their customers' customers?

   Make it a win-win situation. You've got to invest in those partnerships as much as they invest in you. Each party has got to see value in the relationship. Tycoons never lose sight of this critical success factor.

2. Keep people (suppliers, investors, financiers, staff and customers) regularly in the loop and up to date in order that they gain confidence in what you are doing. Confidence begets support. Keep the lines of communication open and invest time in all key relationships to get the most out of them.

3. Network. Get connected, access fresh ideas, share and solve problems faster. The benefits of networking when building your business are plenty. It's about connecting with people you'd never ordinarily meet and then building new and productive relationships. Networking helps to find the missing link in the chain to fulfil your own objectives or provide the missing link via your own business to help someone else to achieve their goals. People buy from people first, so you need to get out there if you want to get far in business. If you lack time initially to attend networking events, go online instead. Sign up to an online networking group on the Web. You can evaluate which topics generate the most interest and response; introduce yourself by posting a topic; consider synergies and develop connections. You could introduce your own contacts to relevant people and get introductions to others to expand your own network. People love to give advice, so ask for it and give it where you can. Refer,

match-make and collaborate. Connect before you sell. Networking will help you and your business build credibility and develop contacts and information, crucial success factors of building a promising future for you and your team.

STEP 8: Focus on Customer Service

'It is high time the ideal of success should be replaced with the ideal of service'
ALBERT EINSTEIN

In each of the businesses I'm involved with, a focus on top-quality service to generate loyalty, value and sustainable success are key components. Building loyalty among customers is vital to Tycoons. It's how Tycoons achieve greater success than the average entrepreneur. In industries where customer service is poor, there is no loyalty. This is where many successful Tycoons have leveraged an idea, by entering a market where providers are not delivering, where customer service is poor and where customer loyalty is low. By providing a new choice and backing it up with great customer service, these businesses have profited hugely. I should know: Phones International Group is one of them.

'Your most unhappy customers are your greatest source of learning'
BILL GATES

Listen Carefully

The vital element is to listen very carefully to any customer who provides you with negative feedback. All businesses suffer with the occasional customer complaint. It's how you deal with negative feedback that's important. Customer retention comes down to honesty. Tell your customers exactly how it is. For example, if we haven't got a product available and it's not coming in, rather than lead a customer to believe it's going to be here,

217

we'd rather be honest. This can mean losing a few customers, but it works out far better in the long run.

Spend time regaining the trust of customers who've complained. By listening and acting on their complaints and feedback, you can turn dissatisfaction into loyalty.

Tycoons always deliver on the promises they make. And, on the rare occasions they do let a customer down, they do their very best to deal with complaints. This goes back to putting the right people and training in place and resourcing staff by giving them the right tools for the job.

It costs less to generate business from your existing customerbase than it does to attract new ones. Therefore customer retention is vital when it comes to building your business. Furthermore, happy customers like to share their good news and will recommend your business to others. They'll refer business your way. As a small growing business, that's a godsend. You won't have a huge budget to market your brand, so you'll need as much help as you can get, and your customers are one of the most helpful assets to help you spread the word. Go the extra mile to turn a complaint into a compliment, an objection into an order, and you're already thinking like a Tycoon; you'll go far in business.

Establish a reputation for outstanding customer service and your business is likely to succeed and grow. This is one of the best things you can do to sustain your future success. Consider how you might go the extra mile, from adding the personal touch to your service, handwriting a thank-you note or being honest and helpful where others in your industry aren't.

TYCOON TIP: Treat people as you wish to be treated. When I say 'people', I mean both those who work for you and those who buy from you.

Tycoons do everything in their power to ensure that their relationships with their customers are enduring. Tycoons encourage customer participation and interaction; they create two-way conversations. They live up to their customers' expectations because they communicate with them.

In my businesses, customer communication has been crucial to our success. Running amazing marketing promotions that clearly explain the benefit of dealing with your company can create incredible customer loyalty. We spend huge amounts of time and effort on targeted and effective marketing. My telecoms business designs and develops in-house marketing adverts, mail-shot campaigns, customer incentives and initiatives continuously. Let me give you an example of how creative you can be: one year, we ran a competition for 12 months and selected our top 200 customers, inviting them to take part in a special *Who Wants to Be a Millionaire?* event, that was filmed and produced as if it was going to be broadcast on TV. Afterwards we sent all 200 parti-cipating customers a personalised DVD. Yes, that's right. We hired the exact studio, the man himself, Chris Tarrant, and they all played 'fastest finger first' for the chance to sit in the hot seat and win £1 million. One person actually won £125,000 and it was the industry's best ever dealer promotion, bar none. We generated a 20 per cent uplift in sales and more than covered the cost of the promotion. A great example of creative marketing. It also won an industry award for Best Marketing Initiative of the Year.

Think Service and Loyalty to Generate Repeat Custom

- Be transparent and give customers respect. In doing so, you'll be granted the same respect and honesty. Never make false promises; they'll catch up with you.
- Exceed expectations: don't just deliver on time, delivery early; include extra product and follow up promptly.
- Train staff. Allow adequate resources and time to do this effectively and make sure they smile – smiling costs nothing.
- Create and maintain a positive and lasting impression and you'll find it so much easier (and far less costly) to sell to those customers than to attract, persuade and convert prospective customers into actual loyal customers. This is particularly true if

you are trying to get a product into a supermarket. Getting your product into the hands of the right buyer (who may then leave, anyway) and getting your product on to the shelves is only half the battle: you need to make sure that product sells enough to create a good impression with the supermarket stocking your goods, a good enough impression to warrant a repeat order.

- Focus on selling additional products and services to your most valuable customers, those who've bought the most from you or have developed the best relationship with you. Give them incredible service and make that your mission. I first did that while running my computer business (see p.24). I went the extra mile by providing an outstanding service to my best client, and it paid great dividends.

STEP 9: Don't Rest on Your Laurels

OK, so here you are, you've achieved success, you're retaining and satisfying customers who are generating repeat business; you are running a profitable business and growing in the right direction; you're evaluating the results you gain, embracing change and doing rather well for yourself. Fantastic! So you can take a step back, relax and rest on your laurels, right? Wrong! Tycoons never rest on their laurels. They know (sometimes from their own personal experience) that complacency in business is very dangerous.

So, a word of warning: no matter how successful your business becomes, never start to believe that you have a magic touch and success is guaranteed at whatever you turn your hand to. The truth is, even the most successful Tycoons make mistakes, sometimes big ones, and no amount of successful ventures can ever guarantee that the next one will be a success, even if we've learned from our mistakes.

In reality, the next business could just as easily be an enormous failure that engulfs all the successes you have ever had before it. You have to treat every venture as a new venture. No one has the golden touch, and anyone who thinks whatever they do is inevitably going to turn to gold is foolishly mistaken.

The Tycoon's journey is ongoing, constantly seeking ways to do things differently and evaluating what still needs work. It's a journey of continuous learning and requires an openness to fresh perspectives and new ways of doing things.

> *'I never see what has been done; I only see what remains to be done'*
> MARIE CURIE

Seek out what still needs to be done and work at it, while focusing on what is working well too. Avoid complacency and comfort levels. Sometimes, when everything is working out and results are being achieved, entrepreneurs can find an element of complacency setting in. Don't let that happen to you. Complacent entrepreneurs will be overtaken by their competition, just like the hare in the fable. Instead, keep up the momentum. Look at other areas. Look at how to enhance what you already have and build upon what's already working.

My Mindset

When I started up my restaurant in Windsor, I had already established a couple of businesses and I thought I knew what I was doing. I was in my late twenties and I thought I could do anything. I didn't know the first thing about the restaurant business, but, because I had built a business before, I thought it would be easy to make a success of it. I thought I was a good enough entrepreneur to do anything I wanted to do. I was so confident that I didn't bother writing a detailed business plan with a cash-flow forecast and sales analysis; I didn't study the market and I didn't look at the competition. In fact, I didn't do any preparation, research or evaluation. I was so very wrong. As I revealed earlier in this book, the business was a complete failure, and, despite a promising start (which only fuelled my complacency), within two years I had lost all my money. I knew nothing about how to run a restaurant, and that lack of experience showed. I really should have known that this outcome was inevitable. I thought it was going to be easy, and, boy, I got it wrong.

TYCOON TIP: Stay humble. Success is earned, not given. Always consider what remains to be done. Stay aware, keep working hard and never get complacent.

STEP 10: Continue Listening and Learning

Listen. Tycoons never stop learning. An openness to learning is crucial to continued and sustainable success. It's a vital part of the Mindset of a Tycoon.

I've got a very open mind, and, for me, every day is a chance to learn something new. I'm very inquisitive, I ask a lot of questions, but I listen attentively too. On *Dragons' Den*, I'm the one who sits and listens rather than always jumping in, unless something aggravates me. I'm a sponge. I like being a sponge, because that's how you learn. I've achieved success, but that learning mindset won't stop. I don't know it all. I never will. I've still got a lot to learn, so have you. We all have.

I am motivated by achievement, by moving forward, by growing things, by success and sharing a common goal. Learning motivates me and that's why I will always continue to listen and soak up as much as I can.

SUMMARY: HOW TO MANAGE GROWTH EFFECTIVELY

To summarise, here is a Tycoon Checklist for you to work through. If you can answer 'Yes' to the questions below, you are geared up for growth, ready to cultivate your company and see your business evolve.

1. Are you acting like a creative leader should and synchronising your team and making good decisions?
2. Do you have an effective recruitment and loyalty strategy to build a solid team?
3. Have you got solid financial reporting processes in place?

This is vital. When a business runs out of cash, it can be strangled. Making your money work for you is fundamental if you want to grow quickly.

4. Have you arranged the proper finance to support your cash-flow forecasts?

5. Have you pinpointed how to scale growth effectively? Is growth in profits contractual, long term and guaranteed, or seasonal and subject to dips? This will determine whether you seek to minimise costs and absorb profit or reinvest profit (and incur additional staff or premises costs).

6. Are you reviewing company performance systematically and consistently on a day-by-day basis? If you read your figures properly, you really can see into the future of your company.

7. Are you maintaining momentum? Focus on areas that are working, invest in outstanding areas and accelerate growth.

8. Are you building and maintaining relationships? Nurture win-win relationships and think outside of the box to add value for your customers. How can you help them better serve their customers?

9. Are you investing time in relationships with bankers, partners, suppliers, customers and staff to create confidence and loyalty?

10. Are you perpetually open to learning? Are you in 'sponge' mode, ready to soak up the knowledge you need to grow your business effectively?

Now that you are managing the growth of your business effectively and are building your future steadily, there's one more thing to say . . . Well done – you are now thinking and acting like a Tycoon. And, if you are achieving and sustaining success, then you are a Tycoon! Welcome to the club; it's an exhilarating rollercoaster of a ride. I hope this book has helped you to be prepared for every twist and turn along the way. Good luck on your journey!

7

MY TIME ON TV

When I set out on my journey, building businesses, I never thought for one minute that I would be on TV, let alone set up my own TV and media company. Perhaps I've long harboured a dream to encourage others to go into business, but it was buried deep under a plethora of pitches, deals and other objectives. It was only when the opportunity came my way that I was able to dust off the cobwebs and hone in on that goal.

I never expected to be voted Britain's top TV business pundit in a recent poll, just above Sir Alan Sugar. In fact, I have to admit that my early initial daydream of running my own business did not include any plans to enter the world of showbiz. However, just as I mentioned in the very first chapter, as Tycoons visualise new and expanding opportunities, our goals shift too. Literally, as one horizon is reached, a new horizon is revealed. So, in achieving the results I set out to achieve, I've created new opportunities that led to better horizons and have widened the goal posts to enable even greater success.

Reaching one goal flicks the switch for the next opportunity. For example, if the BBC hadn't approached me to participate on the panel of *Dragons' Den*, I may not have been bitten by the TV business bug and might not have had the subsequent idea for *American Inventor*, or I might have still had the idea, but not had the contacts in the TV world, or the knowledge, to take it further. But that single programme idea stimulated the idea for Peter Jones TV, which then prompted the idea for *Tycoon* and the deal with ITV. Reaching one horizon revealed another.

In those three years since I first stepped in front of the camera, a 'new ideas movement' has been growing, bubbling away across all corners of Britain. Now, in 2007, there's a sense that business reality TV is the new rock 'n' roll. I think that TV has undoubtedly helped people learn a lot more about business and gain an improved insight of what's actually involved. TV shows like *Dragons' Den* aren't totally off the mark in terms of reality, but are more factual entertainment than reality TV. As such, they are powerful learning tools, feeding the viewer with knowledge. It obviously isn't the way investors work in terms of timescale and due diligence, but it does give the viewer insight – a keyhole view of what it's like to pitch, to convince someone to invest and the importance of knowing your numbers as well as your business.

In recent years there's been a boom in alternative programming that is factual or educational. From the rise in home improvement and property programmes to the increase in programmes following someone on a mission, be it Gordon Ramsay with *Hell's Kitchen* or *Ramsay's Kitchen Nightmares* or Ray Mears on his mission to unveil bushcraft. Business is also a hot topic, one that's getting an ample slice of the airwaves. Factual entertainment furnishes viewers with an incredible amount of useful information and feeds people's desire to go out and do something, whether it's improve their home, buy property abroad, campaign for something they feel passionately about or become their own boss.

While promoting my new show, *Tycoon*, I appeared on BBC London's *Breakfast Show* and encouraged listeners to ring in with their business ideas. The production team later informed me that I had managed to crash the phonelines with the sheer volume of calls. Most encouraging! Only a few weeks later, the same occurred on the *Christian O'Connell Breakfast Show* on Virgin Radio. He told me that it had been their biggest ever phone-in response in the history of the station. 'More than Robbie Williams?' I said. 'More than anyone!' Christian said.

Ultimately, television is starting to encourage people to go out and do something with their ideas. In 2007, more businesses are being invested in and more ideas are coming to market than ever before. That's testament to the power of TV and to the spotlight being placed on business and enterprise. I don't believe it's purely as a result of governmental or policy perspectives. TV has been a key component oiling the wheels of an enterprising nation driving towards prosperity.

The new breed of business TV shows has inspired people to give themselves permission to create new ideas and has given them the nous to know where to go and how to go about it. People can now watch and learn from the contestants who fail on *The Apprentice*. They can learn from those entrepreneurs who pitch ideas on *Dragons' Den*. They can see how to do it *and*, perhaps even more importantly, how not to do it. They can watch a business being created on *Tycoon*.

And now, here I am, writing this book. My journey has brought me to this point. As well as directing my companies, I now have an additional mission: to inspire people and give them the tools and guidelines to get out there and start up in business. With this book, with *American Inventor*, with *Tycoon* and beyond, my mission is to uncover the enterprising talent I know exists in the world and encourage entrepreneurs to become Tycoons. That is my key purpose, my vision.

The rest of this chapter is intended to be an extended case study. It's all about demonstrating how the ideas in this book can be applied to take you to the very top.

THE JOURNEY SO FAR: *DRAGONS' DEN*
The Phone Call

My adventures in television all began with a phonecall from Martin Smyth at the BBC, who said he wanted to meet with me to discuss my interest in appearing in a one-hour pilot for BBC2. I was sitting in my boardroom in Loudwater, Bucks, and we met up and discussed the programme. He described the show, which sounded rather like a business documentary – a bit serious and educational – but it did seem to have something. After completing the one-hour pilot, they asked if I would take

part in a six-part series. I agreed and the rest is history –
Dragons' Den is now in its fourth series and has become a hit
show for the BBC.

About the Show: *Dragons' Den*

Dragons' Den first originated in Japan, where a company called
Nippon own the format. They licensed it to Sony, who approached the BBC to make it in the UK. Today, there are many
international versions of *Dragons' Den*, from Australia and New
Zealand to Canada and Israel. In each version, the premise of the
show is that entrepreneurs pitch their business ideas to a panel of
successful wealthy businessmen and women to secure investment
finance, usually between £50,000 and £250,000. The Dragons'
Den is 'where hope meets experience'.

The entrepreneurs each believe they have a viable business
proposition, but lack the funding to take it forward. They need
cash. The dragons have cash, along with highly valuable contacts
(well, most of us, anyway!) and business know-how, but they
need to be persuaded to part with their hard-earned money and
often refuse to invest.

Pitches vary in length, from ten minutes to an hour or so,
although only a few minutes of a select few pitches make the final
edit, and are followed by questions from the dragons to assess the
potential rewards and risks involved in investing in each individual. Negotiations follow, focused mainly on the percentage of
equity in the company that the budding entrepreneur is willing to
give up in exchange for the dragons' investment. Under fire from
the dragons' questions, many contestants reveal a lack of preparation, a lack of knowledge about the market or risks and a lack
of awareness of turnover or profit figures.

The rules of *Dragons' Den* stipulate that if the entrepreneur
does not raise at least the amount of money they've asked for, they
leave with nothing. So if they only raise half the cash, they leave
empty-handed.

Filming: Behind the Scenes

Amazingly, I wasn't nervous about appearing on TV for the first time. It felt OK because I wasn't being asked to act; I could be myself. The easiest thing about my TV appearances is that I am me. Meeting the other dragons was interesting: everyone was very polite, but clearly eyeing each other up and jostling for position, especially when the camera started to roll. There were a lot of egos in the same place at the same time.

Business propositions on *Dragons' Den* have ranged from the crazy notions (remember the knee-rollerskating Super Knees for dads and golf gloves to remind you to drive on the correct side of the road?) to the genuinely imaginative ideas, such as iTeddy, and the exciting investments with solid business proposals, like Reggae Reggae Sauce and *Wonderland*, each of which I've invested in. I have no regrets about the investments I've made, or those I've opted not to back.

For example, one guy came on the show to pitch an idea for a table with a built-in computer, a bit like the Space Invaders table, with cables underneath. It was a complete mess! You'd never, ever buy one of those, especially at his suggested price of £1,000. But this guy was about to remortgage his house and was putting his whole life on the line to pursue this idea. He had a wife and kids. So I said to the producers, 'Stop! We'll finish this segment of filming, but I can't carry on after that until I've spoken to him properly. I've got to convince him not to do this.'

So, behind the scenes, I sat down with him and spent the next half an hour telling him why he shouldn't pursue the idea and what specifically was wrong with it. He said, 'Thank you. I think you've just saved my house. I won't remortgage now.'

Evidently, as much as persistence and belief are critical success factors in business, there is little point persisting or having unwavering faith in an idea that just isn't viable, hence the importance of testing plausibility and collecting evidence to back up your idea, as I've outlined in previous chapters.

It's not always like that, though. There are contestants who come on *Dragons' Den* who can prove the likelihood of their idea working and have certain characteristics a Tycoon should have. Those who stand out are Huw Gwyther, Levi Roots and Imran Hakim.

Huw Gwyther, the first person to persuade me to invest on *Dragons' Den*, clearly used the rules of the Tycoon's Mindset in his pitch. He was concise but precise, well presented in all senses of the word, had confidence in his figures, had taken substantial action to get to this point and had a clear vision and plan of how he intended to reach his goals. As I said in Chapter 3, I used my intuition and decided to invest in his wonderful *Wonderland* magazine concept. It's now breaking even and expanding into various global territories.

Levi (real name Keith Graham) may not be entirely Tycoon-like, but he is no stranger to success. Levi has performed with James Brown and Maxi Priest, and, in 1998, the Brixton-based Levi was nominated for a MOBO Award for 'Best Reggae Performer'. While he hadn't created a sauce empire, he had managed to sell 4,000 jars of his intriguing Reggae Reggae Sauce at Notting Hill Carnival last year and had been selling jerk chicken covered in the sauce, created from his grandmother's recipe, for the past 15 years. What Levi lacks in business acumen, he more than makes up for in spirit. When he pitched to us dragons, he displayed passion, confidence and persistence. He had a vision and painted it clearly for us to share with him. Furthermore, Levi was likeable and investable. Reggae Reggae Sauce is now on shelves in 600 Sainsbury's supermarket stores across the UK, and Levi's winning smile is even wider.

Imran Hakim was very polished. He demonstrated his drive and enthusiasm for his product and confirmed that he had made key changes to his product in only a few weeks. He was very investable in that he knew his target market, had already identified things that needed to be done to his product to enhance it and didn't exaggerate its potential. He researched his market well, and, under some tough questioning as well as one or two objections to his product (which actually were probably only said for TV, because they weren't very appropriate), he handled himself in a composed manner.

In December 2006, I filmed a fourth series of *Dragons' Den*, which was broadcast in February and March 2007. The previous series attracted 4 million viewers and *Dragons' Den* has become cult viewing. TV and radio presenters across the land even chat on air about the previous night's show. The airwaves are abuzz with business.

Every series of filming brings new surprises, and I enjoy negotiating alongside my fellow dragons, quizzing an army of intrepid budding entrepreneurs and investing in winning people and their ideas. Being a dragon, I've got to meet some wacky people and some inspirational people, and it's been really good fun. But, most of all, it's been a brilliant opportunity to encourage people to pursue their dreams.

GOING TO HOLLYWOOD: *AMERICAN INVENTOR*
The Idea

My experience with *Dragons' Den* was about contestants securing investment to start a business, but I had a real interest in inventions. I have always been intrigued by inventions and famous inventors, from Dyson and cat's eyes to the lawnmower and Einstein. My imagination stirred into motion and I thought, 'Why don't we have an invention show?' So many of my friends had ideas for inventions; wouldn't it be great to see different people of all ages pitching their inventions in the hope of winning a large cash prize.

I really believed this could be a great concept for a TV show because at some point in our lives most of us think of an idea that will solve a problem, help us make money or give us a better life. Many people, however, don't feel they have the right opportunities to embrace those ideas and see them through. That is why I created *American Inventor*. I had different working titles for it, including *Big Shot* and *Pitch for a Million*. Once I'd created a vision of the idea in my mind, I committed to that vision. I jotted the concept down on paper and took immediate action.

I described in Chapter 1 how I took my concept to an executive producer who worked for the BBC but was told that it would 'never be a big show' and that I wouldn't get it on the BBC or a mainstream channel, but maybe cable TV or Channel 4 'if you're lucky'. That feedback was useful to receive. I knew the concept would work, not because of any misguided faith or blind arrogance, but because I knew this wasn't a crazy notion. I'd done the groundwork, looked into the idea and decided it was a viable one. This feedback made me even hungrier to prove them wrong. It inspired me to find someone who would share my vision. I thought Simon Cowell might be that person. I knew Max Clifford handled his PR, so I was able to get in touch, via Max, with some people who worked with Simon.

As I said in Chapter 1, I met with Nigel Hall in Max's office and gave him my idea, talked it through and handed him a hard copy of the format document I had written. He agreed to talk it over with Simon Cowell in a week or so.

The Phone Call

After getting my concept to husband and wife team, Siobhan Green (Shu) and Nigel (who I'd met in Max's office), who worked with Simon Cowell, the couple set off to Los Angeles with my format, still then entitled *Big Shot*. They were very excited and couldn't wait to present the idea to Simon Cowell. They believed if Simon saw what they had seen, this could be a winning show. They called me the day they arrived and said they would be sitting down with Simon the very next day. I felt excited and believed that even if Simon didn't think much of it, at least it had a chance. If he said no, I would go to the networks myself, anyway.

While I was having dinner with my friends Bobby Gonzalez, Greg Jones, Simon Williamson, Richard Griffin and Phil Lucas in Cookham (we often meet up and go out for a few beers and a curry – it's become a bit of a ritual), I received a voice message at 10.39 p.m. on 10 March 2005. The mobile reception isn't great in the area so you often get messages late. I wanted to check who it was and so I went out to the car park and listened to the message. It was Simon Cowell. He said, 'Peter . . . Simon Cowell speaking, how are you? I have been given your idea by Nigel and Shu and, to say I'm excited is an understatement . . . I've got some ideas which I think could make the show even better but, more importantly, I think we could have a hit here in the States . . . let alone the UK.'

As I explained in Chapter 1, I didn't quite know what to do or say. I glanced down at my phone a couple of times and then played the message again, just to make sure it really was Simon Cowell. I even played it to my friend for him to listen to, in case it wasn't real. I couldn't believe it. I wanted to call back immediately, but, at the same time, I wanted to savour the moment for a while longer. After 15 minutes or so, I called and spoke to Simon. I knew then that this was indeed genuine. He asked if I could come out to LA within a week and, naturally, I confirmed that I would.

The next day, after a few hours' sleep, I woke up and I still couldn't believe it. My partner, Tara, and I discussed the call, and, later that day, I made arrangements to go and meet Simon in Los Angeles.

The Meeting

A week later we were in LA, the land of dreams. It was a major point in my life and I wanted Tara and my daughter, Natalia, with me. Even though they couldn't attend the meetings, just having them there made the whole experience even more special, as did having two friends, Bobby and Jo, from home with us. We arrived on Saturday and took our first steps in LA, heading straight for Hollywood. We loved it instantly. On Monday night, we arranged to have dinner with Simon Cowell and his girlfriend, Teri. He brought three colleagues with him, including his business and legal affairs man, Clive Rich, Sonny (the man behind Simon's music business), and Siobhan Green (Shu), who is a major inspiration behind many of Simon's shows, a tiny lady with amazing energy who was always excited whenever we talked about the format for *Big Shot*.

I sat next to Simon at dinner, and, from the time we sat down to the time we left, neither one of us stopped talking. His team didn't even get a chance to get a word in.

Towards the end of the dinner, Simon leaned forward. 'Look,' he said, 'this is your idea and we wouldn't have got to hear about it if it wasn't for you. You want a fifty-fifty deal and I think that is very fair.' I was pleased for two reasons. Firstly, I knew Simon brought a lot to the party and had the contacts in the TV industry due to his success with *Pop Idol* and *American Idol*, and, secondly, even though the show was my idea, it wouldn't work as well without his experience as an executive producer.

This was one person I really wanted to do business with and I had a great feeling about working with him. We both agreed that the lawyers could sort out the details but that the deal was a complete 50/50 split down the middle. I agreed, we shook hands and that was the 'deal done'!

I have to say, I related to Simon and really liked him, and I think he liked me. Likeability has always been important to me when it comes to business partnerships, more so than when hiring staff. Simon was genuine, thoughtful, honest and straight-talking – the qualities I've been told I share. We had common ground and similar attitudes, which can be fantastic foundations not only when it comes to doing a deal and working on a project together, but also for building effective partnerships and even friendships.

I used the Golden Rule of influence. I knew I needed someone else to help me make my TV show a reality, and I couldn't think of anyone better. Now, almost two years down the line, Simon is a good friend of mine. He's become a megastar in America and the UK, and I think he deserves the success he's having. He's great on TV and always adds a great dynamic and a clear difference of opinion to the mix. He's a very talented man and it's been fun getting to know him.

The press often refer to me as 'the pinstripe Simon Cowell'. It's interesting how journalists pick that up and say those things. I just tell Simon that's a compliment to him and smile.

Once the deal with Simon had been done, our goal was to get a network interested, so we took action to get the show on air. Our first stop was Fox Network, before moving on to ABC, which absolutely jumped at the opportunity to put the show on air. Step one, we'd got the result we'd set out to achieve – a commission.

Just one year after receiving that initial call from Simon Cowell, auditions were being held across America. National casting calls were held in seven major cities across the country: Los Angeles, San Francisco, New York, Denver, Chicago, Washington, DC, and Atlanta. Thousands of inventors, tinkerers and entrepreneurs of all ages applied. It was really happening! The idea I'd had while I was sitting in my office in Marlow one day, staring out of the window, thinking about how great it would be to have real inventors pitch their contraptions and ideas to a panel of judges had finally come true. Here's what that seedling of an idea grew into:

About the Show: *American Inventor*

American Inventor is the embodiment of the ultimate American dream and follows a search for America's best new invention to celebrate the best in homespun ingenuity. From the Cabbage Patch Kids and the George Foreman Grill to Post-it Notes and the Rubik's Cube, many great inventions have been born from the minds of American people. The show offers 12 finalists development money and then four inventors are chosen to go forward to the final.

Twelve inventors and their products were chosen from a pool of hundreds by four judges. Each of the three semi-finalists received $50,000 to improve their inventions and compete to become one of the four finalists. In the show's live finale, the four finalists presented a 30-second commercial advertisement for their product, with the home audience voting by phone for the winner. The winner received $1 million!

Filming: On Set in LA

I went back out to Hollywood in January 2006 to wear three hats on the project: co-creator, executive producer and judge. In comparison, *Dragons' Den* is a fairly small production, and that's what I had grown acclimatised to. Going over to America and soaking up that whole LA buzz was unbelievable. It was almost like walking out of a nightclub at 3 a.m. after having a few drinks and being hit by that cold air. It was so astonishing. Everything was awe-inspiring. I was even collected from my hotel in a stretch limousine and taken straight to the set, where there were several hundred people milling around in a car-park lot. The crew had taken over an entire mini trading estate to film the show.

A sea of Winnebagos greeted me as I walked over to the production area. There were more producers and directors than a major production company probably has. Everything was huge, very glitzy and high profile. What's more, this time round, I wasn't merely a dragon or judge; I was involved in creating and producing the show too.

Working with the crew was a learning experience for me; I soaked it all up like a sponge: how they set certain situations up, how it all worked and came together, how they put the show out and promoted it.

Being an executive producer and a judge allowed me to work closely with Simon Cowell's team at Syco (his TV company); and with the producers, Fremantle, while also interacting with the people from the network, ABC; the whole experience was fantastic for me. I love to network, to meet and talk to like-minded people, and they were all wonderful characters. They were all strikingly successful in what they do and were a pleasure to work with. Furthermore, I was putting my Tycoon Mindset to work: learning, interacting and networking.

The glitz, glamour and scale of the whole *American Inventor* operation was incredible enough, but so were the people who came and pitched on the show – the contestants. Literally thousands of people pitched. Some ideas were good, some were average, and some were excruciatingly bad. But there was plenty of real emotion in the show, as most of the hopeful inventors have devoted their lives to pursuing their inventions.

Throughout this book you'll have noticed my Ten Golden Rules given credence with examples of how I've gone about my business and how others have gone about theirs. What's interesting is that on my journey into the media business, not only have I put my Ten Golden Rules into practice as I've embarked on this stage of my career, I've also noticed how so many of the people I've met, on both sides of the camera, have displayed Tycoon tendencies.

The people I worked with in the US were fantastic – very inspiring, upbeat and positive. I witnessed a cultural difference there: the Americans fear failure less than the British and put successful people up on a pedestal. And they protect them, because they want them to be an inspiration for their kids. Donald Trump is a very good example of this. He failed quite massively and has been reinvented, and what a massive success he is now. He's a real inspiration to a lot of people and is "The American Dream" personified.

It was while working on a show that epitomised the American dream that I knew I must create a TV show to create the British dream. Sadly, in the UK, when we have successful people, we put them on pedestals and many people take pride in knocking them down or finding reasons to belittle them, instead of using them as the inspiration to drive people to be like them. That's a key cultural difference. I hope that in stimulating the British dream, I can help overcome that attitude and change it to be more about exposing people's successes than focused on their failures.

The inspiration, passion, drive and enthusiasm the *American Inventor* contestants had was admirable. Even though some ideas weren't great ones, the inventors were still so enthusiastic. They had the attitude of 'I'm going to make it, I'm going to do this, and if it isn't this, it'll be something else.' Many contestants had the Mindset of a Tycoon, and I have no doubt that once these people find a workable idea to pursue, they'll succeed in their endeavours.

The finalists included a double-traction bike that features a second seat on the handlebars of the bicycle; a detachable vest that football players and other athletes can wear to train and develop proper catching skills; a new type of child's car seat in the form of a capsule; and the Word Ace game, an electronic tabletop word game for between one and six players, which teaches children spelling and vocabulary skills in a fun, interactive way. Word Ace was one of my personal favourites.

In fact, it was Word Ace that was the eventual runner up. The game was created by Ed Hall, 40, from Chicago, who used his experience as a former elementary- and high-school teacher and coach, and his inspiration from his fifth-grade students, to come up with his invention. From an early age Ed had dreams of playing in the NBA and promised to get his mother a house outside of the rough neighborhood he grew up in. He hoped to make good on his promise, and I hope he still does. He certainly showed vision, confidence and perseverance – promising Tycoon qualities.

In a live episode on 18 May 2006, the first season's winner was declared. The winner of *American Inventor* 2006 was 52-year-old Janusz Liberkowski, a mechanical engineer from San Jose. His winning invention was the Anecia Spherical Safety Seat – a new kind of car seat in which the child sits inside nested spheres. In a collision, the spheres spin and automatically position the child's neck and back so that they are perpendicular to the force of impact, shielding the child from the destructive force of the impact. I was concerned that it was always going to be too big as a concept to get manufactured.

Janusz Liberkowski touched the hearts of a nation when his story was revealed. Janusz and his wife had tragically lost their elder daughter, Anecia, in a car accident seven years previously, which had driven Janusz to create a revolutionary seat in the hope that it would save children's lives even though his daughter wasn't a child when she passed away. Janusz had a unique invention; he had passion to take action and get results; he had purpose, confidence and exceptional commitment. What's more, he captured the hearts of the nation, and won the show.

Of course, there is no shortage of confident people in America. However, sometimes, people can be overconfident and discover all too late that their confidence is actually misguided. For example, one guy who scored ten out of ten for confidence but zero for the viability of his invention was Ortega, a dental hygienist from New York. He thought he'd invented the world's first portable toilet. It was a suitbag with a zip in it, and you'd climb inside it and zip it up. You could then do your business in the attached colostomy bag. When he zipped it up, he looked like Count Dracula. He said it worked because he'd tried it out at the bus stop before he arrived to pitch it us. Ortega told us, 'People looked round and then looked back again, so even they thought it was normal,' to which I replied, 'I think they looked at you because they thought you were a complete wacko!'

Evidently, confidence and belief in an idea needs validation. Unlike Ortega, the finalists' inventions were all within the realms of possibility; they were feasible ideas that could be taken forward.

Another Golden Rule for becoming a Tycoon is the ability to take action. One contestant certainly did that, but he frightened the life out of the judging panel in the process. He came on to demonstrate how he'd made covers for car windows and bodywork. Hailstones can be so big in America that they can dent cars, so he'd created body armour for cars to protect them. He came on with this big stick and started bashing the hell out of this cover. We all jumped out of our skins. He'd taken action, but perhaps a little too forthrightly. As it turned out, his idea didn't make the final because his product covered the whole window and it would have been a small market. I have to say as a character we should have put him through because he embodied all that was great about the American dream. He was a down-to-earth guy with no money, but he had a dream and an idea. Next season, I will stand up for people with that kind of passion and make sure we encourage them and put them through the audition phase (as long as they have a viable invention) giving them a chance that will change their life for ever. After all, the American public ultimately decides, so why not?

American Inventor Airs: From Vision to Reality TV

American Inventor aired on 16 March 2006 and premiered in style. The response has been overwhelming. It became ABC's biggest hit on a Thursday night for more than three years, with more than 14 million viewers. We had exceeded all expectations for the network, an amazing result!

When we saw the actual output of the show, it was incredible; it makes you realise how much work and hours of editing goes into producing a great show.

Being results-driven is another of my Ten Golden Rules to becoming a Tycoon. And that doesn't change when you're in the media business. Our targeted results were to get enough viewers to get the show re-commissioned and sell the rights internationally. Before the live final to America, we were told *American Inventor* would return for a second season.

Within PJTV we want to develop 'prime-time' high-quality shows that are innovative, challenging and compulsive viewing. They need to be real and able to take people on a journey that is fun, educational and inspirational. Our current show for ITV, *Tycoon*, has all these qualities, but re-commissioning is about audience share, the type of demographic, as well as overall numbers of viewers. We will strive, with both *American Inventor* and *Tycoon*, to be successful in all those areas. A challenge, yes, but we are up to it.

I flew out to film the second season of *American Inventor* in March 2007. It was decided by the producers and ABC, the network, that the show needed a new dynamic, a fresh approach and some clever tweaks, so a decision was made not to use the original three judges and hire in new judges to work alongside me.

239

We managed to sign George Foreman – amazing! The other two judges are Pat Croce, a motivational speaker and former president and past owner of the Philidelphia 76ers, and Sara Blakely, who created the Spanx range of ladies' support underwear, like pantyhose. Presenting the show this year is Nick Smith, who is an ABC primetime reporter and TV presenter based in San Francisco. George has been great to work with and he said to me that I was inspirational, which is an amazing compliment coming from a former twice Heavyweight Champion of the world. He thinks I am quite harsh but my reply to him is 'it's not harsh, it's honest.' I really like Pat Croce and think he is just fantastic. We have become great friends. His energy is incredible and, during speeches to the inventors, just before they audition, he describes me as 'Britain's Donald Trump' – quite a comparison to live up to. Sara Blakely is a very attractive, successful woman and I love our interaction on camera. All of us get on brilliantly, which is great.

We may also have a potential worldwide hit on our hands, as the show was well received at MIPTV in Cannes and has been sold to France, Turkey and Russia, with no doubt many more countries to follow: now that it has become a hit in the US, other countries are more than keen to get hold of it. Success really does create a springboard to additional achievement and opportunity.

You'll notice the Tycoon Golden Rules coming into play throughout this tale. After I'd received that far from favourable feedback from that first BBC executive about my show, I could have parked the idea, but I wasn't prepared to give up that easily. I knew I had something. My intuition and research told me so. I believed it would work and had the courage of my convictions to take it forward. I harnessed the Golden Rules of vision: commitment, action, results, perseverance and influence.

MY OWN SHOW: *TYCOON*
The Vision: Peter Jones TV

As I said in Chapter 1, in 2005, soon after I'd received the call from Simon Cowell, I came up with a new vision for a TV company called Peter Jones TV, which would create and manage TV and media formats, developing programmes across different genres and platforms. Watching the mechanics of television production from my position as a judge on *Dragons' Den* had fascinated me. I could also see that given my background in telecommunications and online development, we could have a very strong focus on driving and exploiting opportunities in the digital-media marketplace.

I take nothing for granted, and I appreciate that television is a creative industry where the core requirements are talented, visionary people combined with good ideas and an understanding of what viewers want. Against that background, I felt that there was a chance to take a look initially at the developing genre of business-reality formats, but doing it my way from the very real perspective of someone who had actually been there and done it in the tough corporate world. It is fair to say that business shows on TV have really come to the fore in recent years, and yet I still felt there were stories and angles in that area that were not being covered, which gave rise to my thought process that eventually led to the creation of *American Inventor* and now *Tycoon*. My vision is not to concentrate solely in this area for the long term, as I have a real desire and yearning to create a media business that is strong in producing programming across a wide range of genres, as well as bolstering this with other complementary aspects to the business that enable international sales distribution, proper exploitation of rights and ancillary licensing deals and digital media development.

My plan was to look at the industry and the way it employs and rewards talent, and I felt there was an opportunity to rewrite the rulebook. Currently, the industry relies on a large pool of freelance talent, who move around from production to production. There is no real long-term loyalty or commitment from either employer or employee. And yet, this to me seems a strange way to operate in a world that is so clearly reliant on people and the development of ideas. My plan is to build a business that offers the cream of the industry good jobs and prospects and a reason to stay and work with me for the long term to develop ideas that I can back using my business acumen and access to funding. Just those elements alone would make Peter Jones TV a formidable force in the industry, and we are already well on our way to establishing a long-term business that will deliver significant commercial success in a properly managed and visionary way. The ideas were flowing in my mind about formats and programmes that would help me kick-start this journey and help me turn exciting ideas into a very real business. Like so many things in business, planning for something is vital, but sometimes opportunities just seem to land in the right place at the right time, and my link-up with ABC and ITV was a great example of this.

My vision for the company is that whether it's comedy, documentary or reality, a Peter Jones production will have the hallmark of being intelligent with a hint of irony, fun and inspiration. My goal is to become one of the most respected players in the market by the end of 2008 and help encourage people to make their dreams reality through the medium of television. The company's first output was *American Inventor*, and we are co-producing the second series for ABC in the US with Fremantle North America and Syco TV, and the show is set to air in June 2007.

However, during my time filming *American Inventor*, I wanted to achieve a UK commission; I wanted to spearhead and advocate the British dream, so I put the wheels into motion by getting in touch with a contact I had who was moving to ITV.

In April 2006, I signed a deal with ITV to produce *Tycoon*. This was a show which saw me put my own money on the line as I went on a quest to find – and invest in – Britain's next Tycoon. This show started where programmes like *Dragons' Den* and *The Apprentice* end. It added a completely new dimension to business television and gave would-be Tycoons the chance to build the company they have always dreamed of creating with my help and guidance.

The Idea

I thought it would be great to find Britain's next Tycoon. Everything starts with an idea and I felt it would be great to capture this on TV, and even better if viewers could get to see the development of the business from scratch. *Dragons' Den* is about investing in a business; *American Inventor* is about finding the next Dyson. This time, I wanted to find someone not just to invest in or run one of my companies, not to pursue an invention, but to set up and run their own company, with my backing, mentoring and guidance. Taking a business, building it and making it a success – ultimately finding Britain's next Tycoon.

I believe Britain is an innovative and entrepreneurial nation at heart but we don't do enough in this country to nurture talented people and help them turn their business dreams into reality. This show would be a way to achieve that objective; not just to help the six finalists and the contestant crowned Tycoon at the end of the series, but to also help the viewers at home and encourage them to think, 'Do you know what? I can do that!'

The Meeting

I approached Paul Jackson, who had previously worked for Granada USA and had a meeting with him in LA while I was filming *American Inventor*. He loved the idea for *Tycoon*, informed me that he was now working for ITV, which was the channel I hoped would take the show and said he'd like to commission it. He not only commissioned *Tycoon*, but also offered me a two-year talent deal to be ITV's face of business, which will see me appear in at least two new programmes for the network. It's incredible how quickly something can happen if you give it your attention and focus.

My first step from there was to build a tremendous team of people to help drive my vision forward. My business affairs lawyer, Jonathan Groves, who worked on the contract for *American Inventor*, handled all the contractual side of things. I then started to research who the best producers were in the UK

243

market. And, with help from ITV's controller of alternative programming, to whom I owe so much, Layla Smith, managed to get some useful contacts that resulted in me hiring some great producers, including Michelle Langer, who had previously worked on shows like *I'm a Celebrity Get Me Out Of Here* and *Big Brother*, and ex-ITV2 controller, Daniella Newman. We've really built a big powerbase of some seriously top producers. What's great is, once you get one great person, other people follow; it's as simple as that. We're now surrounding ourselves with the best people in the business. That way, as long as our ideas are good, we know we're going to make great television.

About the Show: *Tycoon*

Summer 2007 saw Britain's budding entrepreneurs battling it out to win my backing when I put my money on the line to find our nation's next *Tycoon*.

During the show, I challenged the successful entrants to follow my methods in order to turn the initial investment into a huge profit within weeks.

It was a show about people with passion, drive and energy, and, for one person at the end, there was a magnificent reward for succeeding: the chance to own the business they always wanted and become Britain's next Tycoon.

Tycoon was about finding Britain's next big business success story. I wanted to show that anyone can succeed if they have a good idea and follow my methods for maximum success.

This is for anyone who has dreamt of running their own business. I also wanted the public to have the chance of owning shares in the winning Tycoon's business, and so for the first time on television, we ran a competition that gave hundreds of people that chance.

Filming: the Search

My search to find Britain's next Tycoon took me across the land, scouring the nation to seek out men and women of all ages and from all walks of life who believe they have an outstanding idea. My promotional activities included appearances on a variety of programmes, from Sir David Frost's *Frost Tonight* and *Loose Women* to Jo Whiley's BBC Radio One show and Christian O'Connell's Virgin Radio show.

Around the same time as all my promotional activity, ITV launched a website displaying the details (www.itv.com/tycoon), and from 6 January 2007 applications began to flood in.

Eventually the show was won by Iain Morgan, whose company Bladez Toyz imported a fantastic toy helicopter which has become a bestseller!

My life so far in television has been an exhilarating rollercoaster ride, and one of the most memorable moments has to be when I had to present an award at the National TV Awards at the Royal Albert Hall in 2006. In front of millions I presented an award for the 'Most Popular Factual Programme' to *Top Gear* and Jeremy Clarkson came on to the stage to collect the award – a great moment. Tara was there with me in support and even she said she couldn't believe it – businessman to TV man in just two years. After the event, we went out for dinner (a curry in Cookham) with Katie Price (Jordan) and Peter André. Who would have thought two years ago I would be going out with them for dinner? Oh, how life changes – almost in a heartbeat!

Who'd have guessed that seven-year-old 'dreamer' would decades later be invited to the Beckhams' house for the party of the year, and count the likes of Simon Cowell, Jay Kay from Jamiroquai, Paul McKenna, Gordon Ramsay and Gok Wan, among his friends? I certainly would never have thought it either. It's been amazing! I am now working on many other TV related projects that will continue to challenge people's views on business, whether it is helping youngsters create a new consumer product or giving people the self-belief that you can do it if you possess the right mindset. My world now gives me access to many different people, whether they are famous celebrities, mega successful business people or even the Prime Minister, but one thing will remain the same . . . me. I am still the same person that sat in my father's chair at the age of just seven, dreaming of what might be and I am still the same person today who dreams about what will be. My TV work will continue to play a major part in my life but the many businesses that I own or invest in today are still part of the making of who I am. I love business and am really pleased that it has become the new 'rock and roll'. Tycoons grow economies. They always have and becoming one has never been more exciting. I have been right int he middle of that and it makes me happy to know there will be many more thousands of great business leaders tomorrow because of the wider access and knowlege that is available today. Well, that's one side of my life and now, back to my other world – business.

So, after becoming a Tycoon multi-millionaire and enjoying a happy family life, what's next? Well, one of my great dreams is to open a Tycoon academy. This would be a place for people who want to start in business to study and learn about becoming an entrepreneur. It would be like no other academic establishment because, rather than just equipping people with paper qualifications (which it will do), it will provide a gateway for people to become successful entrepreneurs. Whatever happens next, I'll be sure to take my own advice and keep following my Golden Rules.

Remember the Tycoon Tips for Success about how to persevere from Chapter 1? (See pages 51–2.) They apply to how I made *American Inventor* happen to the deal with ITV and are relevant to any idea that needs taking forward.

1. Set your goal, visualise the successful end result and write down what needs to be done to achieve that goal within a set timescale.
2. Give yourself credit. You've already visualised your dreams, set goals and planned actions; you've made a commitment, so it's worth persevering with it.
3. Keep moving forward, always. Take action to get the results

you want. Get yourself heard by the right people. Persist in doing so.

4. Persevere. Stay determined. Never give up unless circumstances dictate and you need to regroup.

5. Stay flexible enough to adjust actions accordingly when necessary. Sometimes you'll need to venture down a different path to reach your destination. In business, you need to be prepared to take a detour.

6. Believe and you *will* achieve.

FINAL WORD

The only person who can write the conclusion to this book is you, because only you know your vision; only you know your planned endgame. You hold the key to unlocking your own potential; you're at the controls. Your vision may be vivid, but your future is not set in stone. The possibilities are endless! One thing is certain, though: your future is in *your* hands, and you have a greater chance of carving out the future you want for yourself if you focus on being the best you can be and develop the Mindset of a Tycoon.

In these pages, I have effectively given you a blueprint of my mindset. I have shared with you a unique glimpse into the thought processes and characteristics of a Tycoon and revealed how I have succeeded personally, where I have not and how I have bounced back and persevered to succeed again. I have asked you to open your mind to the prospect of not succeeding, to welcome change and harness the power of your imagination, and I've provided you with checklists, resources and tools to guide you in the right direction. Hopefully now you understand how I see the world, how I make decisions, what inspires, drives and motivates me, and how you can use all of this information to your own advantage.

You now know how a Tycoon thinks, acts, behaves and why. Ultimately, you've learned the cycle of success, starting with the initial moment of creativity and spark of imagination, which fires up the vision, which leads to action and strategy, plans and motivation, which leads to results, which bring success and learning. The knowledge and contacts then spark more ideas and thus the Tycoon circle continues.

You know that a Tycoon's temperament is focused, engaging and intent on results. You are well aware that being a Tycoon, being successful creatively and financially, requires the right attitude and the right thought processes. You know how a Tycoon's attitude creates opportunities where others might miss them and subsequently sets him or her up for success. You know how a Tycoon's visualisation of good fortune brings good fortune. Perception is vital. If you perceive yourself as lucky, or if you think and behave like a Tycoon, your good fortune will increase, you will create opportunities for yourself, and your behaviour will become rooted firmly in reality. By thinking, 'I can do this. I *will* do this,' you'll create a self-fulfilling prophecy and prove yourself right. Ultimately, if you want to be a big shot, you have to give it your *best* shot.

I've learned these lessons and adopted these Tycoon techniques over 25 years running businesses. I didn't read them in a book. You have a head start. How you use the insight provided is your prerogative. You write the script to your own life, just as you write the plan for your business.

You have learned how to approach your idea, which outlook to adopt when building your team and which Tycoon tendencies to bring to the fore when growing or selling your company. You know what a Tycoon is inclined to do and think when it comes to taking an idea from vision to fruition.

In wrapping up this book, it is worth revisiting those crucial Ten Golden Rules that make up the core sensibilities of a Tycoon's Mindset. Ask yourself:

RULE 1: Do you have a vision?

RULE 2: Are you ready to use your influence to get others on board and learn from them?

RULE 3: Do you feel confident in your idea, purpose and abilities?

RULE 4: Have you made a commitment?

RULE 5: Are you ready to take action now and keep taking action until you achieve the success you have visualised?

RULE 6:   Do you know what results you aim to achieve and how you intend to achieve them?

RULE 7:   Are you sure it is the right time to start this journey?

RULE 8:   Do you know how far you are prepared to go? Are you willing to persevere?

RULE 9:   Have you adopted a caring attitude towards your team, partners and yourself?

RULE 10:   Are you paying attention to your in-built intuition? Is your instinct button switched to 'on'?

These are your building blocks toward the summit of success. If you answer 'yes' to these Golden Rule questions, you are well on your way to understanding and adopting the Mindset of a Tycoon.

I hope this book has given you a useful and gratifying insight into my business approach, philosophy and mindset. Thanks for sticking with it. I hope you have soaked up the tips, techniques and temperament outlined in the previous pages, and have been sponge-like in your digestion of my words. If so, you are effectively programmed and rewired for success.

What you do with the knowledge I have shared with you is up to you. The truth is, nobody can force anyone to become an entrepreneur. Many people go into careers they don't necessarily want to go into. They've been persuaded to become a doctor or a lawyer. People can go through the motions of being accountants and lawyers without particularly wanting to be accountants and lawyers. Yet an entrepreneur cannot unwillingly go through the motions of being an entrepreneur. The fact is, you have to want it; you have to be hungry for it. You can only become a successful entrepreneur, a Tycoon, if you genuinely and deeply want to and then take action to make it happen.

I began this book by saying that we all potentially have it within us to become Tycoons if we want to. We all have 'it' – we just have to wake up the sleeping giant inside us to unleash it. So where does that leave you? Do you think you have what it takes to become a Tycoon? Well, the fact that you have bought and read this book is a very promising start. You've taken the first step on your journey. Now it's time to take the next step. It's time to get down to business.

Be bold! Commit to your dreams. In doing so, you'll release the shackles in which hesitancy enslaves us. Of course, committing wholeheartedly to your dream doesn't just involve a solitary commitment at the beginning; you need to keep committing to take action daily, even when the obstacles seem insurmountable.

As well as committing to action, to results and to success, you also need to commit to learning. In my experience, the one thing all Tycoons have in common is the desire to learn, a constant thirst for knowledge – not academic knowledge, but practical knowledge that comes from listening, observing and learning from life itself. As I said earlier, I have always been extremely inquisitive. In fact, ever since I was a child I have gone out of my way to soak up information and knowledge. If only we can open ourselves up to new ideas and new ways of thinking, the world really is our oyster. You can learn a lot from simply listening and being attentive. As an old Native American proverb advises, 'Listen or thy tongue will keep thee deaf.' Listening is vital in business. We have two ears and two eyes but only one mouth. Maybe we were always meant to do more listening and observing than we were talking.

'A wise old owl sat on an oak. The more he saw, the less he spoke. The less he spoke, the more he heard. Why aren't we like that wise old bird?'

As you embark on your adventure in realising your dreams, that journey will be paved with obstacles and potholes and littered with luck and opportunity. I truly hope your journey is a fruitful one. Certainly, as long as you absorb feedback, stay focused and stay open to learning and new experiences, your journey will be enjoyable and prosperous. And if things don't work out as you'd hoped, you'll have learned enough to turn it round or make it work next time.

'Courage is what it takes to stand up and speak; courage is also what it takes to sit down and listen'
WINSTON CHURCHILL

Another common characteristic that Tycoons share is the importance they place on networking. It is vital that you get out there in the market amongst people, listen to them and strike up relationships with them. Get out there in the thick of things. Tycoons are not shrinking violets. Influence, contacts and knowledge are important tools in a Tycoon's toolbox that bring everything together to help grow a business, so Tycoons make themselves known and get involved. Networking is a Tycoon's social cement.

I don't believe there is one Golden Rule of being a Tycoon that outweighs the others. Each has equal importance and power. Without a vision, there'd be no action; without action, there'd be no results; and without a caring attitude, there'd be no team. However, one rule that all truly successful people from all walks of life have in abundance is perseverance. So perhaps the final question to ask is, how far are you prepared to go? Again, the only person who can answer this question is you. But if you intend to reach for the stars, you need to be prepared to go the extra miles to get there. Becoming a Tycoon requires sacrifice, commitment and, sometimes, stress and heartache. You need to think long and hard about where you draw the line in the pursuit of bringing your dream to life. Dream pursuance can drain all your money, sap all your energy and adversely affect your family and loved ones.

Indeed, running your own business can become an obsession, and, like all obsessions, you need to keep a check on reality to ensure that passion, devotion and obsession do not drown out logic, common sense or intuition. At some point, you need to stand back and ask yourself the difficult question: 'Can I really keep on going when the going gets tough?' Going to the absolute brink in order to make something happen is not for everyone, but, I believe everyone can do it. You need special qualities to find the personal energy to make quitting a no-go area. You might also find that although you have no intention of giving up, circumstances or other people are dictating that you must. You need to be able to stand back, assess whether you are pouring money down a black hole or whether what you have built is worth persevering with. If those around you support your dream and encourage you to keep on going, you're very lucky, and should harness the power of that support network to build momentum. It all boils down to what kind of person you are, and what you have to lose. Only you can decide when enough is enough.

That said, it is perseverance and confidence that drive exceptional growth. 'Keep on keeping on' is a mantra that Tycoons are inclined to follow. You rise, you fall, you rise again. It's all part of the rollercoaster entrepreneurial experience. Stay motivated by addressing your progress and performance to give you a sense of direction and perspective. Stay determined with the right attitude. Don't give up until you've done everything possible to achieve what you set out to do. Persevere!

Before I end this book, let me share two final Tycoon Tips that I have mentioned to you already but will definitely swing the scales in your favour:

- Look after yourself and invest time in your health and well-being. There is little point in building an empire and a fantastic future if you grind yourself into the ground in the process. Nourish your body and brain with fresh and healthy food and regular exercise. This in turn will help feed your imagination and keep your creativity levels topped up. I find this tough myself, and should practice what I preach. So this is not just a goal for you, but a continuing one for me.
- Involve those close to you in what you are doing if possible.

Keep them especially informed about your end goal, the bigger picture, the wider vision. This act of sharing, in itself, can inspire more support and encouragement from the people around you and limit the impact of long hours in pursuit of business goals. It creates a sense of togetherness. Sharing your vision can be very positive for family and friends, and it can make the difference between giving up or sticking with it. The more vivid and detailed your vision is, the more likely you are to realise it, so share it with your family to give it even more credence and make it even sharper.

So, are you ready to realise your dreams? Success is available, but most people don't grab it because the risk of failure is too much to bear. That's what makes the difference. The majority of Tycoons don't see failure like that. They see failure as an opportunity to learn. Remember, failure is feedback.

Not succeeding is a possibility for everyone, but if you don't try, you've already failed. Just as I said at the very beginning of this book, if you don't try, you cannot even hope to succeed. By changing the way you view failure, by shifting your perception and seeing it as feedback, you will learn, move forward faster and be more prepared to take the risks that all Tycoons take. The truth is that everyone will experience successes and failures in their business life. All you can hope for is that you are able to tip the balance in favour of the former. The good news is, if you follow the Golden Rules, the balance will be on your side.

> 'Success is going from failure to failure without loss of enthusiasm'
> WINSTON CHURCHILL

And it is never too late to become your own boss. Ray Krokc, founder of McDonald's, was in his sixties when he started the business. Many successful Tycoons didn't start up until their early forties.

'It's never too late to be what you might have been'
GEORGE ELIOT

As I said earlier in this book, my dream of starting my own academy is getting closer and I was invivted to 10 Downing Street to talk about it with the Prime Minister and the Secretary of State who have given their full commitment and support to the project. What a weird and yet unbelievably wonderful world we live in, especially if you are one of those who believe in seeing your vision come alive and making it happen. My Tycoon Academy will be part of the Peter Jones foundation and will work with 16–19 year olds (25% of whom will come from underprivileged backgrounds) and will produce many successful Tycoons of tomorrow, employing tens of thousands of people! It is time for me to say farewell now and end with the fact that no one ever said that setting up a new business and becoming an entrepreneur would be easy. Indeed, becoming a very successful entrepreneur, a Tycoon, is even tougher. But just because something is tough isn't a good enough reason not to try. One thing I can absolutely promise you is that if you do take the plunge and follow your dream, the rewards will be incredible. Not just the tangible rewards you will achieve from success, but the incredible freedom, satisfaction, sense of achievement and immense joy you will experience on your travels to the top. And that journey starts right now! Go on, follow your dream, enrich your life, put your best foot forward and unlock your potential. Truly, I can think of no better way of living. Here's to your future success! I hope you make your dreams a reality! I have and there is absolutely no reason why you can't now. Good luck and enjoy the journey. Here's to your dreams.

www.tycoon.com
www.peterjones.tv

TYCOON TOOLKIT:
USEFUL RESOURCES AND INFORMATION

Using Your Imagination and Creativity

Creative Ideas and Innovation Tools
www.tycoon.com

The Big Idea

Tycoon
www.tycoon.com

American Inventor
www.americaninventor.tv

Dragons' Den
www.bbc.co.uk/dragonsden

Growth From Knowledge NOP Research Group
www.gfknop.co.uk

Intellectual Property Office
The trademark and patent register.
www.patent.gov.uk

Ipsos MORI (Market and Opinion Research International)
www.ipsos-mori.com

Peter Jones TV
www.peterjones.tv

Jupiter Research
www.jup.com

Securing Investment

British Venture Capital Association (BVCA)
www.bvca.co.uk

GrantsNet
Searchable database of UK grants, loans and funding schemes.
www.grantsnet.co.uk

J4b Grants
Searchable database for government and European funding, grants and so on.
www.j4b.co.uk

National Endowment for Science, Technology and the Arts (NESTA)
www.nesta.org.uk

Northwest Regional Development Agency (NWDA)
www.nwda.co.uk

Small Business Service/ Regional Venture Capital Fund (RVCF)
www.sbs.gov.uk/finance

The Small Business Start-Up Workbook
www.smallbusinessworkbook.com

Making It Happen

To download my business-plan template, visit
www.peterjones.tv and www.tycoon.com.

Companies House
www.companieshouse.gov.uk

Health and Safety Executive
www.hse.gov.uk

HM Revenue and Customs (Inland Revenue)
www.hmrc.gov.uk

Information Commissioner's Office
The data-protection register.
www.ico.gov.uk

Building Your Future

British Chambers of Commerce
www.chamberonline.co.uk

Business Link
www.businesslink.gov.uk

Communications and Wireless
www.wirelesslogic.co.uk

Department of Trade and Industry
www.dti.gov.uk

Institute of Directors (IOD)
www.iod.co.uk

Investors in People
www.investorsinpeople.co.uk

Recruitment

www.celcius.co.uk

Staff Incentives

www.redletterdays.co.uk